African Americans in the Spanish Civil War

"This Ain't Ethiopia, But It'll Do"

John Hunter, Abraham Lincoln Brigadist, somewhere in Spain, 1937.

African Americans in the Spanish Civil War

"This Ain't Ethiopia, But It'll Do"

A Project of
The Abraham Lincoln Brigade Archives
Brandeis University, Waltham, Massachusetts

Danny Duncan Collum, Editor
Victor A. Berch, Chief Researcher

G.K. Hall & Co.
New York

Maxwell Macmillan Canada
Toronto

Maxwell Macmillan International
New York Oxford Singapore Sydney

This project was supported by a grant from the Ford Foundation.

G.K. Hall & Co.
Macmillan Publishing Company
866 Third Avenue
New York, NY 10022

Maxwell Macmillan Canada, Inc.
1200 Eglinton Avenue East
Suite 200
Don Mills, Ontario M3C 3N1

Macmillan Publishing Company is part of the Maxwell Communication Group of Companies.

Library of Congress Catalog Card Number: 91-31899

Printed in the United States of America

printing number
10 9 8 7 6 5 4 3 2

Library of Congress Cataloging-in-Publication Data

African Americans in the Spanish Civil War: "This ain't Ethiopia, but it'll do" / Danny Duncan Collum, editor; Victor A. Berch, chief researcher.
      p. cm.
   "A project of the Abraham Lincoln Brigade Archives, Brandeis University, Waltham, Massachusetts."
   Includes bibliographical references and index.
   ISBN 0-8161-7378-8:
   1. Spain – History – Civil War, 1936-1939 – Participation, Afro-American.
   2. Afro-Americans – Biography. 3. Afro-Americans – Spain – Biography.
   I. Collum, Danny Duncan. II. Berch, Victor A. III. Abraham Lincoln Brigade Archives.
   DP269.47.A45A38   1991
   946.081 – dc20   91-31899
                                                                           CIP

The paper used in this publication meets the minimum requirements of American National Standard for Information Sciences – Permanence of Paper for Printed Library Materials, ANSI Z39.48-1984.   ∞™

CONTENTS

CONTENTS

PART 4   Testimonies

PREFACE

The story of the Spanish Civil War, and of the American role in it, has often been ignored or discounted in treatments of twentieth-century American history. From 1936 to 1939 the democratically elected government of Spain waged a bitter struggle for survival against rebellious right-wing elements of its own armed forces. These forces were led by Spain's future dictator Francisco Franco and were supported by troops from Hitler's Germany and Mussolini's Italy. Approximately 3,000 Americans traveled to Spain and there took up arms against the rising fascist threat. They came to be called the Abraham Lincoln Brigade. Among their number were approximately 90 African Americans. Two decades before the end of segregation in the U.S. armed forces, these brave black volunteers fought side by side with white compatriots in the first fully integrated (albeit unofficial) American fighting force. One of these African Americans, Oliver Law, served as military commander of the Lincoln-Washington Battalion until he was killed in battle at Brunete.

The impetus for this sourcebook came from the lack of available documentation regarding the special role of African Americans in the Spanish Civil War. Before this publication, not even a single scholarly article was devoted to this topic. Given rising popular interest in African-American history, and especially in African-American military history, the relative silence around this important episode seemed especially distressing. The Abraham Lincoln Brigade Archives (ALBA) is proud to offer this volume as a starting point in the reconstruction and preservation of this heroic story.

ALBA was founded in 1979 by some veterans of the Abraham Lincoln Brigade and by scholars with a special interest in the Spanish Civil War. ALBA is dedicated to the preservation of historical materials relevant to the Spanish Civil War and committed to encouraging study and understanding of that conflict. It is especially interested in American participation in that war. The physical archives of ALBA are housed with the special research collection on the Spanish Civil War in the Special Collections Department of the Brandeis University Libraries in Waltham, Massachusetts. It was there that this sourcebook was conceived and compiled.

The ALBA/Brandeis Spanish Civil War collection is one of the most extensive of its kind in the United States. It consists of more than 5,000 books and pamphlets on all aspects of the Spanish Civil War, a few thousand photographs from the war itself, and more than 200 propaganda posters used during the war by the democratic government of Spain and the various political parties to communicate with and to inspire the Spanish people in their fight. The collection also contains the surviving records of the Veterans of the Abraham Lincoln Brigade (VALB), which include the papers, correspondence, and memorabilia of many individual veterans of the war in Spain. ALBA has also compiled oral histories of more than 100 veterans. In addition, a videotaped oral history collection compiled by Lincoln veteran Manny Harriman has been placed with ALBA at Brandeis. Also at Brandeis are the archives of the Abraham Lincoln Brigade Film Project, which in 1990 produced the acclaimed documentary film *The Good Fight*.

This volume begins with an introductory essay by Robin D. G. Kelley that sketches the historical context of the war in Spain and outlines the American social and political movements from which the African-American volunteers emerged. The next part of the book lists alphabetically all known African-American veterans of the Spanish Civil War, along with a biographical sketch of each. The list of veterans includes information on their passage to and from Spain, including passport numbers. This information comes from VALB records and government documents stored at Brandeis. Following the roll of veterans is a group of reprinted essays and articles published during the war years. They are here to give readers a more immediate sense of the events and issues attending the war that were of particular significance to African Americans. The fourth part of the book includes excerpts from some of the ALBA/Brandeis collection's oral histories of African-American Lincoln veterans. The recollections of these black veterans, now advanced in age, bring the reader as close as possible to a personal understanding of the reasons such men decided to join the battle in Spain. Also included in part 4 are the testimony of black Lincoln veteran Crawford Morgan before the Subversive Activities Control Board in 1954 and a selection of poetry by black veteran Ray Durem.

The source material at the back of the book lists information sources on the subject of African Americans in the Spanish Civil War identified by ALBA in a search of the collections at Brandeis, the records of the Veterans of the Abraham Lincoln Brigade, major African-American and left-wing newspapers of the time, and the U.S. National Archives. The materials are listed by the names of the individual veterans to whom they pertain. A topical listing is also included on the support of, and interest in, the Spanish cause from African-American communities on the homefront. This material provides the basis for the biographical sketches in part 2.

The publication of this sourcebook only breaks the ground in the process of uncovering and preserving the story of these almost-forgotten African-American heroes. Our hope is that it will open the way for other authors, scholars, and researchers. For instance, the known record of the postwar lives of most black Lincoln Brigade veterans is very sketchy. We hope that schools or other institutions in veterans' home towns will be able to explore their backgrounds more completely. Passport records, which remain closed for 75 years after the date of application, will eventually prove an important source of information. Records can, however, be opened before the 75-year period expires with the permission of surviving relatives. We at ALBA will continue to collect and compile resources on this topic and look forward to hearing from interested relatives, friends, and others who can offer additional information.

DANNY DUNCAN COLLUM
Editor, Executive
Director, ALBA

VICTOR A. BERCH
Chief Researcher,
Archivist, ALBA

ACKNOWLEDGMENTS

We wish to convey our appreciation to a few of the many persons who made this publication possible. First, we thank the Ford Foundation and program officer Sheila Biddle for the grant that funded this project. Thanks also go to Bessie K. Hahn, Director of Library Services, and Dr. Charles Cutter, Head of Special Collections for Brandeis University Libraries. Brandeis generously provided us with the necessary space, equipment, and access. Thanks also to the Interlibrary Loan Office for its help in locating and obtaining newspaper microfilm.

This project was supervised by a working committee appointed by the ALBA Board of Governors. Members of that project committee are Professor Daniel J. Czitrom, Mt. Holyoke College; Professor Maurice Isserman, Hamilton College; Marc Crawford, Adjunct Professor of Writing, New York University; and William Susman, veteran of the Abraham Lincoln Brigade. Joseph Perkins, a graduate student in the English Department at Brandeis, served as research assistant for the project.

Last but far from least, thanks go to the Veterans of the Abraham Lincoln Brigade, individually and collectively, for their assistance and inspiration.

DANNY DUNCAN COLLUM
Editor, Executive
Director, ALBA

VICTOR A. BERCH
Chief Researcher,
Archivist, ALBA

CHRONOLOGY

1923-1930	Spain under the dictatorship of General Primo de Rivera.
1929	Wall Street crash marks start of Great Depression.
1931	Second Republic proclaimed April 14; King Alfonso XIII goes into exile. Manuel Azaña becomes prime minister in October.
1933	Depression deepens. Massive unemployment in the United States, Great Britain, and Germany. Right-wing parties win national elections in Spain in November.
1934	Adolf Hitler becomes Fuhrer of Germany in August. Workers' October uprising in Asturias crushed by Army of Africa units commanded by General Franco. Uprisings in Madrid and Barcelona fail. Severe repression follows.
1935	Italy invades Ethiopia in October.
1936	Popular Front coalition wins February 16 elections in Spain. Socialist Leon Blum becomes head of France's Popular Front government in June. Military uprisings in Spain and Spanish Morocco July 17-20. Hitler agrees to aid military rebellion in Spain. Airlift of Army of Africa forces to Spain begins July 30. International Brigades of volunteer sympathizers formed in October to aid Spanish Republic. Madrid threatened by insurgents in November. People's defense, helped by International Brigades, turns back Franco's forces.

German Nazi Condor Legion in action in Spain.
Italian fascist troops land in Spain December 22-23 to join Franco's forces, now called "Nationalists."
First American volunteers of the Abraham Lincoln Brigade leave New York for Spain December 26.

1937   Battle of Jarama takes place in February. Renewed Nationalist assault on Madrid turned back.
Battle of Brunete fought in July outside Madrid.
Republican offensive at Belchite in August.
Republican offensive at Teruel begins in December.

1938   Battle of Teruel ends with Nationalist victory in February.
Nationalist offensive in Aragon takes place in March.
Barcelona bombed by Italian planes.
Republican offensive in July along the river Ebro.
Battle of Ebro ends in October. International Brigade volunteers withdraw from Spain.
Nationalist offensive in Catalonia begins in December.

1939   Britain and France recognize Franco regime February 27.
Nationalists enter Madrid March 27.

1953   Veterans of the Abraham Lincoln Brigade (VALB) declared a subversive organization by the U.S. Attorney General's Subversive Activities Control Board (SACB).

1965   U.S. Supreme Court decision reverses SACB action.

1975   Franco dies November 20.

1977   Spain's first democratic elections since 1936 take place in June.

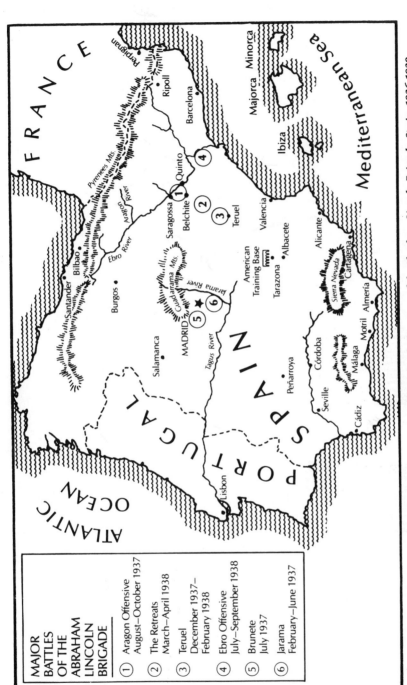

MAJOR
BATTLES
OF THE
ABRAHAM
LINCOLN
BRIGADE

1. Aragon Offensive
   August–October 1937
2. The Retreats
   March–April 1938
3. Teruel
   December 1937–
   February 1938
4. Ebro Offensive
   July–September 1938
5. Brunete
   July 1937
6. Jarama
   February–June 1937

Reprinted from Alvah Bessie and Albert Prago, eds., *Our Fight: Writings by Veterans of the Abraham Lincoln Brigade: Spain, 1936–1939* (New York: Monthly Review Press, 1987), 12.

African Americans in the Spanish Civil War

"This Ain't Ethiopia, But It'll Do"

I had been more than ready to go to Ethiopia, but that was different. Ethiopia, a Black nation, was part of me. I was just beginning to learn about the reality of Spain and Europe, but I knew what was at stake. There the poor, the peasants, the workers and the unions, the socialists and the communists, together had won an election against the big landowners, the monarchy and right-wingers in the military. It was the kind of victory that would have brought Black people to the top levels of government if such an election had been won in the USA. A Black man would be Governor of Mississippi. The new government in Spain was dividing its wealth with the peasants. Unions were organizing in each factory and social services were being introduced. Spain was the perfect example for the world I dreamed of.

–James Yates
From Mississippi to Madrid: Memoir of a Black American in the Abraham Lincoln Brigade

*All you colored peoples
Be a man at last
Say to Mussolini
No! You shall not pass*

–Langston Hughes
"Ballad of Ethiopia"

PART 1

African Americans in the Spanish Civil War:
An Introduction

"This Ain't Ethiopia, But It'll Do"

ROBIN D. G. KELLEY

Four decades ago, radical activist and Lincoln Brigade veteran Steve Nelson predicted that "someday, the working class of America will properly acknowledge the role [the] brave Negro Communist [Oliver Law] played in the fight for freedom." A native of Southside Chicago, Oliver Law died fighting for freedom in the Spanish Civil War (1936-39), the last great cause of the 1930s, in which about 3,000 men and women from the United States risked life and limb to defend the legally elected Spanish Republic against a fascist takeover. Like the rest of his comrades from the states, Law was a member of the Abraham Lincoln Brigade – the contingent of volunteers who participated in the Lincoln Battalion, the George Washington Battalion, the John Brown Field Artillery Battery, the Auto Park, and the American Medical Bureau.[1] Before he was killed at Brunete, Spain, in 1937, he was promoted to commander of the Lincoln Battalion, thus becoming the first black officer ever to command a predominantly white battalion. Fifty years later, the city of Chicago proclaimed Oliver Law Day on November 21, 1987.[2]

Oliver Law Day was indeed a wonderful tribute, but as a gesture toward restoring the martyred commander or other Lincoln veterans to our nation's historical memory, Chicago's day of recognition fell far short of Nelson's prediction. Few local residents had ever heard of Oliver Law

---

The title of this essay is taken from a line in Oscar Hunter's short story "700 Calendar Days," published in *The Heart of Spain*, edited by Alvah Bessie (New York: VALB, 1952), 29. In it, a wounded black soldier explains why he volunteered: "I wanted to go to Ethiopia and fight Mussolini. . . . This ain't Ethiopia, but it'll do." (Also quoted in Alan Guttman, *The Wound in the Heart: America and the Spanish Civil War* [New York: Free Press, 1962], 100.)

5

or the war in which he fought. That the populace remains ignorant of the events in Spain, despite the presence of a rich body of literature on the subject,[3] should not be surprising. The Spanish Civil War has the dubious distinction of being the only twentieth-century military conflict that has been virtually erased from our collective memory. Cold warriors tried their best to turn a noble example of democratic liberalism into a vile act of subversion, and when that failed, history textbooks and social science teachers simply ignored the Lincoln Brigade. Why? Because those who volunteered were labeled subversives – they were "premature antifascists." Many were, in fact, Communists and independent radicals, but their greatest crime was to fight fascism on Spanish soil before our nation's leaders were prepared to go to battle.

The power of anticommunism notwithstanding, it is perhaps more surprising that historians of the African-American experience have not yet confronted the significance of Oliver Law and his black com-rades – numbering about 90 – on the Spanish battlefield. Although there is a substantial body of work on African-American responses to Mussolini's invasion of Ethiopia in 1935, historians have ignored black support for, and participation in, the Spanish Civil War. The struggle in Spain was not simply another "white man's war," but an extension of the Italo-Ethiopian conflict. "By fighting against Franco," poet Langston Hughes observed, "they felt they were opposing Mussolini."[4] The fact that African Americans regarded the Spanish Civil War as inseparable from the antifascist struggle in Ethiopia and the antiracist struggle at home suggests that black volun-teers were motivated by black nationalism and Pan-Africanism, in addition to a commitment to radical internationalism. Thus, like the American-Jew-ish volunteers whose cultural and national identities constituted a central element of their radical politics,[5] they found that ethnic nationalism and internationalism were not mutually exclusive. On the contrary, the black Left in general and the black volunteers in particular saw nationalism and internationalism as two sides of the same ideological coin. African-Ameri-can volunteers were as much the creation of American communism as of black nationalism, as much the product of African-American folk culture as of Euro-American radical thought. In order to understand what prompted nearly 100 African Americans to leave the relative safety of home for the Spanish battlefields, we must begin by examining the complex social, political, and cultural milieux of the black Left.

2

African Americans in the Lincoln Brigade, with very few exceptions, com-prised part of a small but significant black communist Left that came of age sometime between the First World War and the economic crisis of the

1930s. During World War I black working people experienced changes that would eventually lead to a resurgent militancy in America's cities. Between 1916 and 1918 a steady migration of black Southerners (and a few West Indians) streamed into America's northern industrial centers, some finding their way into the American labor movement despite the racism and exclusionary practices of the American Federation of Labor. When the war came to an end and many black industrial workers were laid off, a few cursed themselves for having come North in the first place. Black war veterans were even more disappointed upon their return, for they had fought in Europe with the belief that a victory for democracy abroad would also apply to the home front. It was an apocryphal vision, indeed. Postwar recession, black disillusionment, and white backlash contributed to the eruption of racial violence in cities such as Chicago, East St. Louis, and Tulsa, Oklahoma.[6]

The war and its aftermath led to the formation of several black nationalist organizations, the most powerful being the Universal Negro Improvement Association (UNIA), founded in 1916 by Jamaican activist Marcus Moziah Garvey. Viewing the plight of blacks through the prism of Pan-Africanism, Garvey sought to build ethnic pride and self-confidence through black capitalism and a variety of quasireligious, race-centered signs, symbols, and rituals. Like many of his nineteenth-century predecessors, Garvey believed that emigration to a black-controlled Africa was the key to emancipation. Nevertheless, during his formative years in England (1912-16), Garvey articulated a much broader conception of internationalism, inspired in part by his links to Irish nationalists.[7]

To the left of Garvey was a small but significant cadre of black radicals who had been deeply touched by events in Russia. They kept abreast of the Bolshevik Revolution in 1917 and watched with interest as radical working-class movements throughout Europe, the United States, and parts of Africa, Latin America, and Asia followed the Soviet lead and pledged their allegiance to Third International, thus giving birth to the world communist movement. While this chain of events did not propel large numbers of African-American radicals into the American Communist party (CPUSA), it did reinforce their belief that socialist revolution was possible within the context of a complicated matrix of "race politics" and working-class unity. Perhaps the most enigmatic group among the postwar black Left was the African Blood Brotherhood (ABB), a secret underground organization of radical black nationalists led largely by West Indian immigrants. Founded in 1918 by Cyril Briggs, the ABB advocated armed defense against lynchings, the right to vote in the South, the right to organize, equal rights for blacks, and the abolition of Jim Crow laws. At its height it claimed 2,500 members at 50 posts in the United States, the West Indies, and Latin America. A unique experiment in black Marxist organization, the ABB was short-lived; it was killed off by its own internal logic. By the early 1920s its Marxist leadership, having decided that an interracial proletarian party would be a more effective form of organization, opted to join the CPUSA. A similar effort was launched by black activists A. Philip Randolph and Chandler Owen. They attempted to build African-American support for the Socialist Party of America (SPA) by emphasizing class-specific as well as race-specific goals, but the Socialists' official position regarded racist oppression secondary to the class struggle and held steadfastly to the idea that socialism was the only way to solve the problems of blacks.[8]

Like the Socialists before them, American Communists initially regarded black radicalism as merely a subset of the class struggle. The Party's 1921 program asserted that "the interests of the Negro worker are identical with those of the white." Two years later, communist leadership recognized that black people in the United States constituted an "oppressed race" but considered black nationalism a retrograde tendency. The Party's 1923 platform declared nationalism "a weapon of reaction for the defeat and further enslavement of both [blacks] and their white brother workers." Pressure from the Communist International (Comintern) and popular support for black nationalist movements within African-American working-class communities, however, compelled the CPUSA to seriously reconsider its approach to the "negro question." Even before the Bolshevik seizure of power in 1917, Vladimir Lenin explored the idea of national self-determination in order to reckon with pervasive nationalism and ethnic sentiment inside Russia. At the Second Congress of the Comintern in 1920, Lenin (along with Indian Communist M. N. Roy) insisted that the "communist parties give direct support to the revolutionary movements among the dependent nations and those without equal rights (e.g. Ireland, and among American Negroes), and in the colonies." One year later Lenin assailed American communist leadership for neglecting the plight of African-American workers.[9]

Despite opposition from American communist leadership, Lenin's views prevailed. The Fourth Congress of the Comintern in 1922 adopted a set of theses that described blacks as a nationality oppressed by worldwide imperialist exploitation. Because black workers' struggles were now considered inherently anti-imperialist, American Communists were obliged to view Garveyism and other notable nationalist movements anew. Although the Party continued to criticize Garvey's rhetoric of racial pride and espousal of repatriation to Africa, by 1925 communist leaders believed the UNIA could be transformed into a revolutionary movement "fighting for the class interests of the Negro workers in the United States." The CPUSA's newfound respect for Garvey's appeal came a bit too late, however, since the UNIA was already on the verge of collapse. The Party responded by forming the American Negro Labor Congress (ANLC) in 1925, an organization led chiefly by former ABB leaders whose primary purpose was to build interracial unity in the labor movement. Chapters were to be established throughout the United States, particularly in the South, but because of poor leadership and planning, the ANLC never gained popular support.[10]

Organizational weaknesses notwithstanding, the Communists' inability to attract the kind of following Garvey had once enjoyed, particularly in the 1920s, can be partially attributed to the fact that the Comintern promoted a vision of internationalism that went beyond Pan-Africanism and/or racial solidarity. While Comintern officials recognized differences between anticolonial and European working-class movements, peasants and proletarians, they still insisted that their struggles be united under the same banner. Even the Comintern's conferences emphasized an international unity that few Americans, black or white, could ever imagine. In 1927, for example, African-American delegates were invited to attend a conference in Brussels held under the auspices of the League against Colonial Oppression. Organized in 1926 by the German Communist party (KDP) to combat procolonial sentiments emerging in Germany, the league was an important step toward coordinating various struggles for national liberation in the colonies and "semicolonies," and it served as an intermediary between the Comintern and the anticolonial movement. It was at this conference that former ABB leader Richard B. Moore witnessed Europeans, Asians, and Africans pass a general resolution that proclaimed: "Africa for the Africans, and their full freedom and equality with other races and the right to govern Africa." It was indeed a remarkable sight for anyone who believed the struggle for African freedom was *only* an African struggle.[11]

Most African Americans drawn to the Communist party, therefore, developed an advanced internationalist outlook alongside their militant, race-conscious nationalism. Knowledge of this vision is crucial to understanding why most blacks who went to Spain came out of the communist Left. Ironically, this same internationalist vision sometimes hindered their work in the black community. For example, black delegates from the Workers (Communist) party and the ABB attending the first All-Race Conference in 1924 were treated with suspicion when they attached to their proposal for armed self-defense and working-class organization a statement endorsing the "Internationale" as the "anthem of Negro Freedom." Similarly, at the ANLC's first mass meeting in Chicago, hundreds of black workers in attendance became disenchanted with the Congress during the entertainment: a Russian ballet and a one-act play written by Pushkin, performed entirely in Russian! Organized by Lovett Fort-Whiteman, a high-ranking black Communist who was often seen traipsing through Southside

Chicago draped in a Russian *rabochka,* the Congress was emblematic of the kind of cultural internationalism for which few black working people were prepared.[12]

At the Sixth World Congress of the Comintern in 1928, a resolution was passed asserting that African Americans in the "black belt" counties of the American South constituted an oppressed nation and therefore possessed an inherent right of self-determination. Not surprisingly, the resolution met fierce opposition from white and some black Party leaders. For many black Communists, however, particularly those in the urban North, the resolution on black self-determination indirectly confirmed what they had long believed: that African Americans had their own unique revolutionary tradition. As historian Mark Naison observes, "By defining blacks as an oppressed nation . . . the Comintern had, within the Leninist lexicon of values, endowed the black struggle with unprecedented dignity and importance." Black Communists published dozens of articles in the Party press supporting the idea that blacks have their own identifiable, autonomous traditions of radicalism. "Aside from the purely Marxian analysis," wrote one black Party organizer, "the Negro's history is replete with many actual instances of uprising against his exploiters and oppressors."[13]

The self-determination slogan might have inspired a few black intellectuals already in the Party, but it was not the key to building black working-class support. The horrendous conditions brought on by the Great Depression, the Party's defense of the Scottsboro Nine (young black men accused of raping two white Georgia women) and Angelo Herndon (a black communist organizer tried for sedition in Georgia), its vigorous denunciation of racism, and its unrelenting fight for the concrete economic needs of the poor attracted a considerable section of America's submerged black working-class and intelligentsia, many of whom were former Garveyites or Pan-Africanist ideologues. This rich matrix of radical traditions, born of racism and joblessness and reinforced by the Comintern's interpretation of black cultural nationalism, found its clearest expression in the pages of the *Liberator,* the newspaper of the communist-sponsored League of Struggle for Negro Rights. The *Liberator* became the mouthpiece for black internationalism, a journal of black news tailor-made for the African-American community, and a forum for lesser-known black left-wing writers. The essays, poems, and stories combined class consciousness with prevailing Pan-African ideas. One contributor borrowed an old nineteenth-century slave song to create a humorous parody entitled "No Mo', No Mo.' " The tune epitomizes the sort of secular radicalism for which the Communists were famous, yet reconstructs a prophetic vision of an insurmountable black revolutionary movement:

No mo' KU-KLUX KLAN with
  their burnin' crosses.
No mo' chain-gangs, we's no
  dogs no' ho'ses.
The NAACP, God no' Moses
  Can stop us blackies fightin' the
    bosses. . . .

Negroes ain' black – but RED!
Teacher Lenin done said
Brothers all oppressed an' po.'
Ain't it so? Sho! . . .[14]

The chorus leaves one with an image of an all-black army of militants poised for a battle against racism, yet guided by the "teachings" of Lenin. J. Thompson, another grass-roots black radical, used verse to appeal for black unity and resistance. His poem "Exhortation" not only resonates with the spirit of Garveyism but also contains echoes of Claude McKay's celebrated poem of 1919, "If We Must Die":

Rise, Afric's sons with banner
  red.
Freedom's path we too must tread.
We've fought for it and bled.
  Black men, United! . . .

Face the lynchers, the Southern
  Cossacks.
Face the demons. Strike them
  back.
Face them dying but striking back.
For our right.[15]

Thompson's "Exhortation" could have been a manifesto for African Americans in the Lincoln Brigade. It is perhaps the clearest expression of the radical traditions from whence they came. Although they were a diverse bunch that included Northerners and Southerners, college-trained and semiliterate people, unemployed workers and self-styled intellectuals, most were Party members or supporters who interpreted communism through the lenses of their own cultural world and the international movement of which they were a part. They joined the movement out of their concern for black people, and thus had much in common with the black nationalists and mainstream black political figures whose leadership they challenged. On the other hand, they were part of an organization that encouraged black-white unity without completely compromising black nationalist politics and that introduced them to an entirely different inter-pretation of the way the world worked. The Party, in short, offered African Americans a framework for understanding the roots of poverty and racism, linked local struggles to world politics, and created an atmosphere in which ordinary people could analyze, discuss, and criticize the society in which they lived. As one black volunteer noticed when he arrived in Spain, "the ideas of all the Negroes from the United States were practically the same though these men did not know one another."[16]

These words were spoken by Mack Coad, an illiterate steel worker originally from Charleston, South Carolina, who had joined the Party in Birmingham in 1930. Although Coad was never singled out for his heroics in Spain, he had known war in the South. In March 1931 he was sent to Tallapoosa County, Alabama, to organize the Communist-led Share Croppers' Union (SCU). In the abandoned houses of rural Alabama, Coad discovered local militants who were quite comfortable combining communist and folk cultures. These grass-roots leaders had established a tradition of singing before and after gatherings, which grew out of the rural church services after which they had patterned their meetings. In addition to adopting standards such as the "Internationale" and "Solidarity Forever," rural blacks in and around the Party transformed popular spirituals into political songs with new messages. "We Shall Not Be Moved" and the ever-popular "Give Me That Old-Time Religion" were stock musical forms used to create new Party songs. In the latter, the verse was changed to "Give Me That Old Communist Spirit," and Party members closed each stanza with "It was good enough for Lenin, and it's good enough for me."[17] Unfortunately, because Tallapoosa landlords would not tolerate a surreptitious organization of black tenant farmers and agricultural workers, Coad and other union recruits were caught in a shootout with police within weeks of the SCU's founding. When it was all over, SCU leader Ralph Gray lay dead and Coad was forced to flee the state. The following year Coad was sent to the Lenin School in the Soviet Union, where his sense of the world and knowledge of international politics expanded immensely, although he still could neither read nor write when he left. After he returned to the South in 1934 he resumed Party work in Raleigh, North Carolina, in Birmingham, and rural Alabama before heading to Spain in 1937.[18]

There were other Southern-born blacks who went to Spain, but most of them left the South at rather young ages and became acquainted with left-wing causes in Northern cities. Abe Lewis, born and raised in Alabama, joined the Communist party in Cleveland. A struggling laundry worker, Lewis always remained firmly grounded in black community institutions, having been active in the Future Outlook League, the local NAACP, and the black church. He was a prime mover behind the Cleveland Scottsboro Defense Campaign and a consistent contributor to the local black press. Vaughn Love, a native of Tennessee who had begun working in the coal mines at 14, made his way to New York in 1929 and became acquainted with the Communist party through the League of Struggle for Negro Rights.[19] James Yates, about whom more is known, was born in 1906 in Quitman, Mississippi. He was nourished on stories of how African Americans enjoyed democracy during Reconstruction; was taught by a schoolteacher who insisted that one day America would have a black president; was touched by the vision of his Garveyite uncle, who eventually moved to the all-black town of Boley, Oklahoma; and was told over and over again about his other uncle, who had armed himself to defend his family from the Klan, and of the Irish immigrant neighbor who had assisted him by providing ammunition. In the small town of Quitman, Mississippi, the young Yates witnessed not only countless episodes of racism and violence but also stark examples of internationalism, black nationalism, Pan-Africanism, and interracial solidarity. Quitman was apparently an appropriate place to raise a black antifascist.[20]

Yates arrived in Chicago in 1923, during the height of the Garvey movement. Even his boss at the stockyards was a member of the UNIA. Although Yates himself never joined, he was clearly impressed by Garvey's overall message and the idea of black self-organization. By the time the Depression hit home, Yates discovered in the streets and parks of Southside Chicago an even more impressive bunch of men and women, some of whom would eventually join him in Spain. They were activists in the Communist party and/or the unemployed councils. It is not clear whether Yates joined the Party or not, but he was unmistakably a part of the unemployed movement and even began organizing dining-car waiters in Chicago and New York. During his first mass demonstration – a march to Springfield, Illinois, that had been organized by the Party – he came to realize the international significance of the Communist party's struggle for jobs, relief, and equality: "I was a part of their hopes, their dreams, and they were a part of mine. And we were a part of an even larger world of marching poor people. By now I understood that the Depression was world-wide and that the unemployed and the poor were demonstrating and agitating for jobs and food all over the globe. We were millions. We couldn't lose."[21]

One of the leaders of the Springfield demonstration was Oliver Law, a native of the Southside and undoubtedly the most celebrated African American to have served in Spain. After spending six long years in the U.S. Army and never having surpassed the rank of corporal, Law left the service and became a building-trades worker. By the time the Great Depression hit Chicago and left most construction workers jobless, he was sufficiently disillusioned with American capitalism to join the Communist party. Like Mack Coad, he not only rose through the Party's ranks quite rapidly, becoming chairman of the Southside chapter of the International Labor Defense and a principal leader in the "Hands off Ethiopia" campaign, but also found himself engaged in a war at home. He was hospitalized in 1930 after being severely beaten by police for his role in leading a demonstration of unemployed workers.[22]

In addition to James Yates and Oliver Law, an unusually large number of black Spanish Civil War veterans came through the Communist party in Chicago's Southside.[23] This should not be surprising; the Party there attracted a substantial following in the black community and thus offered a large pool of candidates. The black cadre on the Southside, however, was an unusual group of individuals who probably had more in common with the black nationalists than with their white comrades. Their culture enveloped the Party at the grass-roots level. The local comrades punctuated dry theoretical discussions with their rendition of "Give Me That New Communist Spirit," and on one occasion a black Chicago Communist replaced James Weldon Johnson's lyrics to "Lift Every Voice and Sing" (often referred to as the black national anthem) with his own:

> Sing a song full of the strife that the dark
>   past has taught us.
> Sing a song full of the hope Communism has
>   brought us.
> Facing a Red! Red! Sun of a new day begun
> Let us fight on till victory is won.[24]

The meetings in which African Americans predominated generally resembled Sunday-morning church services. As one observer noted, "At mass meetings their religious past becomes transmuted into a communist present. They follow every word of the speaker with real emotion; they encourage him, as at a prayer meeting, with cries of 'Yes, yes, comrade' and often there is an involuntary and heartfelt 'Amen!' "[25]

Despite white Communists' intentions, race relations within the Chicago Communist party were not always smooth. Oscar Hunter, a black Party member who served in Spain, was constantly being criticized by local Party leadership for his views on race. "I was *always* in trouble," he recalls; "I didn't have the correct line, I didn't have the correct approach." And to make matters worse, his white comrades thought they knew "more about blacks and the history of blacks [than] I did." He vividly remembers one Southside meeting at which he made the mistake of referring to blacks as "my people" while appealing to the Party to adress the high rate of illiteracy among black Chicagoans. For uttering those words he was attacked by the leading cadre, who, according to Hunter, "give [another black Communist] the job of putting me in my place . . . so he comes right out and says what's this shit MY PEOPLE. . . . There's no such a goddamn thing."[26]

Hunter's problem with white Party leadership probably had more to do with his background and education than his unreconstructed black nationalist politics. Hunter was born in 1908 to a working-class family in Orange, New Jersey. He and his brothers and sisters had to practically raise themselves after their father left and their mother died. At 14 Hunter dropped out of school and moved to Cleveland in search of work. Soon after he arrived, a friend offered to send him to Hampton Institute, where he became involved in student politics and met a radical religion teacher who introduced him to Marxist literature. He went on to West Virginia State and then, on the suggestion of another professor, continued his education at Brookwood Labor College in Katonah, New York. Impressed by some of the Communists he met at Brookwood, Hunter eventually moved to Chicago and joined the Party. As an independent black intellectual whose training in Marxism predated his membership in the Party, Hunter's vocal presence threatened a number of leading cadres in the Chicago area, both black and white. Nevertheless, he continued to pursue his intellectual interests at Northwestern University's School of Journalism and at the lively meetings of the local John Reed Club, which were attended by the likes of Richard Wright and Nelson Algren. Yet, despite his intellectual training, Hunter never took the movement as seriously as did his leaders. "I joined the party, and I don't think I was the best communist in the world, I know I wasn't. I think that I had certain corruptions. I liked women, I liked to drink now and then, I liked to have fun."[27]

Oscar Hunter was not the only African-American volunteer whose left-wing roots predated his membership in the Communist party. Admiral Kilpatrick, whose background is as unique as his name, was born in Colorado in 1898 to a socialist family. His mother had been born a slave in Kentucky and his father, an American Indian from Oklahoma, had been a member of the Socialist party since the turn of the century. Having grown up around radicals, Kilpatrick was about 19 when he joined the Industrial Workers of the World. Like many of his comrades, he was influenced by the Russian Revolution and the Sacco and Vanzetti case, and he was a victim of antiradical repression in 1919 under the direction of Attorney General A. Mitchell Palmer. He eventually joined the Communist party in 1927 and went to the Soviet Union in 1931 to study at the Lenin School.[28]

By the mid-1930s, a combination of events had radicalized a segment of the African-American community. Nine young black men had been falsely accused of, and incarcerated for, the rape of two white women near Scottsboro, Alabama, and Claude Neal had been lynched in Florida. The passage of much-heralded New Deal legislation left millions of blacks still jobless and landless. A callous economic system still kept over half the black population in some cities unemployed. And across the nation groups like the Klan, the American Nazi Party, the White Legion, and the Black Shirts beat, raped, and humiliated black people without compunction. So when Mussolini invaded the only independent black African nation in 1935, the simmering anger of African Americans turned to outrage.

The defense of Ethiopia did more than any other event in the 1930s to internationalize the struggles of black people in the United States. Also known as Abyssinia, this particular section of the Horn of Africa held considerable historical, religious, and cultural significance for black communities throughout the world. Under Emperor Menelik II, the Ethiopians had managed to maintain their independence while the rest of Africa was being carved up by Europeans.[29] Ethiopia had become known as the cradle of civilization; it was among the first countries in the world to adopt Christianity. In the black Christian world, Ethiopia has remained a principal icon and is in some ways perceived as an African Jerusalem. As historian William Scott explains, many African Americans, particularly the followers of Ethiopianism, believed that "Ethiopia had been predestined by biblical prophecy to redeem the black race from white rule." Their point of reference, of course, was the biblical passage "Ethiopia shall stretch forth her hands unto God" (Psalm 68:31). The best known institutional manifestation of Ethiopianism in the United States was perhaps Harlem's own Abyssinian Baptist Church, founded in 1809. During the 1930s, Abyssinian's pastor, Adam Clayton Powell, Sr., developed a reputation for his radical race-conscious sermons and strident support for Ethiopian resistance to Italy. The Garvey movement, whose official anthem was entitled "Ethiopia, Thou Land of Our Fathers," made constant reference to this African nation in its songs, rituals, and symbols. Likewise, the Star Order of Ethiopia, founded by Grover Cleveland Redding, went so far as to advocate emigration there. The movement was deemed subversive by authorities in Chicago when one of its leaders "burned an American flag to symbolize the surrender of allegiance to the United States and the assumption of allegiance to Ethiopia." While Redding's organization was unable to persuade African Americans to move to the mother country, the Ethiopian ambassador to the United States was slightly more successful. By 1933 the African-American community in Ethiopia numbered between 100 and 150.[30]

In some ways the African-American response to the Italian invasion resembled the Left's response to Franco's rebellion in Spain. Almost overnight an array of support organizations were formed, mainly in New York, Chicago, and Los Angeles, to raise money for relief and medical aid; men from across the nation volunteered to fight in Ethiopia. Individuals such as Walter J. Davis of Fort Worth, Texas, and organizations such as the Pan-African Reconstruction Association (PARA), headed by Samuel Daniels, initiated efforts to recruit men for Emperor Haile Selassie's army.

According to Daniels, his organization had already mobilized an estimated 1,000 volunteers in New York, 1,500 in Philadelphia, 8,000 in Chicago, 5,000 in Detroit, and 2,000 in Kansas City. While these figures are undoubtedly exaggerated, the overwhelming response from black men suggests a potential volunteer army equal to, and perhaps greater than, the number of Americans who joined the Lincoln Brigade. Initially, Selassie was willing to accept African-American combatants, but pressure from the U.S. government compelled Ethiopia to cease all recruitment efforts. Furthermore, potential volunteers were warned that they would be in violation of a federal statute of 1818 governing the enlistment of U.S. citizens in a foreign army. If convicted, they would face a maximum three-year prison sentence, a $2,000 fine, and loss of citizenship. Despite the law, the Garveyite Black Legion allegedly established a training camp in upstate New York for some 3,000 volunteers, while another group made plans to purchase a freighter to carry black men to the Horn of Africa. None of these efforts came to fruition, however. According to most accounts, only two African Americans ever reached Ethiopia – airmen John C. Robinson of Chicago's Southside and Hubert F. Julian of Harlem.[31]

Most mainstream black political figures opposed sending a brigade of black troops to Ethiopia and counseled young men against breaking the law, but the League of Nations' refusal to protect Ethiopia left many feeling disillusioned with any form of legal recourse. Indeed, black nationalists generally believed that indifference on the part of Western nations (most of which had their own African colonies to contend with) was nothing short of an act of racism. The invasion of Ethiopia was merely the first skirmish in what they viewed as a worldwide race war. Robert Ephraim, founder and president of the Negro World Alliance, stated in the summer of 1935 that "the refusal of the United States to throw its influence against Mussolini . . . can only be taken as an indication that the white races are lining up definitely against the black."[32]

This racial interpretation of the invasion created a dilemma for the Communist party and other left-wing movements because most of the leading black nationalists refused to work with whites. With the help of a few friendly Garveyites, black Communists in Harlem created the Provisional Committee for the Defense of Ethiopia (PCDE), which worked tirelessly to redirect antiwhite and anti-Italian sentiment toward antifascism. With solid support from the American League against War and Fascism, the PCDE waged a lively "Hands off Ethiopia" united-front campaign in several black communities across the country. But the Party's efforts were weakened by its opposition to the idea of recruiting African Americans for the Ethiopian army and by the Soviet Union's weak stand vis-à-vis the invasion. During a League of Nations meeting in April 1935, for example, Soviet delegate Maxim Litvinov did not condemn Italian aggression in

Ethiopia. Even more damaging to the Soviet's reputation was a *New York Times* article the following September, claiming that the USSR had sold coal tar, wheat, and oil to Italy below market price. Both events outraged black supporters of the Hands off Ethiopia campaign.[33]

The Soviets' initial vacillation resulted in a loss of confidence in the PCDE, and a few organizations, such as the Ethiopian World Federation, were created expressly to counter communist influence. But the majority of African Americans who had supported the Hands off Ethiopia campaign learned to distinguish between Soviet interests and the genuine antifascist politics of rank-and-file Communists. Moreover, a contingent of black Leftists had always treated Italy's aggression as something more than a race war. When the Comintern and the Republican government asked for volunteers to come to Spain, African Americans who responded to the call regarded the Spanish Civil War as an extension of the Italo-Ethiopian conflict. At the same time, black volunteers did not forget racism and poverty in America; for them Spain had become the battlefield to revenge the rape of Ethiopia *and* part of a larger fight for justice and equality that would inevitably take place on U.S. soil. In the words of Mack Coad, "I was interested in going to Spain because I wanted to wake the Negro up on the international field. I spoke to Negroes about helping Ethiopia and many of them would say 'I'm not an Ethiopian; I'm an American free-born Negro' which I knew was not true. So I thought here was a chance to show the Negro what role he had to play on the international field against fascism, which would give him a better understanding on how to fight against fascism on a national scale which means at home."

Lincoln veteran Crawford Morgan, a native of North Carolina, expressed similar sentiments: "I felt that I had a pretty good . . . idea of what fascism was and most of its ramifications and [was] aware [of] . . . what the Fascist Italian Government [had] done to the Ethiopians." Morgan linked the events in Ethiopia with "fascist tendencies" in the United States, mainly the fact that "Negroes have been getting lynched in this country by mobs." Vaughn Love, who had collected medical supplies for the Hands off Ethiopia campaign, simply defined fascism as "the enemy of all Black aspirations."[34]

By early 1937 the Party had adopted the slogan "Ethiopia's fate is at stake on the battlefields of Spain" and asked that material aid that had been collected for Ethiopia be passed on to Spain after the Ethiopian government could no longer receive shipments of supplies. While many nationalist leaders attacked the slogan and fiercely rejected the idea that Spain and Ethiopia were part of the same battle, a number of black intellectuals and artists adopted the Spanish cause as their own. Black newspapers, most notably Pittsburgh's *Courier,* Baltimore's *Afro-American,* Atlanta's *Daily World,* and Chicago's *Defender,* unequivocally sided with the Spanish Republic and occasionally carried feature articles about black participation in the Lincoln Brigade. Several black medical personnel from the United Aid for Ethiopia (UAE) offered medical supplies and raised money in the community; Harlem churches and professional organizations sponsored rallies on behalf of the Spanish Republic; black relief workers and doctors raised enough money to purchase a fully equipped ambulance for use in Spain; and some of Harlem's greatest musicians, including Cab Calloway, Fats Waller, Count Basie, W. C. Handy, Jimmy Lunceford, Noble Sissle, and Eubie Blake, gave benefit concerts sponsored by the Harlem Musicians' Committee for Spanish Democracy and the Spanish Children's Milk Fund. Besides the few who volunteered for service or helped collect money and supplies, a number of prominent contemporary cultural figures became involved. Paul Robeson, the great black renaissance man of modern times, actually visited Spain during the height of the war. So moved by the black men of the Lincoln Brigade was Robeson that he planned to make a film about war hero Oliver Law, but he was unable to obtain sufficient backing. Poet Langston Hughes, who was also deeply touched by the black men he had met at the front, had intended to publish a book of essays entitled "Negroes in Spain." The war even gripped the imagination of a 12-year-old Harlem boy named James Baldwin, whose first published essay was a short story "about the Spanish Revolution," which appeared in a local church newspaper. Although Baldwin later could not remember the story's content, he did recall vividly that it had been "censored by the lady editor."[35]

Among the nurses and doctors who had turned their efforts from Ethiopian relief to Spanish relief, two actually went to Spain as part of the American Medical Bureau. Caribbean-born Arnold Donawa, a graduate of Harvard University and former dean of Howard University's dental school, had developed a reputation as a brilliant oral surgeon. In Spain, Donawa became the head of Oral Surgery in the Medical Corps. Although it is not clear where he stood in the political spectrum, especially in relation to the Communist party, he had been among the first UAE members to redirect relief efforts to Spain. He also persuaded a young nurse from Harlem Hospital, Salaria Kee, to volunteer for service in Spain. Originally from Ohio, Kee was a recent graduate of the Harlem Hospital Training School – not the school of her choice, but the only one that would accept blacks into the nursing program. Upon completing her training in 1934, she was given an undesirable position as head nurse in a tuberculosis ward. Soon thereafter she found herself working with a group of Harlem nurses who collected medical supplies and helped organize a 75-bed field hospital for Ethiopia's troops. After talking with Dr. Donawa and reading bits and pieces of information about the Spanish Civil War, she tried to volunteer through the Red Cross, but that organization made it absolutely clear that it would not accept black nurses. The International Brigades gladly accepted her, however, and she set sail for Spain on March 27, 1937.[36]

In essence, African Americans who went to Spain shared with black nationalists a moral and political obligation to come to Ethiopia's defense, a sense of duty shaped by their daily confrontation with racism at home. But this is where the similarity ends. Most black Lincoln Brigade soldiers saw the world in terms of rich and poor, not just black and white. They even approached the contemporary social and political situation in Ethiopia far more judiciously than did their black nationalist counterparts.

While "race" scholars praised Abyssinia for its ancient civilizations, its written language, and its rulers' proud claim of direct lineage from Solomon and the Queen of Sheba, black Leftists discussed a mountainous peasant region in the Horn of Africa ruled by a dying monarchy that did not believe in land reform. Indeed, it was one of the few regions on earth where slavery persisted well into the early 1930s. In 1931 black Communist George Padmore (a.k.a. Malcolm Nurse) described Abyssinia as a feudal oligarchy under a reactionary emperor and called for an internal revolution against "the reactionary religious hierarchy and the feudal system." Soon after the invasion, black Communist leader James Ford similarly characterized Africa's only independent nation as "a feudal state, under the rule of powerful native feudal lords," but insisted that the "the war of Ethiopia against Italian aggression must be regarded as a national (liberation) war. . . . The international proletariat must regard the struggle of Ethiopia as a just war, as a national defensive war, and support the Ethiopian people." This is a critical observation, for it helps us understand why the Comintern never deployed International Brigades to Ethiopia. Racism alone has never been an adequate explanation.

The fact is that the ruling class in Ethiopia was promonarchy and virulently anticommunist, and it governed a country in which most peasants were landless and most of the wealth was concentrated in the hands of a few.[37] Spain was different. It was a nation experimenting with a radical democracy in which peasants, workers, and women had the right to vote and in which Socialists and Communists held positions of power in government. More important, Spain was one of the few examples of the Popular Front in practice.

3

Though their motivations were as diverse as their ranks, the Lincoln Brigade volunteers went to Spain primarily to fight the fascist threat. The more observant among them, as well as most perceptive historians, have come to realize that the conflict was much more than a struggle against fascism; it was several wars rolled up in one. The roots of the civil war can be found in Spain itself, in time-honored battles between the Catholic church and anticlericalists, between ethnic regionalists from Catalonia and the Basque provinces and Castilian centralists, between urban workers and Spain's few capitalists, and most important, between landless peasants and the old agrarian ruling class. Class struggles in the countryside were inevitably at the heart of the matter. Peasants on the huge landed estates in the south fought fiercely for land reform, and agricultural laborers demanded better wages. Big landholders turned increasingly to conservative Catholic political organizations and relied on legal and extralegal terrorist activities to keep their estates intact. By 1931 two million agricultural workers owned no land, whereas about 50,000 of Spain's landed gentry owned half of Spain's acreage. The differences were even sharper in provinces such as Seville, where 5 percent of the landowners owned 72 percent of the land, and Badajoz, where 2.75 percent owned 60 percent of the land.[38]

Meanwhile, the military had become a powerful influence in Spain's political life, particularly after World War I. By 1921 the army's humiliating string of defeats at the hands of the Rif people of Morocco had created a political crisis for the government. But the Rif wars were just the tip of the iceberg. Frustrated by peasant insurrections, radical working-class opposition, the intransigence of Spain's capitalists in their refusal to compromise with organized labor, the militancy of Basque and Catalanist movements for autonomy, and the overall inability of liberals to build a meaningful political alliance, a military junta under the leadership of General Primo de Rivera seized power in 1923 with the encouragement of King Alfonso XIII. As dictator, Primo de Rivera set out to resolve the political crises that had plagued Spain since the end of World War I, but the experiment was a dismal failure. After seven years of mass strikes by students and workers and small mutinies within the army, the king had no choice but to succumb to mass pressure and dismiss Primo de Rivera. When municipal elections were finally held on April 12, 1931, a coalition of liberal and socialist parties defeated the monarchists, thus paving the way for the creation of the Second Republic.[39]

On April 14, 1931, the Second Republic was proclaimed, with a new constitution declaring that the new government was "a republic of workers of all classes." But given the broad political spectrum within this coalition, few agreed as to what the Republic should look like. Initially, some of the changes marked a dramatic break from the past. In addition to granting Catalonia and the Basque provinces limited autonomy, the Republic took a few halting steps toward social and economic reform. The Minister of Labor, Socialist Largo Caballero, supported some land reform, but Republican initiatives fell far short of peasants' expectations. Not only did the state fail to break up the great landed estates of the south and south-west; under Azaña, only 45,000 hectares were redistributed, and fewer than 7,000 families benefited from these limited measures. Moreover, the new government's efforts at secularizing education and minimizing the power of the church and army eventually inspired a revolt of high-ranking officers in August 1932. Although the government easily suppressed the uprising, it was a foreshadowing of things to come.

After two years, popular support for the Republican government had begun to diminish. Its land and labor reforms were not enough to satisfy Spain's workers and peasants, and the military, the church, pro-monar-chists, and the bourgeoisie believed the government had gone too far. Riding the crest of clerical reaction, the Confederación Española de Derechas Autónomas (CEDA), led by José María Gil Robles, built an elec-toral alliance with other right-wing groups, narrowly defeated the left-wing coalition, and promptly dismantled social and economic reforms: wages were reduced, clerical control over schools was reinstated, land reform came to a standstill, and the central government in Madrid began to whittle away at the Catalan autonomy. By 1934 radical and moderate Republicans feared that Gil Robles and the CEDA would lead the nation down the road to fascism. Thousands of urban industrial workers, already outraged by cutbacks in wages and benefits under the right-wing republi-can government, were poised for a showdown.

In October 1934, led by Socialists, Left Republicans, Communists, and a few anarchists, workers attempted a general strike that quickly turned into an insurrection in Barcelona and Asturias. Workers proclaimed a socialist republic in Asturias, ran mines and factories by council, and established a "Red army" militia. The workers did not know it then, but the Asturian uprising (also known as Spain's October Revolution) was a dress rehearsal for the civil war that was to follow. Acting on the advice of General Francisco Franco, the state used the Foreign Legion and Moroccan troops rather than Spanish conscripts to crush Asturian resistance. Hundreds were massacred, about 40,000 were imprisoned, and whatever autonomy Catalonia still enjoyed was suspended.[40] The vicious suppression of the October Revolution and the reversal of social and economic reforms created another political crisis in 1935. The left responded by building a Popular Front coalition that defeated the right wing in the 1936 elections. Their platform centered largely on their promise to release the prisoners of 1934.[41]

The Popular Front government can hardly be called radical, and Communists played a very minimal role during the months prior to the outbreak of the civil war. Indeed, the new government had intended merely to continue some of the mild reforms implemented during the first two years of the Second Republic. Needless to say, for the conservatives – especially in the military – the Popular Front still constituted a considerable threat. Soon after the elections, a group of army officers calling themselves the Unión Militar Española insisted that Spain had succumbed to a Communist-controlled government and set out to rid the country of the Red menace, restore law and order, and save the Catholic church from ruin. With support from the CEDA and the Falange, a handful of junior officers stationed in Morocco revolted against the Republican government on July 17 and 18, 1936. The rebels were soon joined by nearly half the Spanish army based in the north, west, and extreme south of the peninsula. General Francisco Franco and General Emilio Mola, the principal leaders of the revolt, expected a swift military victory within a month, but stiff resistance from Loyalist Republican supporters, particularly in Madrid, Barcelona, and most of Catalonia, Valencia, and the Basque provinces, put a wrinkle in their plans. The government provided whatever arms were available to workers' militias, which defended Madrid with tenacity.[42]

The issues that brought on the officers' revolt were undeniably rooted in Spanish history and politics, but the civil war was not merely a national ordeal. Franco's forces might have been easily defeated at the very outset had it not been for German, Italian, and Portuguese intervention. Antonio de Oliveira Salazar, Portugal's dictator since 1926, offered critical support to Spain's insurgents at the outbreak of the war. Portuguese transportation and communications facilities were vital ingredients in the Nationalists' war effort, and at least 18,000 Portuguese men enlisted on Franco's side. The rebels' military might rested largely with the Army of Africa, which was stranded in North Africa at the time of the officers' uprising. Adolph Hitler saved the day for the Nationalist rebels, providing Morocco with twenty Junkers 52 transport planes, which were used to transport the Army of Africa to the mainland. Military and material aid from Hitler and Mussolini clearly shifted the balance of power in the Nationalists' behalf. Even with the support of the Spanish Foreign Legion and the Army of Africa, Franco could have assembled only approximately 250,000 men. Mussolini not only dispatched over 50,000 troops to Spain before February 1937 but also provided the Nationalists with more than 700 aircraft, 6 submarines, 2 destroyers, at least 10,000 automatic weapons, and 950 tanks. Hitler's contribution included some of the most up-to-date antiaircraft guns, aircraft, and tanks, and about 10,000 "advisers," most of whom were specialists in the Condor Legion. Anticipating a larger European conflict, both Hitler and Mussolini used the Spanish Civil War as a testing ground for their modern weapons.[43]

While Franco enjoyed massive assistance from fascist countries, the legally elected Republican government was literally abandoned by the leading Western capitalist nations. The governments of the United States and Britain invoked the argument of nonintervention as an excuse for

23

refusing to sell arms to the Loyalists (yet at the same time Texas Oil Company extended long-term credit to the Nationalists). Their decision to remain "neutral" with respect to Spain has its roots in U.S. and British foreign policy during the 1930s, which consistently viewed the spread of communism as a greater evil than the spread of fascism. Indeed, both countries had shown hostility toward Spain, beginning with the Second Republic, and the Popular Front drew even more hostile opposition. The American and British stand compelled the French Popular Front government, under Socialist Leon Blum, to place a ban on all war materials to Spain in August 1936. While sympathetic to the Republicans, Blum did not wish to ruin relations with Britain, especially since Nazi expansion across the Rhine River threatened France's security. Nonetheless, Blum did try to neutralize outside support for Franco. His efforts eventually led to the nonintervention agreement requiring all foreign powers to withdraw military support and supplies, but Germany and Italy simply ignored the pact.[44] Initially, the USSR abided by the decisions of the nonintervention committee, offering only food and other nonmilitary supplies to the Republic. But when it became evident that Italy and Germany would continue to arm the Nationalists, the Soviet Union and the Comintern came to the defense of Spain. In fact, with the exception of Mexico, the USSR was the only country to offer military and other material aid to the Spanish Republic, although Soviet assistance never equaled Italian and German aid to Franco.[45]

Thus, the conflict that had been brewing for decades between workers and employers, landlords and peasants, regionalists and centralists, anticlericalists and the Catholic church, the army and the state, conservatives and radicals, suddenly became a grand international struggle against the rise of fascism in Europe. The Comintern called for volunteers throughout the world to make Spain "the grave of European fascism." Altogether, an estimated 35,000 people from over 50 countries and colonies volunteered for the International Brigades.[46]

The first contingent of U.S. volunteers left New York Harbor on the day after Christmas 1936, aboard the SS *Normandie*, bound for Le Havre, France. Among this first group of 96 were 2 black Communists – Alonzo Watson, an artist from New York, and Edward White of Philadelphia. For Watson, Spain – specifically the battlefields of Jarama – would be his final destination (ironically, he was one of the first African Americans to go to Spain and also the first to die). These volunteers knew full well that their chances of returning home in one piece were slim, yet they continued to come. Within a month, the next few shipments of volunteers included Walter Garland, Oscar Hunter, James Roberson, Tomas Diaz Collado, Oliver Law, and Douglas Roach. By late summer of 1937 nearly 80 black men had arrived in Spain, anxious to confront fascist troops on the battlefield.

Just getting to Spain, these men soon found out, was a battle in and of itself. First, enlisting in the International Brigades was made difficult by bureaucratic hurdles, security screenings, and the Communists' genuine fear that working-class struggles in the United States would suffer if too many Party members volunteered. Some excellent organizers were turned down because they were considered indispensable to the CPUSA and/or the labor movement. In short, the number of willing volunteers from both black and white communities far exceeded the number of participants accepted into the Lincoln Brigade. Besides, few women were allowed to volunteer unless they were part of a medical unit, and none were allowed to fight.

When a volunteer was accepted into the ranks, he still might need to come up with money to purchase equipment. As historian and Lincoln Brigade veteran Arthur Landis notes, "During this period, and in the months to follow, there was to be quite a run in New York [Army-Navy surplus] stores on sheepskin coats, heavy boots, khaki shirts, pants, army blankets, ammunition belts, and any serviceable equipment that could be packed in a simple suitcase." Given the fact that most of the volunteers were industrial workers, many of whom were unemployed, or Works Progress Administration workers, raising money to go to Spain was no easy task.[47]

Once a volunteer obtained a passport and secured passage to France, he or she still faced a difficult ordeal just to get into Spain. The U.S. government not only was prepared to punish volunteers for violating the federal statute of 1818, which made it unlawful for any U.S. citizen to enlist in a foreign army; it also placed restrictions on travel to Spain soon after the State Department discovered that Americans were joining the brigades. After March 4, 1937, all U.S. passports were stamped Not Valid for Travel in Spain. Thus, in order to enter Spain, volunteers had to pass through France and embark upon a treacherous climb over the Pyrenees mountains, whose steep and rugged slopes were a formidable challenge for even the most physically fit. More often than not, the men had to drop their "knapsacks, coats, blankets; anything to lighten the load. They even took off their socks and flung them into the darkness." As if the ascent was not arduous enough, most volunteers had to climb by night in order to avoid being arrested by the French border patrol.[48]

Black men survived the climb and the bureaucratic hurdles with a determination reminiscent of southern slaves struggling to get to Union lines during the American Civil War. In some ways their mission was similar. Spain offered black men what the Union army had offered them over 70 years earlier: guns, ammunition, and an opportunity to fight their oppressors. For Oscar Hunter, the war finally gave him "a chance to at least not have a goddamn cop on a picket line, you know, but that I'd have a gun against a gun." Crawford Morgan felt the same way: "I got a chance to fight [fascism] there with bullets and I went there and fought it with bullets. If I get a chance to fight it with bullets again, I will fight it with bullets again." Walter Garland viewed Spain as a rare and historic opportunity for black men to fight back and regain their manhood: "You know, in a measure, we Negroes who have been in Spain are a great deal luckier than those back in America. Here we have been able to strike back, in a way that hurts, at those who for years have pushed us from pillar to post. I mean this – actually strike back at the counterparts of those who have been grinding us down back home." Of course they were not literally fighting American landlords, policemen, and industrialists on Spanish soil, but like their emancipated ancestors, who saw the entire Confederate army rather than their individual masters as the embodiment of the slave system, these black volunteers regarded Franco, Mussolini, and Hitler as representatives of their oppressors back home.[49]

After crossing the border into Spain, the volunteers were shuttled from the Catalan town of Figueras, through Barcelona and Valencia, and to the International Brigade headquarters at Albacete. There they enjoyed a rare opportunity to shower, received mismatched uniforms and whatever supplies were on hand, filled out questionnaires, and were given assignments based on their previous military experience and special skills. Because virtually all newly arrived volunteers wanted to get into the action, those who received noncombatant assignments were often disappointed. James Yates served in the motor pool; 52-year-old Council Gibson Carter, a native of Carbonville, Utah, apparently too old for combat duty, was assigned to an ambulance, as was Howard University medical student Thaddeus Battle; Kanute Frankson, a black auto worker from Detroit, was appointed chief mechanic at the Auto Park for the International Brigades; and Burt Jackson's knowledge of maps and artistic talent landed him a job as topographer for the Brigade Commissariat. The International Brigades even attracted three black pilots – James Peck, Paul Williams, and Patrick Roosevelt. Their presence in Spain was remarkable in light of the fact that fewer than eight years earlier there had been only five licensed black pilots in the Unites States. Williams was an aviation engineer with considerable flying time, and Peck, who had studied two years at the University of Pittsburgh, learned to fly privately after he was denied entrance to both the Air Corps and Navy flying schools. Both men were among the last American pilots to serve in the Spanish air force, and Peck was decorated for heroism. The third black airman, Patrick Roosevelt, never had the opportunity to fly. His day-to-day confrontation with racism as a commercial pilot in New York led him to the Communist party and to the struggle in Spain. He eventually served in the infantry and lost a leg during a battle in the hills of Sierra Cabals.[50]

Newly arrived volunteers could not help but notice the multinational character of the International Brigades. As soon as they reached Albacete they met volunteers from all over the world, including Germans in the Thaelmann battalion and Italians in the Garibaldi battalion who had fled fascism in their own countries. African-American brigadists whose Pan-African sensibilities contributed to their decision to come to Spain were especially inspired by the presence of Africans and other people of African descent. In addition to a handful of Africans from Spain's colonies, one Ugandan, black volunteers from England and Latin America, and at least five black Cubans who were attached to the 15th Brigade, about a dozen Ethiopians made their way across the Pyrenees to engage Mussolini on a different terrain. Most, like the son of Ras Imru, were the European-educated children of the ruling class. Realizing that Ethiopia was in no position to defeat Italy, he chose to enlist in the People's Army of the Republic as a rank-and-file soldier. "Madrid is not Addis Ababa. There we had nothing but our justified hatred. Here we have guns, tanks, and aeroplanes." Overall, we do not know how many Africans and people of African descent participated in the war, but the presence of a Pan-African force within the International Brigades is a historical landmark in the history of the black world that deserves further examination.[51]

Building a volunteer army among American radicals was no easy task. Most of the recruits had never even shot a gun before coming to Spain, and only a very tiny minority had any military experience. Although the infantry received some training at a base in Tarazona, proper training was impossible with so few weapons, so little ammunition, and so little time. Some recruits had only fired their weapons four or five times before going into battle. To make matters worse, the Russian- and Mexican-made rifles the Loyalists relied on jammed periodically, and few volunteers knew how to remedy the problem. Second, the Communists and independent radicals were unaccustomed to, even disdainful of, military life. The deference that accompanied the salute and the hierarchical relationship between officers and men of lower rank recalled the class system they had grown to hate. Nonetheless, thanks in part to a system of commissars whose purpose was presumably to explain the political significance of important military decisions, and a conscious effort to play down differences by rank, this tension was not nearly as evident among the International Brigades as it was among the Spanish anarchists or combatants in the anti-Stalinist POUM (Workers' Party of Marxist Unification).

The Lincoln battalion had its first and most bitter taste of war in the Jarama Valley in the spring of 1937. At Jarama the poorly trained, poorly equipped American volunteers paid a heavy price for their role in the defense of Madrid. Of the 400 American troops, 127 were killed (including Alonzo Watson), and over 200 were wounded. For the early black volunteers, Jarama was more than a baptism by fire; it was a test of courage and endurance that most passed with flying colors. Oliver Law, who commanded a machine-gun crew under 120 days of heavy fire, was promoted to captain and subsequently rose to the rank of battalion commander, becoming the first African American in history to command a predominantly white military unit. Walter Garland's performance earned him promotions to commander of a machine-gun company and the rank of lieutenant. Two lesser-known black heroes at Jarama were Doug Roach and Oscar Hunter of the Tom Mooney machine-gun company. Roach, a native of Provincetown, Massachusetts, and a graduate of Massachusetts Agricultural College, where he lettered in wrestling and football, was barely five feet tall. Having been a member of the Communist party since 1932, he was among the first volunteers. Together, Roach and Hunter dug trenches and directed a barrage of machine-gun fire at the enemy until their outmoded machine gun became inoperable. "The way Doug and I solved our problem," Hunter later recalled, "was, as people died, we took their rifles . . . we had about ten guns and we just kept loading them and firing them."[52]

The soldiers of the Lincoln Battalion, now under Oliver Law's command, had barely rested up before they were ordered to take part in the Brunete offensive in July. The purpose was to divert Franco's forces from the northern front in order to mitigate pressure on Madrid. The American volunteers were supplemented by fresh arrivals from the States who composed the newly formed George Washington Battalion. Altogether, each of the battalions consisted of about 500 men, including a handful of Canadian, Cuban, and Irish volunteers. Both groups were practically annihilated during the Brunete offensive, however, and the survivors (numbering little more than 250) ended up merging into one battalion as part of the 15th International Brigade. Most of the black recruits at Brunete were injured, including Roach and Garland, and their new commander, Oliver Law, was killed leading an assault up the hills of Villanueva del Pardillo.[53]

The high rate of casualties and the increasing number of wounded men (most of whom recuperated at overcrowded military hospitals perpetually short of supplies) did not deter the flow of American volunteers to Spain. Nor did the horrors of war keep the 15th Brigade out of the critical battles. A month after the Brunete offensive, the Lincoln Brigade fought Franco's forces street by street, house by house, in order to take Quinto and Belchite. During the unbearable winter of 1937-38 they battled both the enemy and the elements in the hills of Teruel until rebel artillery and aerial bombs forced them to retreat to Belchite. When they discovered that Belchite was also under siege they had to endure a longer, more difficult retreat under fire. Among the Lincoln volunteers captured by enemy forces were Edward Johnson and Claude Pringle, two African Americans who, at ages 47 and 44, respectively, were among the oldest at the front. (Coincidentally, both men were born in Virginia, served in World War I, and moved to Ohio, where they became involved in radical politics.) By the time the Lincoln soldiers regrouped at Mora la Nueva in April 1938, their numbers had dwindled from 500 to 100.[54]

African-American volunteers took part in all of these battles, and many distinguished themselves under fire. Commander Milt Wolf witnessed several remarkable instances of black courage at the front: "[Walter] Garland pulling the wounded Leo Kaufman off a hill and himself being wounded in the process, is a scene burned into my memory; him shouting for us to take cover as he lifted the frail Kaufman in his arms, a sniper peppering the exposed crest, bringing Leo safely into the waiting arms of Sanidad and then Walter tying a handkerchief around his own wound and leading us on." In a letter to home, volunteer Leo Gordon praised Milton Herndon for not even hesitating when he was ordered to lead his gun crew "thru a hail of fire up a slope in front of the enemy trenches." Gordon was also awed by Otto Reeves, a black Young Communist League (YCL) organizer from Los Angeles who "rode atop our tanks up to the enemy lines. With a bullet thru his arm, he managed to drag a wounded comrade two kilometers back to a first aid station."[55]

The endless stories of black courage and heroism were told over and over again in letters, speeches, and journalistic observations from the front, which the black press seized upon with enthusiasm. A few white observers from the Unites States were genuinely surprised, for no matter how progressive and antiracist they were, they were raised to believe that cowardice and mental inferiority were part of the Negro's genetic makeup. The performance of black volunteers proved how ridiculous it was for the United States to segregate its armed services and to limit African Americans to noncombat duties. During a tour of the front, black Party member and International Workers' Order secretary Louise Thompson emphasized this point during a radio broadcast from Madrid: "These Negro soldiers are not in the work battalions, as was the case of the Negroes who fought in France during the World War. They occupy any military position for which they are qualified." Although Thompson's remarks are slightly overstated, given the numerous examples of distinguished black combat service in previous U.S. wars,[56] her observations accurately describe the experiences of most African-American servicemen, particularly those who had served in the armed forces before joining the Lincoln Brigade. While visiting the front with her husband, Paul, Eslanda Goode Robeson jotted down a revealing conversation between Oliver Law and a colonel from the U.S. Army who was visiting Spain. The somewhat puzzled colonel asked Law why he was wearing a captain's uniform, to which he responded,

"Because I am a Captain. In America, in your army, I could only rise as high as corporal, but here people feel differently about race and I can rise according to my worth, not according to my color!"[57]

Although Party publications and the black press waged noble propaganda effort, African-American volunteers were not always heroes. Like other soldiers, they exhibited moments of cowardice, fear, and incompetence. Some cracked under pressure, and there is evidence that at least one deserted. Perhaps the least-respected black officer was Harry Haywood, who earned the rank of political commissar largely because he was a leading member of the Communist party. In addition to personal conflicts with commanders of the 15th Brigade, Haywood had had numerous run-ins with other black volunteers during his brief stay in Spain. Although we may never know the details of Haywood's experiences in Spain, his memoirs tell us that his biting criticism of the 15th Brigade's high command was the cause of his difficulties and the reason for his early withdrawal. Some of his black comrades tell a different story, however. Mississippi-born Communist and brigade member Eluard Luchell McDaniels had a clear image of Haywood in Spain: "He spent most of his time around women and dressed up and stuff like that." Oscar Hunter will never forget the day Haywood came to Jarama "with a pretty little suit on." When enemy fire became too heavy, "he got the hell out of there real quick . . . he was a real mess for us blacks up there." A few weeks after Haywood returned to the Unites States, Hunter and his comrades were dumbfounded when they received the most recent *Daily Worker* and discovered a photograph of Haywood at "Madison Square Garden, dressed up in this natty goddamn uniform. You should have heard the roar all along that goddamn line."[58]

Like their white compatriots, black troops at the front did not always follow the rules. Occasionally they faced charges of insubordination, but in most instances their tiny acts of rebellion were ad hoc responses to helpless situations and occasionally made for some light-hearted moments. Black volunteers sometimes relied on cunning and wit to get themselves out of a jam – an aproach that some might argue had been learned from their enslaved ancestors. Leo Gordon described with admiration and humor Milton Herndon's problem-solving abilities when food and supplies were running low:

> There's a Negro section leader in my company who is very popular. Very intelligent . . . and a born leader. Once while marching down a road we passed a vineyard. All the fellows looked at the grapes longingly but in vain. There are certain restrictions about picking fruit. Sort of protect property if you know what I mean. Coming back we walked thru the same field. Suddenly Milt blew his whistle – an airplane signal! The entire mob dived into the bushes out of sight. Presently we heard the

recall signal. Everybody emerged grinning widely – with peculiar bumps protruding out of their shirts.

In a similar fashion, Doug Roach, along with three other machine gunners, decided to "organize" a horse during the Brunete offensive. When Commissar Steve Nelson discovered the horse and found out how it had been obtained, he administered a well-deserved tongue-lashing: "Don't you know this is no way to act in a Republican army – stealing horses?" The culprits apologized, but kept the horse.[59]

The Lincoln volunteers went to Spain exclusively to fight Fascists, but very few could have remained oblivious to the workers' and peasants' revolution taking place around them. Anarchists, POUMists, and rank-and-file trade-union members had begun to seize land, run factories by council, dismantle churches, and reorganize local politics – in short, they were attempting to revolutionize Spanish society in the midst of war. The Communist party of Spain, the Comintern, and the majority of Spanish Socialists and liberals, on the other hand, decided that the military conflict had to take precedence over the revolution. The only way to win, they argued, was to defend the bourgeois republic and fight a very conventional war. Indeed, on a few occasions the Loyalist government suppressed the revolutionary process outright.[60] African-American volunteers generally supported the "war first" policy, but they were also impressed with the social and economic transformations taking place around them, particularly in the Spanish countryside. They had come to Spain armed with an unusually broad interpretation of fascism that included all forms of racist and class oppression. The system of sharecropping and tenant farming, for example, was often described as fascist, since it not only exploited rural folk economically but also denied southern blacks their civil rights and used extralegal violence to punish those who stepped out of line. Walter Garland once said, "We can't forget for one minute that the oppression of the Negro is nothing more than a very concrete form, the clearest expression, of fascism. . . . In other words, we saw in Spain . . . those who chain us in America to cotton fields and brooms." The analogy was extended to the Deep South, in particular. After reading about a lynching in the *Daily Worker* during a lull in the fighting, one American volunteer observed, "Hitler uses bombs to destroy the people of Spain; Our Dixie Hitlers use rope."[61]

Even if a black volunteer knew virtually nothing about the revolution taking place around him, he certainly noticed the difference in the way he was treated by the Spanish people. There were no Jim Crow laws or racial barriers, or even restrictions on dating Spanish women. Visiting celebrities Paul Robeson and Langston Hughes repeatedly remarked on how the Spanish "lack all sense of color prejudice." "Spain was the first time in my life," recalled company sergeant Tom Page, "I was treated as a person. . . . I was a man! A person!" Having grown up in the South, Crawford Morgan was not used to living in a country where practically everyone he came in contact with treated him as an equal: "I felt like a human being, like a man. People didn't look at me with hatred in their eyes because I was black, and I wasn't refused this or refused that, because I was black." Nevertheless, while Spaniards might not have looked with hatred, they did *look*, especially if one had dark skin. African Americans were sometimes treated as curiosities. Luchell McDaniels remembers always being "the center of attraction," and whenever Doug Roach entered a Spanish village, "the children would crowd around [him], attracted by his dark color."[62]

That African Americans were treated better in Spain than they were back home does not mean that Spaniards were free of racism. What many black Lincoln volunteers failed to realize was that the respect and admiration bestowed upon them had more to do with their status as volunteers than anything else. The same Spanish Loyalists felt utter hatred for the Moroccans fighting on Franco's side – a hatred whose roots go back at least a millenium. All Spanish schoolchildren learned about the age of "Moorish domination," when Muslims from North Africa ruled Spain from the eighth century until the fifteenth century. Only the Christian crusades, they were taught, had saved Spain and the rest of Europe from this heathen menace to civilization. Moreover, Spanish society had been shaped immeasurably by the transatlantic slave trade, the exploitation of black labor on plantations in the so-called New World, colonialism in Africa, and the recent Rif wars. Race, as well as a thousand years of history, undeniably complicated the way in which Republican Spain viewed Franco's Army of Africa. According to historian Allen Guttman, North African troops fighting for Franco were "usually shown in Loyalist posters as very black," a distortion that exaggerated the image of the Moors as an evil race of people. In fact, a tiny minority within the African-American community was hesitant to support the Republic because Loyalist propaganda directed at North African troops was so venomous that it was interpreted as racism pure and simple. Given these racial dynamics, being black in Spain complicated matters. On numerous occasions African Americans were shot at by Loyalists who had mistaken them for Moors. Eluard Luchell McDaniels had to take precautions in certain sections of Spain in order to defuse any hostility from the crowd: "When we went in a town, I was called upon to make a speech . . . so they could see me. So I'm not a Moor. Black yes, Moor no. I'm a friend of theirs."[63]

Franco's use of Moroccan troops was disheartening to black volunteers whose Pan-Africanist and pro-Ethiopian sentiments brought them to Spain in the first place. Why would their darker brethren, laboring under the yoke of colonial oppression, fight on behalf of the Fascists? Black novelist Richard Wright summed it up this way: "The fascists have duped and defrauded a terribly exploited people." Langston Hughes, who probably devoted more energy to understanding the role of North Africans in the conflict than any other contemporary observer, agreed with Wright and further noted the irony of Franco's sending Muslim troops·on a crusade to rid Christian Spain of communism. Yet he was most interested in the dilemma of blacks fighting on both sides. In fact, part of his rationale for going to Spain as a correspondent was to explore this relationship: "I knew that Spain once belonged to the Moors, a colored people ranging from light dark to dark white. Now the Moors have come again to Spain with the fascist armies as cannon fodder for Franco. But on the loyalist side, there are many Negroes of various nationalities in the International Brigades. I want to write about both Moors and Negroes." Although his investigative reporting offered more questions than answers, Hughes beautifully captured the confusion many black brigadists felt in a poem entitled "Letter From Spain":

We captured a wounded Moor today.
He was just as dark as me.
I said, Boy, what you been doin' here
Fightin' against the free? . . .

Of course, the problem was much more complicated. Some radicals called on the Republican government to grant independence to North Africans under Spanish rule, arguing that such a measure was not only politically correct but would in effect undercut Franco's forces. However, Prime Minister Largo Caballero and his successor, Juan Negrin, would not even consider it. On the contrary, the Caballero government went so far as to offer territorial concessions to France and Britain in exchange for Western support. "Its desire not to offend the Western powers," wrote historians Pierre Broue and Emile Temime, "now led it deliberately to renounce, not only the principle of self-determination for colonial peoples, but also a real chance to strike at the heart of Franco's power." The Communist party of Spain, while supporting this policy, tried to improve relations by helping to bring about the Hispano-Moroccan Anti-Fascist Association. Its purpose was to win North African support for the Republic and to educate Spaniards about racism and colonial oppression, but it failed miserably to win large numbers of Moroccans to the Republican side.[64]

While African-American volunteers rarely experienced discrimination from their Spanish hosts, they had occasional bouts with racism within their own ranks. During their visit to the front, Paul and Eslanda Robeson were told by a white officer in the Lincoln Battalion that blacks had "quite a time at first with some of the southern white Americans and the British on this Negro question . . . the really difficult ones [are] the British. They refuse to eat in dining rooms with the Negroes, etc., and have to be drastically educated, because neither the Spaniards nor the International Brigade will tolerate such heresy."[65]

This sort of blatant racist behavior was very rare, however. The majority of white volunteers had come out of movements in which racism was simply not tolerated. But American volunteers, white as well as black, tended to overestimate the level of interethnic harmony and cultural integration within the International Brigades. The black Lincoln volunteers always remained a very small minority within their own battalion and a minuscule presence among tens of thousands of International brigadists and millions of Spaniards. Though they certainly felt a strong sense of camaraderie with other Lincoln soldiers, the black volunteers occasionally felt a tinge of alienation from the social and cultural life of the brigade. James Yates's ruminations on life as a volunteer, though not intended to illustrate the more subtle side of cultural isolation, are revealing nonetheless. He recalls, for example, the joy of "humming tunes I did not know" during group singing. Perhaps there is significance in the fact that as black sergeant Joe Taylor was being carried away on a stretcher with a bullet lodged in his shoulder, he "hummed an old Negro folksong, 'The Preacher Went Down to the River to Pray.' " Even more revealing is Yates's recollection of his experience as a driver for Ernest Hemingway and two other white journalists, from Britain and the United States, respectively. These three men conversed among themselves about the war and never thought to ask Yates, a participant, his opinion.

Volunteer Ramon Durem probably understood this sort of invisibility better than anyone. A native of Seattle, Washington, born of mixed parentage, Durem was 14 years old when he dropped out of school and ran away from home. After a brief stint in the U.S. Navy, Durem became involved in a number of left-wing causes (he probably joined the Communist party) and at 22 boarded the SS *Aquitania,* bound for Spain. Durem's skin color and features enhanced his invisibility – he easily passed for white. In a preface to a collection of his poems, written 25 years after he left for Spain, he tried to explain how his "whiteness" gave him a unique insight into racism: "Since I was ten years old I have been conscious of the venality, hypocrisy, and viciousness of the criminal system in the United States, built on racial hatred. I am descended from a mixed family, but my appearance is that of a white man. For this reason white people in the United States (and they are all racists in varying degrees) talk and act very freely in front of me, thus giving me an insight into their mentality seldom achieved by a dark negro who puts them on their guard." One cannot help but wonder if Durem was treated any differently by his comrades in the International Brigades.[66]

Although we know virtually nothing about the social and cultural life of black volunteers, it is possible that they developed a special sense of camaraderie among themselves, alongside their strong feelings of international solidarity. As we have seen, most black volunteers came out of a communist/nationalist political culture that discouraged separatism on the one hand, but encouraged members to gravitate toward issues affecting the African-American community and to anchor themselves in local community institutions. If such a community existed in Spain, few black volunteers would have admitted it; indeed, few would have been conscious of this kind of cultural bonding. It is fitting, even ironic, that the people who recognized a sense of community among African-American volunteers were often the individuals who felt alienated from such a community. Eluard Luchell McDaniels, for instance, felt like an outsider in relation to other black Lincoln soldiers. Although he was a preacher's son born in Lumberton, Mississippi, he ran away from home at a very young age (seven, he claims) and was raised in California by radical photographer Consuela Kanaga, who literally discovered him roaming along the beach. "I hadn't been used to associating with too many Negroes," McDaniels admitted. When he began associating with black brigadists in Spain he "seemed a little out of place," since he lacked "all the habits that the rest of them have. . . . I couldn't . . . sound like a Negro."[67]

If McDaniels felt out of place among his fellow African Americans, how did African Americans feel among their white fellow Americans, particularly in a social setting? For that matter, how comfortable were they with white European International brigadists for whom language served as a major barrier? To what extent were they treated as objects (i.e., representatives of a race and examples of an ideal) as opposed to thinking, feeling subjects? Only future scholarship will answer these and other questions about the lives of black Lincoln Brigade members. Such answers are crucial, since African Americans did not necessarily take the same road to Spain as their white comrades. And as we shall see, neither did they take the same road home.

4

By the spring of 1938 the collapse of the Aragon front and the ensuing nightmare of a retreat left the Lincoln Brigade in a shambles. "They were unshaven and filthy," writes historian Robert Rosenstone, "their clothes torn, their bodies full of lice, their feet swollen and bloodstained. Command had broken down, and for several days the Americans were less a military unit than a mob of homeless men." The combined forces of Mussolini, Hitler, and Franco had overwhelmed the Republican armies. The Lincoln Brigade alone had lost 70 percent of its men to fatal wounds and

Franco's prisons, and a few to desertion. Meanwhile, in March, France and England watched silently as Hitler's tanks rolled into Austria and formally annexed it to the German Reich. By this time, most Lincoln volunteers believed that defeat was inevitable. Their wounds, fatigue, and hunger pangs told them that the fascist forces were militarily superior and that the inaction of Western powers had sentenced the Spanish Republic to death. Except for the most recent arrivals and a handful of zealots, the Lincoln brigadists longed to go home.[68]

The slow collapse of the Republic was not entirely due to Western indifference. Internal problems had begun to weaken the government as early as May 1937. At that time, Prime Minister Largo Caballero had been forced to resign for refusing to outlaw the POUM even after some of its members, along with militants from the Confederación Nacional de Trabajo (CNT), rose up against the Republican government in Barcelona. Juan Negrin, a moderate Socialist and a staunch supporter of the "war first" policy, became prime minister. Meanwhile SIM (Servicio de Investigación Militar) – literally a political police force within the army – set out to crush anyone who disrupted the war effort. The new regime of "national unity" even alienated some of the Republic's most important supporters when it began to encroach on Catalan autonomy. By the winter of 1937 essential food and supplies began to dry up in the Republican zone, and the number of desertions increased dramatically.[69]

It was under these taxing circumstances that the Republic launched its last offensive across the Ebro River on July 25, 1938. This major sweep into Nationalist territory was supposed to relieve pressure on Valencia. But after early Loyalist successes, Franco's forces followed up with a ferocious counterattack and turned back the offensive.

Soon rumors began to circulate among the troops that the International Brigades were going to be withdrawn. The rumors turned out to be true. On September 21, as Franco's troops transformed the Loyalist advance into the Ebro defensive, Prime Minister Juan Negrin announced before the League of Nations that the Spanish government would withdraw all foreign volunteers. Negrin had hoped that international pressure might force Franco to withdraw Italian and German troops and compel members of the Nonintervention Committee to lift the embargo on war materials. Negrin's act of diplomatic goodwill was of no avail, however: nine days later the French and British signed the Munich agreement, giving Hitler the green light to invade Czechoslovakia. In light of this act of appeasement to Hitler, few could still have expected the West to defend Spain. On December 23, 1938, Franco invaded Catalonia, crushing the Republican army in the process. Barcelona fell on January 26, 1939, and two months later a coup led by Republican Colonel Lopez Casado and moderate Socialist Julian Besteiro gave General Francisco Franco what he wanted – an unconditional surrender.[70]

Those who survived the Ebro offensive and could still walk received an emotional farewell from the Spanish people on October 29, 1938. They marched through the streets of Barcelona in the crisp autumn weather with mixed emotions, saddened by the defeat, burdened with a guilt-laden sense of abandonment, and ecstatic that they were finally going home. By December most of the Americans were well on their way, except for a handful still caught behind enemy lines, rotting in Franco's prisons. Among the last group of Lincoln volunteers to make it back to the states were four African Americans: Kansas native Tom Brown and three Ohio residents, Abe Lewis, Claude Pringle, and Edward Johnson. Lewis arrived home in early February 1939, but Brown, Pringle, and Johnson were not released from Franco's prisons until April of that year. Otherwise, most of the black volunteers either found themselves on the SS *Paris* or the SS *Ausonia*, bound for home in time for Christmas.[71]

As these men gathered in small groups on deck, with the wind off the Atlantic Ocean striking them with the reality of their return, we can only wonder what was going on in their minds. Of course they had grown weary of life in the trenches and were anxious to see loved ones, sleep in a warm bed, communicate in a language they knew, and enjoy some down-home cuisine. But they were coming back to second-class citizenship, racial epithets, Jim Crow lines, and liberal condescension. This struggle against fascism hadn't changed America, and they knew it. Several African-American volunteers showed little interest in returning home. War hero Tom Page "hated to come back [to the United States]." Luchell McDaniels wrote from the front, "I would rather die here than be slaved any more." Alpheus Prowell, who *did* die in Spain, had once written, "I was miserable in L.A. Here I'm happy."[72]

Most of the returning black veterans probably had the same immediate experience as James Yates – a war hero's welcome from the American Left, followed by a slap in the face by American racists. On his first night home in New York, buoyed by the kisses and handshakes he received at the docks, Yates was denied a room at the hotel his comrades had planned to stay in. Although the white veterans checked in without a problem, when Yates stood before the registrar, the clerk simply looked at him and said "No Vacancy": "Inwardly I winced. So soon? I had hardly left the boat and here it was. After having experienced being welcomed in cafes and hotels in Spain and France, I was doubly shocked to be hit so quickly. The pain went as deeply as any bullet could have done [*sic*]. I had the dizzy feeling I was back in the trenches again. But this was another front. I was home." Needless to say, his comrades promptly gave up their accommodations and moved on.[73]

The transition to civilian life was not easy for the veterans, black or white. Even before touching U.S. soil, many Lincoln brigadists were harassed by the FBI and had their passport privileges revoked. Furthermore, they came home in dire need of medical attention, a place to stay, and employment of some kind. By 1939 the United States was still in the throes of the Depression, and jobs were scarce. Although a number of black veterans resumed their activities on behalf of the Communist party, very few (e.g., Harry Haywood) could expect sufficient financial support from the Party. In lieu of a Veterans Administration, they turned to the newly created Friends of the Abraham Lincoln Brigade. Composed of ex-Lincoln soldiers and their supporters, the FALB raised money to bring some volunteers back to the States, provided small stipends to unemployed veterans during the winter of 1938-39, paid medical bills, and assisted in any way it could to rehabilitate returning veterans. The FALB, for example, provided Crawford Morgan with a pair of eyeglasses and a new suit, and paid for a medical examination and minor dental work. Oscar Hunter was particularly useful to the FALB by making arrangements with the Cook County Hospital in Chicago to provide beds for incoming wounded.[74]

Nevertheless, despite personal hardships, most black veterans retained their enthusiasm for the "good fight." They returned to the burgeoning trade union movement, organized WPA workers, participated in antifascist demonstrations, and spoke to anyone who would listen about the Spanish tragedy. This sort of collective action led to the formation of the Veterans of the Abraham Lincoln Brigade (VALB). More than a radical version of the American Legion, the VALB was conceived as an activist organization to protest fascism and other forms of injustice in the United States as well as in the rest of the world. But because the VALB was labeled a communist front, it also had to fight for its very existence. It not only made Congressman Martin Dies's Un-American Activities hit list but also came under attack from liberals and anti-Stalinist leftists when the veterans joined the Communist party in supporting the Nazi-Soviet Pact. Signed in August 1939, this nonagression pact cleared the way for the Nazi invasion of Poland and simultaneously enabled Russia to invade Finland. Almost overnight, Spanish Civil War veterans who had supported the agreement dropped the old antifascist slogans and launched a campaign to keep America out of the "imperialist war." The Soviets' action was undoubtedly embarrassing and disheartening, but the veterans' own experiences in Spain indicated that had Germany invaded the Soviet Union, the Western capitalist nations would have done nothing; indeed, they would have applauded. Stalin's compromise could not be compared with the Munich agreement or the Nonintervention Commission, they argued, since he at least tried to fight fascism on Spanish soil.[75]

The VALB's political isolation came to an end when Germany invaded the Soviet Union, thus breaking the nonaggression pact. Three years after returning from Spain, most of the physically able veterans were anxious to engage the Fascists once again in World War II. Soon after Japan's attack on Pearl Harbor, VALB Executive Secretary Jack Bjoze wrote President Franklin Roosevelt and offered the services of the Lincoln Brigade as a unit of experienced combatants. Roosevelt declined the offer, of course, but many veterans enlisted in the armed forces anyway. Within a few months an estimated 500 were back in uniform. Despite their combat experience and willingness to put their lives on the line, some of these "premature antifascists" were hounded by military intelligence and punished by their superior officers because they had gone to Spain.

Black Lincoln veterans who enlisted faced the double burden of regular military racism as well as anticommunist persecution. All branches of the U.S. armed services enforced racial segregation, denied African Americans combat duty until 1944, relegated black servicemen and women to menial tasks, and banned black newspapers from military posts until 1943, to name but a few of the federally sanctioned indignities with which black soldiers had to live. To add insult to injury, physical and verbal assaults by racist white servicemen were almost commonplace, and in several instances black soldiers in the United States were treated worse than German and Italian war prisoners.

Lincoln veteran James Peck, an experienced pilot who had fought Hitler's Luftwaffe in Spanish skies, offered his services to the U.S. Army Air Corps. He was not only turned down for combat duty but rejected as a possible instructor at the segregated aviation-training program for black cadets at Tuskegee, despite the fact that he was better qualified than many of the other instructors. Crawford Morgan, who had reached the rank of sergeant in the U.S. Army, witnessed racism and violence against black soldiers firsthand. "Not only were we Jim Crowed . . . but all of the nasty jobs, all of the worst jobs were handed to the majority of the Negroes." While stationed in Mississippi, he complained, "the 'Crackers' shot us up, and never did the Government do nothing about it." Is it possible that his efforts to make the government do something about conditions in the army could have led to Morgan's demotion to corporal? Was he regarded as a greater threat than other black soldiers because of his Spanish Civil War background? James Yates enlisted in the Signal Corps, but for some strange reason he was pulled from his unit just before they were about to go overseas. He was then placed "in charge of a unit doing dirty work for the medics" at Bushnell Hospital in Utah. Soon thereafter, the Spanish Civil War veteran contracted an infection during a routine tooth extraction and had to be hospitalized for three months. He accepted an honorable discharge and finished out the war as a civilian.[76]

The veterans who could not get into the military or who were discharged early continued their fight at home. Black opposition in particular had intensified during the war. African Americans were entering the industrial labor force in greater numbers; black union membership rose from 150,000 in 1935 to 1.2 million by 1945. Civil rights organizations recruited tens of thousands of new members (the NAACP, for example, had grown tenfold during the war), and black leadership had adopted an uncompromising stance vis-à-vis the war effort, insisting on a "double victory" against racism at home and fascism abroad. In short, black working-class militancy was on the rise again, and it seemed as if A. Phillip Randolph's March on Washington Movement was the catalyst. Although the march never actually took place, Randolph had threatened to lead 100,000 black people to the nation's capitol unless Roosevelt issued an executive order eliminating racial discrimination in hiring and segregation in the armed services. Randolph accepted a compromise, however, that led to the formation of the Fair Employment Practice Committee, though the armed forces continued to segregate its troops.

Ironically, wartime black militancy and the Double V slogan created a dilemma for black Lincoln Brigade veterans who were still members of, or close to, the Communist party. The Party essentially opposed the Double V campaign, arguing that too much black militancy could undermine the war effort. Yet the Party's "war first" policy did not mean giving up the black struggle entirely. Rank-and-file Communists as well as Lincoln veterans continued to fight on the civil rights front throughout the war. In fact, the VALB was at the forefront of a campaign to create a mixed combat unit to be known as the Crispus Attucks Brigade, and Adam Clayton Powell, Jr., frequently pointed to the Lincoln Brigade as an example par excellence of a successful integrated military unit. Nevertheless, in spite of these measures, the Party's opposition to the Double V slogan left many African Americans feeling that it had abandoned them for the sake of the war.[77]

The VALB's decision to adopt the policy that the war take precedence over the "Negro revolution" probably embittered a few of the more nationalist-inclined black veterans. This seems to be the case with Ramon Durem, who had once "hoped that by building left-wing organizations without respect of colour, we could do away with the rank injustice in the United States. At the end of World War Two, I discovered that even the white radicals were not interested in a radical solution to the Negro Question." Durem's shift to black nationalism does not seem to have dampened the internationalist outlook that had brought many black radicals to Spain in the first place, though for him internationalism was limited to Third World solidarity. As early as 1962 he had anticipated the rise of urban black nationalism as "part of the general world colonial revolution."[78] His poem "Hipping the hip" is even more telling. A critique of the Beat Gener-

ation and its false claim to radicalism, the poem suggests looking to Africa
and China for possible alternatives:

Juice
is no use
and H
don't pay

I guess revolution
is the only way

Blues - is a tear
bop - a fear
of reality.
There's no place to hide
in a horn

Chinese may be lame
but they ain't tame

Mau Mau only got a five-tone scale
but when it comes to Freedom, Jim -
they wail!

dig?[79]

Oscar Hunter, who was kept out of the war because of hypertension,
had his own problems with the Party over the issue of race. During the
immediate postwar period, Hunter became wedded to the underground
world of bebop, the music and counterculture that represented the latest
in black urban militancy. His attachment to this cultural world – a world
with which few white Communists were familiar – eventually led to his
break with the Party. One Chicago club owner, whom Hunter claimed was
a gangster, occasionally helped him raise money for the Party by having
small jazz concerts and running gambling games. Hunter's alleged gangster
friend never knew "what the hell I was up to but that there was a lot of
good music and a lot of beautiful broads. . . . But that didn't satisfy the
party." He eventually faced disciplinary action by the Party as a result of
his lifestyle, but quit before the Chicago cadre had a chance to expel
him.[80]

Most black veterans, however, remained staunch supporters of the
VALB and held fast to their radical convictions, even at the height of
McCarthyite repression. Some veterans were dismissed from their jobs
because of their politics, hounded by the FBI, and barred from unions
they had helped to build. Very few of the Lincoln veterans subpoenaed by
the House Un-American Activities Committee (HUAC), and later by the
Subversive Activities Control Board (SACB), willingly cooperated with the
government. Indeed, not one single black Lincoln veteran who was

brought before the HUAC or the SACB turned informant. Some, like black Philadelphia Communist Sterling Rochester, refused to answer almost every question. Others, such as Crawford Morgan and Admiral Kilpatrick, skillfuly turned their inquisitions into a forum for indicting U.S. foreign policy abroad and domestic racism at home. When asked by the SACB what the VALB's policy was with respect to U.S. recognition of Franco, Crawford had this to say: "Well, we thought it was one of the most terrible things our government had ever done for the simple reason [that] we were the first Americans that felt fascism and later on a great section of the world was fighting it, including America. Thousands of our sons and daughters died over on the other side fighting fascism, and now our government is embracing it, and because we don't want to embrace it with them they are persecuting us for it."

As a former Wobblie who had survived the Palmer raids in 1919, Admiral Kilpatrick was no neophyte when it came to government repression. "In the class struggle," he reflected, "you can't stay in it when it's good and jump out and leave it when it's bad. You go all the way." When he testified before the HUAC, he neither cooperated with the committee nor took the First or Fifth amendments. "I didn't take no Fifth Amendment. What the hell am I going to take the Fifth? They knew who I was, I didn't give a damn. . . . I've been trying to take the 13th, 14th, and 15th Amendment all my damn life and got nowhere."[81]

Black veterans emerged from the postwar Red scare as militant and committed as ever, although the struggles they chose to engage in were as diverse as they were. Abe Lewis remained a leading Communist in Cleveland until his untimely death in 1949. Together, Burt Jackson and Walter Garland formed the United Negro Allied Veterans of America and fought tirelessly for the rights of African-American vets. James Yates was elected president of the Greenwich Village-Chelsea chapter of the NAACP during the early 1960s and raised money for civil rights activists in Mississippi. Oscar Hunter joined most of the surviving veterans in demonstrating against the Vietnam War. Ramon Durem became a militant nationalist whose ideas, articulated in poetry published in the late 1940s and early 1950s, anticipated positions Malcolm X would espouse nearly a decade later. Like Malcolm, Durem had forseen the black power movement of the late 1960s, but he did not live long enough to see the end result. He died of cancer on December 17, 1963. Not surprisingly, Admiral Kilpatrick remained a committed Marxist–so committed that he insists he was expelled from the CPUSA "because I wasn't going to go along with the fact [that] now all of a sudden you can build a Party with all classes." His problems with Party leadership had begun during the Popular Front. The very idea that the Party "was carrying on the traditions of Lincoln, Jefferson, and Douglass," in Kilpatrick's opinion, was "a lot of bull."[82]

That these men turned out to be long-distance runners in the struggle against racism and injustice has a lot to do with their experiences in Spain. It was one of the few places on earth where black and white, Jew and gentile could use guns to battle forces that threatened their individual and collective security, though they paid a dear price for the opportunity. More important, the particular historical road that African Americans had traveled before arriving on Spanish soil gave them a unique vantage point. Black Lincoln volunteers knew class oppression and racism, shared with one another a dual identity rooted in an African and an American past, and were willing to put their lives on the line in Spain partly to revenge the rape of Ethiopia. Of course, not all the African-American veterans were Communists, but all accepted the Communists' vision of internationalism and interracial unity – a vision that allowed them to retain their nationalism and to transcend it. Volunteers like Oscar Hunter, Oliver Law, James Yates, Walter Garland, and Salaria Kee were fighting not simply *the* "good fight" but several "good fights" rolled into one. Like Crispus Attucks in the American Revolution or Martin Delany in the American Civil War, African Americans in the Lincoln Brigade believed that their people's struggles were inextricably intertwined with the larger conflict. Neither patriotism nor a desire to save the Union brought former slaves and the sons of slaves into the Union Army; rather, they put their lives on the line with the intention of destroying the system of slavery once and for all.

But this is where the analogy ends. Whereas black Union troops fought in segregated units under white command, often accompanied by indifferent or confused white men, the black Lincoln volunteer waged war in an army that did not divide troops by skin color, whose members shared for the most part a singularity of purpose, and whose principal commander for a brief time was a black man from Southside Chicago. The documents in this volume begin to tell this story in the words of the participants. Theirs is an important chapter in American history that must be examined, not merely to celebrate what was undeniably an heroic past but also to enhance our understanding of American radicalism during the 1930s. The materials gathered herein should open new doors to the social and cultural history of the Abraham Lincoln Brigade, the contested meanings of nationalism and internationalism, the very elusive world of African-American radical consciousness, and the ways in which race, class, and culture shaped the development of the American Left.

NOTES

1. Soon after the Brunete offensive, the two U.S. battalions merged.

2. Steve Nelson, *The Volunteers* (New York: Masses and Mainstream, 1953), 151; *Chicago Tribune*, December 7, 1987; *In These Times*, December 9, 1987.

3. The literature on the International Brigades is voluminous on both the Left and Right. See, for example, Arthur Landis, *The Abraham Lincoln Brigade* (New York: Citadel Press, 1967); Robert Rosenstone, *Crusade of the Left: The Lincoln Battalion in the Spanish Civil War* (Lanham, Md.: University Press of America, 1980); Marc Crawford and William Katz, *The Lincoln Brigade* (New York, 1989); Alan Guttman, *The Wound in the Heart: America and the Spanish Civil War* (New York: Free Press, 1962); Soviet War Veterans' Committee, *International Solidarity with the Spanish Republic, 1936-1939* (Moscow: Progress Publishers, 1975); E. H. Carr, *The Comintern and the Spanish Civil War*, ed. Tamara Deutscher (New York: Pantheon, 1984); and Vincent Brome, *The International Brigades: Spain, 1936-1939* (Morrow, 1966). More conservative interpretations include R. Dan Richardson, *Comintern Army: The International Brigades and the Spanish Civil War* (Lexington: University Press of Kentucky, 1982); Cecil Eby, *Between the Bullet and the Lie: American Volunteers in the Spanish Civil War* (New York: Holt, Rinehart and Winston, 1969); and David T. Cattell, *Communism and the Spanish Civil War* (Berkeley: University of California Press, 1955). The best film on the subject is Noel Buckner, Mary Dore, and Sam Sills's *The Good Fight: The Abraham Lincoln Brigade in the Spanish Civil War* (1984), distributed by First Run Features and Kino International. Important memoirs of participants, oral histories, and documentary collections include Alvah Bessie, *Men in Battle: The Story of Americans in Spain* (1939; reprint New York: VALB, 1954; San Francisco: Chandler and Sharp, 1975); Alvah Bessie and Albert Prago, eds., *Our Fight: Writings by Veterans of the Abraham Lincoln Brigade: Spain, 1936-1939* (New York: Monthly Review Press, 1987); Nelson, *The Volunteers*; Steve Nelson, James R. Barrett, and Rob Ruck, *Steve Nelson: American Radical* (Pittsburgh: University of Pittsburgh Press, 1981), 183-239; Edwin Rolfe, *The Lincoln Battalion: The Story of the Americans Who Fought in Spain in the International Brigades* (1939; reprint, New York: VALB, 1974); Louis Fischer, *Men and Politics* (New York: Duell, Sloan and Pearce, 1941); and Joe North, *Men in the Ranks* (New York: International Publishers, 1939). John Gerassi's collection of oral histories, *The Premature Antifascists: North American Volunteers in the Spanish Civil War, 1936-1939: An Oral History* (New York: Praeger, 1986), is suspect. The excerpts he includes in the book do not always match the transcribed interviews he claims to have used, which are now at the Abraham Lincoln Brigade Archives at Brandeis University. In many cases, the published statements have been altered significantly from the original transcript. Besides, many of the stories included in the volume contradict evidence from other accounts, which apparently were not consulted or considered.

4. Langston Hughes, *I Wonder as I Wander* (New York: Holt, Rinehart and Winston, 1956), 354. For a sampling of work on African Americans and the Italo-Ethiopian conflict, see footnotes 33 and 34.

5. Over one-third of the volunteers were Jewish. Although most Jews who volunteered were assimilationist or nonreligious, it has been suggested that their decision to fight in Spain was inspired in part by Hitler's genocidal war against Jews in Germany. See Albert Prago, "Jews in the International Brigades," in Bessie and Prago, *Our Fight*, 94-103.

6. See, for example, Carole Marks, *Farewell – We're Good and Gone: The Great Black Migration* (Bloomington: Indiana University Press, 1989); Florette Henri, *Black Migration Movement North, 1900-1920: The Road from Myth to Man* (Garden City, N.J.: Anchor Press/Doubleday, 1976); and Philip Foner, *Organized Labor and the Black Worker* (New York: International Publishers, 1982), 129-57. For a discussion of the attitudes of returning black veterans, see Herbert Shapiro, *White Violence and Black Response: From Reconstruction to Montgomery* (Amherst: University of Massachusetts Press, 1988), 145-48; William Tuttle, Jr., *Race Riot: Chicago in the Red Summer of 1919* (New York: Atheneum, 1970), 216-41; Robert W. Mullen, *Blacks in America's Wars: The Shift in Attitudes from the Revolutionary War to Vietnam* (New York: Monad Press/Pathfinder, 1973), 42-50; and Robert V. Haynes, *A Nightmare of Violence: The Houston Riot of 1917* (Baton Rouge: Louisiana State University Press, 1976).

7. See especially Robert Hill's introduction to *The Marcus Garvey and Universal Negro Improvement Association Papers*, ed. Robert A. Hill, vol. 3 (Berkeley: University of California Press, 1984); Judith Stein, *The World of Marcus Garvey: Race and Class in Modern Society* (Baton Rouge: Louisiana State University Press, 1986); Theodore Vincent, *Black Power and the Garvey Movement* (San Francisco: Ramparts Press, 1972), 101-36; Robert A. Hill, "The First England Years and After, 1912-1916," in *Marcus Garvey and the Vision of Africa*, ed. John Henrik Clarke (New York: Vintage Books, 1974), 38-70.

8. Carl Offord, "Cyril Briggs and the African Blood Brotherhood," (WPA Writers' Project, no. 1), Schomburg Collection, New York Public Library; *Crusader* 2, no. 2 (October 1919): 27; "Program of the African Blood Brotherhood," *Communist Review* (London), April 1922, 449-54; Mark Solomon, "Red and Black: Negroes and Communism, 1929-1932" (Ph.D. diss., Harvard University, 1972), 80-83. For more on the ABB, see Haywood, *Black Bolshevik*, 122-30; Mark Naison, *Communists in Harlem During the Depression* (Urbana: University of Illinois Press, 1983), 3, 5-8, 17-18; Vincent, *Black Power and the Garvey Movement*, 74-85 and passim; Tony Martin, *Race First* (Westport, Conn.: Greenwood Press, 1976), 237-46; Theodore Draper, *American Communism and Soviet Russia* (New York: Viking Press, 1960), 322-32; Foner, *Organized Labor and the Black Worker*, 148-49; Cedric J. Robinson, *Black Marxism: The Making of the Black Radical Tradition* (Totowa, N.J.: Biblio Distribution Center, 1983), 296-301; David Samuels, "Five Afro-Caribbean Voices in American Culture, 1917-1929: Hubert H. Harrison, Wilfred A. Domingo, Richard B. Moore, Cyril Briggs and Claude McKay" (Ph.D. diss., University of Iowa, 1977); Theman Taylor, "Cyril Briggs and the African Blood Brotherhood: Effects of Communism on Black Nationalism, 1919-1935," (Ph.D. diss., University of California, Santa Barbara, 1981). On the Socialist party and African Americans, see Philip Foner, *American Socialism and Black Americans: From the Age of Jackson to World War II* (Westport, Conn.: Greenwood Press, 1977); Jervis Anderson, *A. Phillip Randolph: A Biographical Portrait* (New York, 1973), 85-137; Theodore Kornweibel, *No Crystal Stair: Black Life and the Messenger, 1917-1928* (Westport, Conn.: Greenwood Press, 1975); Henry Williams, "Black Response to the American Left" (Princeton, N.J.: Princeton University History Department, 1971); Robert Allen, *Reluctant Reformers: Racism and Social Reform Movements in the United States* (Washington, D.C.: Howard University Press, 1983), 212-15; Sally Miller, "The

Socialist Party and the Negro, 1901-1920," *Journal of Negro History* 56 (July 1971): 220-39; Lawrence Moore, "Flawed Fraternity: American Socialist Response to the Negro, 1901-1912," *Historian* 33, no. 1 (1969): 1-14; Mark Naison, "Marxism and Black Radicalism in America: Notes on a Long (and Continuing) Journey," *Radical America* 5, no. 3 (1971): 4-10; David A. Shannon, *The Socialist Party of America* (New York: Macmillan, 1955), 49-52; and James Weinstein, *The Decline of Socialism* (New Brunswick, N.J., Rutgers University Press, 1984), 69-70.

9. Workers (Communist) Party of America, *Program and Constitution: Workers Party of America* (New York, 1921), 14; Workers (Communist) Party of America, *The Second Year of the Workers Party of America: Theses, Programs, Resolutions* (Chicago, 1924), 125; V. I. Lenin, "The Socialist Revolution and the Right of Nations to Self-Determination (Theses)," in *Lenin on the National and Colonial Questions: Three Articles* (Peking: Foreign Languages Press, 1967), 5; "Theses on the National and Colonial Question Adopted by the Second Congress of the Comintern Congress," in *The Communist International, 1919-1943, Documents*, ed. Jane Degras (London, 1956), 1:142.

Roy's contribution to the theses, as well as to the general direction of the commission, was quite substantial. Among other things, he recognized the existence of class distinctions in the colonies, and he placed the peasantry in a pivotal position for waging the anticolonial movement. See Manabendra Nath Roy, *M. N. Roy's Memoirs* (Delhi: Ajanta Publications), 378; see also John Haithcox, *Communism and Nationalism in India: M. N. Roy and Comintern Policy, 1920-1939* (Princeton: Princeton University Press, 1971), 14-15; and D. C. Grover, *M. N. Roy: A Study of Revolution and Reason in Indian Politics* (Calcutta: Minerva Associates, 1973), 2-13. Roy's theses appear in V. B. Karnik, *M. N. Roy: A Political Biography* (Bombay: Nav Jagrita Samaj, 1978), 107-10. For Lenin's views on Roy's supplementary theses, see "The Report of the Commission on the National and Colonial Questions, July 26, 1920," in *Lenin on the National and Colonial Questions*, 30-37; and Draper, *American Communism*, 321. As early as 1913, Lenin wrote a short article titled "Russians and Negroes," in which he compared the plight of blacks to that of emancipated Russian serfs (see V. I. Lenin, *Collected Works* [Moscow: Progress Publishers], 18:543-44). And in his "Notebooks in Imperialism," put together in 1916, Lenin was critical of the Socialist party's position on African Americans, as well as of the Mississippi Socialist party's policy of segregation (*Collected Works*, 39:590-91). Lenin's criticism of the American Communists' failure to work among blacks was based on research he had conducted regarding the plight of black sharecroppers and tenant farmers in the United States. In the resulting works, completed in 1915 and 1917, Lenin suggested that blacks constitute an oppressed nation in the United States. ("New Data on the Laws Governing the Development of Capitalism in Agriculture," in *Collected Works*, 22:13-102; "On Statistics and Sociology," in *Collected Works*, 23:276.)

10. Draper, *American Communism*, 320-21, 327-28; Robinson, *Black Marxism*, 304; Roger E. Kanet, "The Comintern and the 'Negro Question': Communist Policy in the United States and Africa, 1921-1941," *Survey* 19, no. 4 (Autumn 1973): 89-90; Haywood, *Black Bolshevik*, 225; Claude McKay, *A Long Way from Home* (1937; reprint, New York: Arno Press, 1969), 177-80; Billings [Otto Huiswoud], "Report on the Negro Question," *International Press Correspondence* 3,

no. 2 (1923): 14-16. The full text of the "Theses on the Negro Question" is available in *Bulletin of the IV Congress of the Communist International*, no. 27 (December 7, 1922): 8-10, and Degras, *The Communist International, 1919-1943*, 1:398-401. On the Communist party and Garveyism, see Vincent, *Black Power and the Garvey Movement*, 211; Robert A. Hill, *The Marcus Garvey and Universal Negro Improvement Association Papers* (Berkeley: University of California Press) 3:675-81; Workers (Communist) Party of America, *Fourth National Convention of the Workers (Communist) Party of America* (Chicago, 1925), 122 (source of in-text quotation) ; James Jackson [Lovett Fort-Whiteman], "The Negro in America," *Communist International*, February 1925, 52; and Robert Minor, "After Garvey–What?" *Workers Monthly* 5 (June 1926): 362-65. On the ANLC, see Haywood, *Black Bolshevik*, 139, 140-46; "Report of National Negro Committee, CPUSA," 1925 transcript, box 12, folder "Negro–1924-25," Robert Minor Papers, Butler Memorial Library, Columbia University; James Ford, *The Negro and the Democratic Front* (New York: International Publishers, 1938), 82; Harvey Klehr, *The Heyday of American Communism: The Depression Decade* (New York: Basic Books, 1984), 324; Wilson Record, *The Negro and the Communist Party* (Chapel Hill: University of North Carolina Press, 1951), 29-33.

11. Willy Munzenberg, "Pour une Conference Coloniale," *Correspondance Internationale* 6, no. 9 (August 1926): 1011; Munzenberg, "La Premiere Conference Mondiale Contre la Politique Coloniale Imperialiste," *Correspondance Internationale* 7, no. 17 (February 5, 1927): 232; Robin D. G. Kelley, "The Third International and the Struggle for National Liberation in South Africa, 1921-1928," *Ufahamu* 15, nos. 1 and 2 (1986): 110-11; Edward T. Wilson, *Russia and Black Africa before World War II* (New York: Holmes and Meier, 1974), 151; *South African Worker*, April 1 and June 24, 1927; "Les Decisions du Congres: Resolution Commune sur la Question Negre," *La Voix des Negres* 1, no. 3 (March 1927): 3.

12. "Resolutions Proposed by Workers Party of America at the Negro Sanhedrin, February 12, 1924," 4, 7, 9, 13, Box 13, and "Report of National Negro Committee, CPUSA," 1925 transcript, box 12, Robert Minor Papers; W. A. Domingo, interview, January 18, 1958, transcript, p. 4, box 21, folder 3, Theodore Draper Papers, Emory University; Ford, *The Negro and the Democratic Front*, 82; Haywood, *Black Bolshevik*, 143-46; Klehr, *The Heyday of American Communism*, 324; Naison, *Communists in Harlem*, 13.

13. Naison, *Communists in Harlem*, 18; Gilbert Lewis, "Revolutionary Negro Tradition," *Negro Worker*, March 15, 1930, 8 (source of in-text quotation). Cyril Briggs published a whole series of essays on this score, such as "Negro Revolutionary Hero–Toussaint L'Overture," *Communist* 8, no. 5 (May 1929): 250-54; "The Negro Press as a Class Weapon," *Communist* 8, no. 8 (August 1929): 453-60; and "May First and the Revolutionary Traditions of Negro Masses," *Daily Worker*, April 28, 1930.

14. *Liberator*, November 14, 1931.

15. J. Thompson, "Exhortation," *Harlem Liberator*, June 24, 1933.

16. *Daily Worker*, February 11, 1939. For an elaboration on the role of Marxist pedagogy among African Americans in the Communist party, see Robin D. G. Kelley, *Hammer and Hoe: Alabama Communists During the Great Depression* (Chapel Hill: University of North Carolina Press, 1990), 93-99.

17. *Daily Worker*, April 7, 1934; *Southern Worker*, July 1936. For examples of adaptations of "We Shall Not Be Moved," see *Labor Defender* 9 (December 1933): 80.

18. Kelley, *Hammer and Hoe*, 40-42, 95; *Daily Worker*, February 11, 1939; Joe Brandt, ed., *Black Americans in the Spanish People's War against Fascism, 1936-1939* (New York: Veterans of the Abraham Lincoln Brigade, 1980), 24; *Southern Worker*, March 21, 1931; Nell Irvin Painter, *The Narrative of Hosea Hudson: His Life as a Negro Communist in the South* (Cambridge, Mass., 1979), 84; Haywood, *Black Bolshevik*, 398; "Testimony of Leonard Patterson," State of Louisiana, Joint Legislative Committee, in *Subversion in Racial Unrest: An Outline of a Strategic Weapon to Destroy the Governments of Louisiana and the United States*, Public Hearings, part 1 (Baton Rouge, 1957), 121.

19. Brandt, *Black Americans*, 14, 25; *Daily World*, February 24, 1979.

20. James Yates, *From Mississippi to Madrid: Memoir of a Black American in the Abraham Lincoln Brigade* (Seattle: Open Hand Publishers, 1989), 15-28.

21. Ibid., 29-55, 72-73.

22. Landis, *The Abraham Lincoln Brigade*, 73; Nelson, Barrett, and Ruck, *Steve Nelson*, 218; Brandt, *Black Americans*, 33-35.

23. Other black volunteers from Chicago included James Roberson, Nathaniel Dickson, Oscar Hunter, Theodore Gibbs, West Swanson, Tom Trent (né Arthur Witt), Daniel Bede Taylor, and Harry Haywood. The other two cities with large contingents of black volunteers were New York and Los Angeles.

24. *Daily Worker*, October 2, 1932.

25. Michael Gold, "The Negro Reds of Chicago," *Daily Worker*, September 30, 1932.

26. Oscar Hunter interview, May 2, 1980, Abraham Lincoln Brigade Archives (ALBA), Brandeis University, Waltham, Mass., 18-19.

27. Ibid., 6-20, 78; Brandt, *Black Americans*, 23.

28. Admiral Kilpatrick interview, June 8, 1980, ALBA.

29. The only other African nation not under direct European colonial rule was Liberia, a colony settled in 1822 by African-American emigrés and the American Colonization Society and that had ostensibly become an independent republic in 1847. Despite the appearance of independence and the symbolic meaning Liberia held for African nationalists, it remained essentially a protectorate of the United States, which pressured the Liberian government to offer Firestone Rubber Company a concession of one million acres – nearly all of its arable land mass – for the cultivation of rubber. Furthermore, the Americo-Liberian elite

exploited the indigenous African population in a manner comparable to that of European authorities in other colonies. In retrospect, few scholars today accept the idea that Liberia constituted a completely independent nation. See especially I. K. Sundiata, *Black Scandal* (Philadelphia: Institute for the Study of Human Issues, 1980); Cedric J. Robinson, "W. E. B. DuBois and Black Sovereignty," in *Pan-Africanism Revisited: Class, Culture, and Nationalism in the African Diaspora*, ed. Sidney J. Lemelle and Robin D.G. Kelley (forthcoming from Temple University Press); Frank Chalk, "The Anatomy of an Investment: Firestone's 1927 Loan to Liberia," *Canadian Journal of African Studies* 1, no. 1 (March 1967): 12-32; and J. Gus Liebenow, *Liberia: The Evolution of Privilege* (Ithaca, N.Y.: Cornell University Press, 1969).

30. William R. Scott, "Black Nationalism and the Italo-Ethiopian Conflict, 1934-1936," *Journal of Negro History* 63, no. 2 (1978): 118-21; Gayraud Wilmore, *Black Religion and Black Radicalism* (Garden City, N.J.: Anchor/Doubleday, 1972), 120-21, 126-28, 160-61; E. Ullendorff, *Ethiopia and the Bible* (London: Oxford University Press, 1968); W. A. Shack, "Ethiopia and Afro-Americans: Some Historical Notes, 1920-1970," *Phylon* 35, no. 2 (1974): 142-55; Bernard Makhosezwe Magubane, *The Ties That Bind: African-American Consciousness of Africa* (Trenton, N.J.: Africa World Press, 1987), 160-65; S. K. B. Asante, *Pan-African Protest: West Africa and the Italo-Ethiopian Crisis, 1934-1941* (London: Longman, 1977), 9-38; Robert G. Weisbord, *Ebony Kinship* (Westport, Conn.: Greenwood Press, 1973), 90-92; Randall K. Burkett, *Garveyism as a Religious Movement: The Institutionalization of a Black Civil Religion* (Metuchen, N.J.: Scarecrow Press, 1978), 34-35, 85-86, 122, 125, 134-35; Arnold Kuzwayo, "A History of Ethiopianism in South Africa with Particular Reference to the American Zulu Mission from 1835-1908" (M.A. thesis, University of South Africa, 1979); George Shepperson, "Ethiopianism and African Nationalism," *Phylon* 14, no. 1 (1953): 9-18.

31. Scott, "Black Nationalism," 121, 128-29; Naison, *Communists in Harlem*, 138-40; Magubane, *The Ties That Bind*, 166-67; Cedric J. Robinson, "The African Diaspora and the Italo-Ethiopian Crisis," *Race and Class* 27, no. 2 (Autumn 1985): 51-65; Weisbord, *Ebony Kinship*, 94-100; and S. K. B. Asante, "The Afro-American and the Italo-Ethiopian Crisis, 1934-1936," *Race* 15, no. 2 (1973): 167-84. Julian never actually saw combat. For more on Robinson and Julian, see Weisbord, *Ebony Kinship*, 94-95; Col. Hubert Julian, *Black Eagle* (London: Adventurer's Club, 1965); and John Peer Nugent, *The Black Eagle* (New York: Stein and Day, 1971). On the war itself, see Angelo Del Boca, *The Ethiopian War, 1935-1941* (Chicago: University of Chicago Press, 1969); George Baer, *The Coming of the Italo-Ethiopian War* (Cambridge: Harvard University Press, 1967); and Esmonde Robertson, *Mussolini as Empire Builder: Europe and Africa, 1932-1936* (New York: MacMillan, 1977).

32. Quoted in Scott, "Black Nationalism," 129; Naison, *Communists in Harlem*, 138-40.

33. Naison, *Communists in Harlem*, 138-40, 155-58, 174-76.

34. Coad quote from *Daily Worker*, February 11, 1939; Subversive Activities Control Board, "Herbert Brownell, Jr., Attorney General of the United States v.

Veterans of the Abraham Lincoln Brigade," Hearings, September 15, 1954, docket no. 108-53, 3202-3; Brandt, *Black Americans*, 14; *Daily World*, February 24, 1979. See also Yates, *Mississippi to Madrid*, 96.

35. *Daily Worker*, March 2, 6, 22, 27, May 29, 1937, November 12, 17, 24, 1938; Naison, *Communists in Harlem*, 196-97, 212; Scott, "Black Nationalism," 127; Martin Bauml Duberman, *Paul Robeson* (New York: Knopf, 1988), 215-220; Rampersad, *The Life of Langston Hughes* (New York: Oxford University Press, 1986, 1:351; Faith Berry, *Langston Hughes: Before and Beyond Harlem* (Westport, Conn.: Lawrence Hill, 1983), 261-63; James Baldwin, *Notes of a Native Son* (Boston: Beacon Press, 1955), 3.

36. *Chicago Defender*, March 26, 1938; *Daily Worker*, September 23, 1938; January 7, 1939; *Baltimore Afro-American*, October 1, 1938; Joseph North, *No Men Are Strangers* (New York: International Publishers, 1958), 126; Yates, *Mississippi to Madrid*, 129; Brandt, *Black Americans*, 18, 23; Naison, *Communists in Harlem*, 197; The Negro Committee to Aid Spain, *A Negro Nurse in Republican Spain* (New York, 1938); *Daily Worker*, March 30, 1937, May 18, 1938.

37. George Padmore, *The Life and Struggles of Negro Toilers* (London, 1931; reprint, San Bernadino, Calif.: Borjo Press, 1986), 77; Ford, *The Negro and the Democratic Front*, 160. On slavery in Ethiopia, see Jon R. Edwards, "Slavery, the Slave Trade and the Economic Reorganization of Ethiopia, 1916-1934," *African Economic History* 11 (1982): 3-14. Soviet leaders probably realized from the outset that Ethiopia could not have defeated Italy under any circumstances. One of the differences between Haile Selassie's situation in 1935 and the circumstances in which Menelik II was able to rout Italian troops at Adowa was that an arms embargo had been imposed on Ethiopia in 1916 and had lasted until 1930. See especially Harold G. Marcus, "The Embargo on Arms Sales to Ethiopia, 1916-1930," *International Journal of African Historical Studies* 16, no. 2 (1983): 263-79.

38. On struggles between the church and anticlericalists, see especially Gerald Brenan, *The Spanish Labyrinth: An Account of the Social and Political Background of the Civil War* (Cambridge, England: The University Press, 1943); Pierre Broue and Emile Temime, *The Revolution and the Civil War in Spain*, trans. Tony White (Cambridge: MIT Press, 1972), 37; Jose M. Sanchez, *Reform and Reaction: The Politico-Religious Background of the Spanish Civil War* (Chapel Hill: University of North Carolina Press, 1962); Frances Lannon, "The Church's Crusade against the Republic," in *Revolution and War in Spain, 1931-1939*, ed. Paul Preston, 35-58 (New York: Methuen, 1984). For more on Basque and Catalonian nationalism, see Norman Jones, "Regionalism and Revolution in Catalonia," in *Revolution and War in Spain*, 85-111; Martin Blinkhorn, "The Basque Ulster: Navarre and the Basque Autonomy Question under the Spanish Republic," *Historical Journal* 17, no. 3 (1974): 593-613. Catalonia was also the center of Spanish anarchism. See Robert W. Kern, *Red Years/Black Years: A Political History of Spanish Anarchism, 1911-1937* (Philadelphia, Institute for the Study of Human Issues, 1978), 1; Murray Bookchin, *The Spanish Anarchists: The Heroic Years, 1868-1936* (New York: Harper and Row, 1976); Sam Dolgoff, ed., *The Anarchist Collectives: Workers' Self-Management in the Spanish Revolution, 1936-1939*

(New York: Free Life Editions, 1974); George Orwell, *Homage to Catalonia* (New York: Harcourt Brace, 1952); Gerald W. Meaker, *The Revolutionary Left in Spain, 1914-1923* (Stanford: Stanford University Press, 1974); Abel Paz, *Durruti: The People Armed* (Montreal: Black Rose Books, 1976). For a more extensive discussion of agrarian struggles, see Broue and Temime, *The Revolution and the Civil War in Spain*, 34-35; Paul Preston, "The Agrarian War in the South," in Preston, *Revolution and War in Spain*, 159-81; E. E. Malefakis, *Agrarian Reform and Peasant Revolution in Spain* (New Haven, Conn.: Yale University Press, 1970); Juan Martinez Alier, *Labourers and Landowners in Southern Spain* (Totowa, N.J.: Rowman and Littefield, 1971).

39. Raymond Carr, *Modern Spain, 1875-1980* (New York: Oxford University Press, 1980), 47-116; Gabriel Jackson, *The Spanish Republic and the Civil War, 1931-1939* (Princeton, N.J.: Princeton University Press, 1965), 3-24; Shannon E. Fleming and Ann K. Fleming, "Primo de Rivera and Spain's Moroccan Problem, 1923-1927," *Journal of Contemporary History* 12 (January 1977): 85-99; Shlomo Ben-Ami, "The Dictatorship of Primo de Rivera: A Political Reassessment," *Journal of Contemporary History* 12 (January 1977): 65-84; Victor Alba, *Transition in Spain: From Franco to Democracy*, trans. Barbara Lotito (New Brunswick, N.J.: Transaction Books, 1978), 49-63; Stanley Payne, *A History of Spain and Portugal* (Madison: University of Wisconsin Press, 1973), 2:578-629.

40. On the history of the Second Republic, see Paul Preston, *The Coming of the Spanish Civil War: Reform, Reaction, and Revolution in the Second Republic, 1931-1936* (New York: Barnes and Noble Books, 1978); Jackson, *The Spanish Republic and the Civil War*; Schlomo Ben-Ámi, *The Origins of the Second Republic in Spain* (New York: Oxford University Press, 1978); Arthur Landis, *Spain!: The Unfinished Revolution!* (New York: International Publishers), 9-97; and Aviva and Isaac Aviv, "The Madrid Working Class, the Spanish Socialist Party and the Collapse of the Second Republic (1934-1936)," *Journal of Contemporary History* 16 (April 1981): 229-50. On the 1934 uprising, see Paul Preston, "Spain's October Revolution and the Rightist Grasp for Power," *Journal of Contemporary History* 10 (October 1975), 555-78; Manuel Grossi, *L'Insurrection des Austries* (Paris: Etudes et Documentations, 1972); Adrian Shubert, "The Epic Failure: The Asturian Revolution of October 1934," in Preston, *Revolution and War in Spain*, 113-36; Kern, *Red Years/Black Years*, 128-30; Jackson, *The Spanish Republic and the Civil War*, 148-68.

41. Paul Preston, "The Creation of the Popular Front in Spain," in *The Popular Front in Europe*, ed. Helen Graham and Paul Preston (London, 1987), 84-105; Robert G. Colodny, "Notes on the Origin of the Frente Popular of Spain," *Science and Society* 31 (Summer 1967): 257-74.

42. The amount of published work on the Spanish Civil War seems infinite. For a sampling of the good English-language scholarship on the conflict, see Broue and Temime, *The Revolution and the Civil War in Spain*; Raymond Carr, *The Spanish Tragedy: The Civil War in Perspective* (London: Weidenfield and Nicolson, 1977); Jackson, *The Spanish Republic and the Civil War*; Hugh Thomas, *The Spanish Civil War*, 4th ed. (1961; reprint, New York: Harper and Row, 1986); Burnett Bolloten, *The Grand Camouflage: The Communist Conspir-*

acy in the Spanish Civil War (New York: Praeger, 1961), the revised version the latter, titled The Spanish Revolution: The Left and the Struggle for Power During the Civil War (Chapel Hill: University of North Carolina Press, 1979); and his final comprehensive history (published posthumously), The Spanish Civil War: Revolution and Counterrevolution (Chapel Hill: University of North Carolina Press, 1990); Brenan, The Spanish Labyrinth; Alba, Transition in Spain: From Franco to Democracy, ; Franz Borkenau, The Spanish Cockpit: An Eye-Witness Account of the Political and Social Conflicts of the Spanish Civil War (1937; reprint, Ann Arbor: University of Michigan Press, 1963); Joan C. Ullman, The Tragic Week (Cambridge: Harvard University Press, 1968); Cattell, Communism and the Spanish Civil War; Robert G. Colodny, The Struggle for Madrid: The Central Epic of the Spanish Conflict (New York: Paine and Whitman, 1958); Vernon Richards, Lessons of the Spanish Revolution (London: Freedom Press, 1983); Stanley Payne, The Spanish Revolution (New York: Norton, 1970); Landis, Spain!; Ronald Fraser, Blood of Spain: An Oral History of the Spanish Civil War (New York: Pantheon Books, 1979).

43. Broue and Temime, The Revolution, 321-65; Payne, A History of Spain and Portugal, 2:669-70; Hugh Kay, Salazar and Modern Portugal (New York, 1960); H. Martins, "Portugal," in European Fascism, ed. S. J. Woolf (New York: Methuen, 1969), 302-36; John Coverdale, Italian Intervention in the Spanish Civil War (Princeton, N.J.: Princeton University Press, 1975); Robert H. Whealey, Hitler and Spain: The Nazi Role in the Spanish Civil War, 1936-1939 (Lexington: University Press of Kentucky, 1989); Raymond L. Proctor, Hitler's Luftwaffe in the Spanish Civil War (Westport, Conn.: Greenwood Press, 1983). The war radicalized a segment of the Portuguese working class; in September 1936 a group of Portuguese seamen mutinied and attempted to join the Spanish Left. Salazar responded by adopting more repressive measures and abandoning what he had called Catholic corporatism for a more blatantly fascist form of government. Ironically, Salazar's downfall was the result of a military coup led by Portugal's version of the Army of Africa in 1974. The officers and troops had become war-weary after fighting anticolonial insurgents in Portugal's African colonies. A left-wing military junta helped usher in a democractic regime in Portugal and independence for Mozambique, Angola, Guinea-Bissau, and the Cape Verde Islands. See especially Barbara Cornwall, The Bush Rebels (New York: Holt, Rinehart and Winston, 1972), 84-87; R. M. Fields, The Portuguese Revolution and the Armed Forces (New York: Praeger, 1976); James H. Mittleman, "Some Reflections on Portugal's Counter Revolution," Monthly Review 28 (March 1977): 58-64; Phil Mailer, Portugal: The Impossible Revolution (London: Solidarity, 1977); and Nicos Poulantzas, The Crisis of Dictatorship (London: Humanities Press, 1976).

44. Douglas Little, Malevolent Neutrality: The United States, Great Britain, and the Origins of the Spanish Civil War (Ithaca, N.Y.: Cornell University Press, 1985); Richard P. Traina, American Diplomacy and the Spanish Civil War (Bloomington, Indiana University Press, 1968); Broue and Temime, The Revolution, 321-65; Dante Puzzo, Spain and the Great Powers, 1936-1941 (New York: Columbia University Press, 1962); David Carlton, "Eden, Blum, and the Origins of Non-Intervention," and M. D. Gallagher, "Leon Blum and the Spanish Civil War," Journal of Contemporary History 6 (January 1971): 40-55 and 56-64.

45. Russian men totaled slightly more than 2,000 during the entire war, including 772 airmen, 351 tank men, 222 army advisers and instructors, and a few hundred specialists, mechanics, radio operators, and interpreters. In fact, there were never more than 600 to 800 Russians present in Spain at any one time. The total military supplies from the USSR consisted of 806 military aircraft, 362 tanks, 120 armored cars, 1,555 artillery pieces, 500,000 rifles, 340 grenade launchers, 15,113 machine guns, over 110,000 aerial bombs, about 3,400,000 rounds of ammunition, 500,000 grenades, 1,500 tons of gunpowder, and numerous torpedo boats, search lights, motor vehicles, radio stations, torpedoes, and tanks of gasoline. Aside from the government, the people of the USSR, through organizations such as the All-Union Central Council of Trade Union's Fund of Aid to Republican Spain, had collected thousands of tons of food, clothing, and other nonmilitary material aid. Also, by 1938 nearly 3,000 Spanish children were living in the Soviet Union as refugees, and the USSR set up homes and boarding schools where they were taught in Spanish (Soviet War Veterans' Committee, *International Solidarity*, 329-30.)

46. Even before the Comintern began organizing the International Brigades, volunteers from Germany, Italy, France, Austria, and Belgium were slowly trickling across the Spanish border within days of the officers' uprising. Among the first group of volunteers were two Americans, Rosario Negrete of the (Trotskyite) Revolutionary Workers' League and engineer Lee Fleischman, both of whom found their way into the ranks of the Republican army before the Lincoln and Washington battalions had been formed (Rosenstone, *Crusade of the Left*, 28-31).

47. Rosenstone, *Crusade of the Left*, 95; Subversive Activities Control Board (SACB), "Herbert Brownell, Jr., Attorney General of the United States v. VALB [Veterans of the Abraham Lincoln Brigade]," September 15, 1954, 3265; Landis, *The Abraham Lincoln Brigade*, 17.

48. Landis, *The Abraham Lincoln Brigade*, 15-16; Rosenstone, *Crusade of the Left*, 122-32. Quote from Yates, *Mississippi to Madrid*, 112, see also 108-12. For descriptions of the climb over the Pyrenees, see especially Bessie, *Men in Battle*, 18-24; Nelson, Barrett, and Ruck, *Steve Nelson*, 199-202; Nelson, *The Volunteers*, 70-77; and Haywood, *Black Bolshevik*, 471-72.

49. Hunter interview, p. 23; SACB, "Brownell v. VALB," 3203; *Daily Worker*, September 29, 1937.

50. *Daily Worker*, September 29, 1937; Hunter interview; Yates, *Mississippi to Madrid*, 131-52, 155; *Daily Worker*, December 23, 1938; Brandt, *Black Americans*, 20-21, 23, 27-30; Arthur H. Landis, "American Fliers in Spanish Skies," in Bessie and Prago, *Our Fight*, 27.

51. Brandt, *Black Americans*, 15, 43; Yates, *Mississippi to Madrid*, 176; Eluard Luchell McDaniels interview with Peter Carroll and Bruce Kaiper, conducted for the Radical Elders Oral History Project, March 13, 1978, 2a-21, 57-58; letter from Victor Berch in the *Volunteer* 12, no. 1 (May 1990): 23; *Daily Worker*, May 21, 1937; *Baltimore Afro-American*, February 20, 1937; *Chicago Defender*, April 3, 1937. On the Ugandan radical who served in Spain, see Ras Makonnen, *Pan-*

Africanism Within, ed. Kenneth King (New York: Oxford University Press, 1973), 176. (I am grateful to Cedric J. Robinson for bringing this to my attention.)

52. *Daily Worker*, September 29, 1937; Yates, *Mississippi to Madrid*, 119; Rolfe, *The Lincoln Battalion*, 53; Nelson, Barrett, and Ruck, *Steve Nelson*, 218; Brandt, *Black Americans*, 8, 33-35; Rosenstone, *Crusade of the Left*, 161-62; Landis, *The Abraham Lincoln Brigade*, 34, 65, 73, 171, 173, 242; Hunter interview, p. 33.

53. Landis, *The Abraham Lincoln Brigade*, 73; Nelson, Barrett, and Ruck, *Steve Nelson*, 218; Brandt, *Black Americans*, 33-35; Rosenstone, *Crusade of the Left*, 184.

54. The most comprehensive account of the battles in which the Lincoln Brigade participated is Landis, *The Abraham Lincoln Brigade*; see also Rosenstone, *Crusade of the Left*, 149-64, 174-212, 230-54, 276-96, 313-33; Bessie, *Men in Battle*; Nelson, *The Volunteers*, 101-88 passim (much of which appears again in Nelson, Ruck, and Barrett, *Steve Nelson*); Rolfe, *The Lincoln Battalion*, 37-293 passim; Brome, *The International Brigades*, 105-18, 195-225, 236-61; Soviet War Veterans' Committee, *International Solidarity*, 340-45; and Richardson, *Comintern Army*, 81-89.

55. Brandt, *Black Americans*, 32; Joe and Leo Gordon, "Seven Letters from Spain," ed. Daniel Czitrom, in Bessie and Prago, *Our Fight*, 196.

56. Thompson quoted in *Daily Worker*, September 29, 1937. While U.S. military policy from the American Revolution through World War II has always remained ambivalent or opposed to placing black troops in combat duty, specific circumstances have always resulted in the suspension of such a policy. For more on the history of blacks in the military through World War I, see Bernard C. Nalty, *Strength for the Fight: A History of Black Americans in the Military* (New York: Free Press, 1986); Jack D. Foner, *Blacks and the Military in American History* (New York: Praeger, 1974); Benjamin Quarles, *The Negro in the American Revolution* (Chapel Hill: University of North Carolina Press, 1961); William Nell, *Colored Patriots of the American Revolution* (1855; reprint, New York: Arno Press, 1968); James McPherson, ed., *The Negro's Civil War* (New York: Pantheon Books, 1967); Arlen Fowler, *The Black Infantry in the West, 1869-1891* (Westport, Conn.: Greenwood Press, 1971); William H. Leckie, *The Buffalo Soldiers: A Narrative of the Negro Calvary in the West* (Norman, Okla.: Negro Universities Press, 1967); Marvin Fletcher, *The Black Soldier and Officer in the United States Army, 1891-1917* (Columbia: University of Missouri Press, 1974); Willard B. Gatewood, *"Smoked Yankees" and the Struggle for Empire: Letters of Black Soldiers, 1898-1902* (Urbana: University of Illinois Press, 1971); Gerald Wilson Patton, "War and Race: The Black Officer in the American Military" (Ph.D. diss., University of Iowa, 1978); W. Allison Sweeney, *History of the American Negro in the Great World War* (1919; New York: Negro University Press, 1969); Robert W. Mullen, *Blacks in America's Wars* (New York: Anchor Foundation, 1973).

57. Duberman, *Paul Robeson*, 217; Dolores Ibarruri, *They Shall Not Pass: The Autobiography of La Pasionaria* (New York: International Publishers, 1966), 265.

58. Haywood, *Black Bolshevik*, 474-87; *Daily Worker*, October 12, 1937; McDaniels interview, 5a-20; Hunter interview, 21, 25. When he was stationed at Murcia, one of Hunter's jobs was to pick up deserters. One was a black man he had known in Chicago (Hunter interview, 55.)

59. Joe and Leo Gordon, "Seven Letters from Spain," ed. Daniel J. Czitrom, 194; Nelson, Barrett, and Ruck, *Steve Nelson*, 219.

60. On the Soviets' role in the Loyalist defense and the tensions between efforts to make a revolution and fight a conventional war, see Bolloten, *The Spanish Revolution*; Broue and Temime, *The Revolution and the Civil War in Spain*, 172-212; Kern, *Red Year/Black Year*, 239-47; Raymond Carr, *Modern Spain*, 137; E.H. Carr, *The Comintern and the Spanish Civil War*, 29-31; and Ibarruri, *They Shall Not Pass*, 270-75. The debate over whether the Communists were wrong in suppressing the revolution for the sake of the war will not be solved here and will probably never be solved. Nonetheless, few can deny that Franco's victory was inevitable because of fascist support and indifference from Western capitalist nations.

61. Guttman, *The Wound in the Heart*, 100; *Daily Worker*, December 2, 1938. There is a slight possibility that a handful of black radicals identified with Basque and Catalan demands for self-determination, but as yet no evidence of such support exists. Perhaps future scholars will explore this question.

62. Duberman, *Paul Robeson*, 219; Rampersad, *The Life of Langston Hughes*, 1:345; Rosenstone, *Crusade of the Left*, 196; Tom Page, "Interview with a Black Anti-Fascist," in Bessie and Prago, *Our Fight*, 56; SACB, "Brownell v. VALB," 3211; McDaniels interview, 5a-23; *Daily Worker*, December 2, 1938. For observations by other black visitors to the front who maintained that Spain was free of prejudice, see William Pickens, "What I Saw in Spain," *Crisis* 45 (October 1938): 321; Edward E. Strong, "I Visited Spain," *Crisis* 43 (December 1936): 358-59; Eslanda Goode Robeson, "Journey to Spain," in *The Heart of Spain*, ed. Alvah Bessie (New York: VALB, 1952), 247.

63. Guttman, *The Wound in the Heart*, 99; Thyra Edwards, "Moors and the Spanish War," *Opportunity* 16 (March 1938): 84-85; Yates, *Mississippi to Madrid*, 127; McDaniels interview, 5a-23.

64. Rampersad, *The Life of Langston Hughes*, 1:349, 351; *Baltimore Afro-American*, October 30, 1937; Hughes, *I Wonder as I Wander*, 327, 351; Berry, *Langston Hughes*, 262; Broue and Temime, *The Revolution and the Civil War in Spain*, 266-67; *Daily Worker*, September 29, 1937.

65. Duberman, *Paul Robeson*, 219-20.

66. Rolfe, *The Lincoln Battalion*, 266; Yates, *Mississippi to Madrid*, 116, 145-46; Ray Durem, *Take No Prisoners* (London: Paul E. Breman, 1971), 3; see also letter from Victor Berch in *Volunteer* 12, no. 1 (May 1990): 23.

67. McDaniels interview, 5b-27 and 28.

68. Rosenstone, *Crusade of the Left*, 313, 314-21; Bessie, *Men in Battle*, 139-94 passim.

69. Bolloten, *The Spanish Revolution*, 403-77; Broue and Temime, *The Revolution and the Civil War in Spain*, 273-315; Carr, *The Spanish Tragedy*, 197-201; Cattell, *Communism and the Spanish Civil War*, 169-78; Graham, "The Spanish Popular Front," 123-26; Kern, *Red Years/Black Years*, 225-33; Alba, *Transition in Spain*, 145-57.

70. On the Lincoln battalion's role in the Ebro offensive, see Rosenstone, *Crusade of the Left*, 324-33; Landis, *The Abraham Lincoln Brigade*, 511-88; Bessie, *Men in Battle*, 213-345; Rolfe, *The Lincoln Battalion*, 258-93; and James M. Jones, "Hold That Position!" in Bessie and Prago, *Our Fight*, 261-68. Among the black volunteers wounded during the Ebro offensive were sergeant Thomas Page of the Third Company, who was shot in the chest, and sergeant Joe Taylor, who took a bullet in the shoulder.

71. Rosenstone, *Crusade of the Left*, 335-38; Rolfe, *The Lincoln Battalion*, 306-10; Ibarruri, *They Shall Not Pass*, 313; Yates, *Mississippi to Madrid*, 158-59; Steck POW Commission files in special collection on the Spanish Civil War at Brandeis University.

72. Yates, *Mississippi to Madrid*, 158-59; Tom Page, "Interview with a Black Anti-Fascist," 56. Prowell and McDaniels quoted in Rosenstone, *Crusade of the Left*, 196.

73. Yates, *Mississippi to Madrid*, 160.

74. Hunter interview, 59-60; Yates, *Mississippi to Madrid*, 160; Rosenstone, *Crusade of the Left*, 338-34; SACB, "Brownell v. VALB," 3213.

75. Kilpatrick interview; Maurice Isserman, *Which Side Were You On? The American Communist Party during the Second World War* (Middletown, Conn.: Wesleyan University Press, 1982), 28; Rosenstone, *Crusade of the Left*, 341-46; SACB, "Brownell v. VALB," 3220-22. On the Communist party's defense of the Nazi-Soviet Pact, see Klehr, *The Heyday of American Communism*, 386-409; Isserman, *Which Side Were You On?* 32-54; and Naison, *Communists in Harlem*, 287-90.

76. Brome, *The International Brigades*, 290-93; Rosenstone, *Crusade of the Left*, 346-47; Eby, *Between the Bullet and the Lie*, 314-15; Isserman, *Which Side Were You On?*, 104-12; Mary P. Motley, *The Invisible Soldier: The Experience of the Black Soldier, World War II* (Detroit: Wayne State University Press, 1987), 194-95; SACB, "Brownell v. VALB," 3234, 3250, 3282; Yates, *Mississippi to Madrid*, 160-64. On racism and African-American participation in the armed forces during World War II, see Motley, *The Invisible Soldier*; Richard M. Dalifume, *Desegregation of the U.S. Armed Forces: Fighting on Two Fronts, 1939-1945* (Columbia: University of Missouri Press, 1969); Shapiro, *White Violence and Black Response*, 305-9; Philip McGuire, ed., *Taps for a Jim Crow Army* (Santa Barbara, Calif.: ABC-CLIO, 1983); Studs Terkel, *The Good War: An Oral History of World War II* (New York: Pantheon, 1984), 149-56; 261-67; 274-79; 365-71.

77. Manning Marable, *Race, Reform, and Rebellion: The Second Reconstruction in Black America, 1945-1982* (Jackson: University Press of Mississippi, 1984), 13-14; Herbert Garfinkel, *When Negroes March: The March on Washington*

Movement in the Organizational Politics of the FEPC (Glencoe, Ill.: Free Press, 1959); SACB, "Brownell v. VALB," 3245; Isserman, *Which Side Were You On?* 118-119.

78. Durem, *Take No Prisoners*, 3.

79. Ibid., 8.

80. Hunter interview, 68-69. On the political significance of the bebop counterculture, see Eric Lott, "Double V, Double-Time: Bebop's Politics of Style," *Callaloo* 11, no. 3 (1988): 597-605; Stuart Cosgrove, "The Zoot-Suit and Style Warfare," *History Workshop Journal* 18 (Autumn 1984): 77-91; Bruce M. Tyler, "Black Jive and White Repression," *Journal of Ethnic Studies* 16, no. 4 (Winter 1989): 31-66; Ben Sidran, *Black Talk* (New York: Holt, Rinehart and Winston, 1967), 78-115.

81. Rosenstone, *Crusade of the Left*, 351-55; U.S. Congress, House Un-American Activities Committee, *Communist Activities in the Philadelphia Area* (Washington, D.C., 1952), 4434-41; SACB, "Brownell v. VALB," 3225; Kilpatrick interview, 64, 68.

82. Brandt, *Black Americans*, 20-21, 25; Durem, *Take No Prisoners*, 3; Yates, *Mississippi to Madrid*, 160-64; Kilpatrick interview, 73.

PART 2

Roll of African-American Veterans

Introduction

This roll of African-American veterans contains an alphabetical listing of all the identified black members of the Abraham Lincoln Brigade. Approximately 2,800-3,000 American volunteers fought for the Spanish Republic. During the war observers estimated that about 100 of these were African Americans.

Precise documentation of the Americans in Spain is difficult to obtain. The records of the brigade were lost or captured in the conflict. A roster of the American volunteers was compiled after the fact using shipping lists. This has been supplemented over the years by the memories of surviving veterans and by subsequent research in Spain and elsewhere. Adolph Ross, himself a Lincoln veteran, has for years compiled and updated the most complete available listing of the volunteers. For this volume, we began our research with a list of approximately 90 black veterans supplied by the Veterans of the Abraham Lincoln Brigade. In the course of our research we discovered some black fighters unknown to the VALB, and we found that a few of the men on the original list were actually white. In the end the number of identified African-American veterans was still about 90. We are sure that more remain unknown, and our search for their identity continues.

In the roll that follows, the name of each veteran is accompanied by biographical information. The amount of information available on each individual varies widely. Some (like Oliver Law and Walter Garland) occupied positions of leadership in Spain. Others (such as Frank Alexander) became important figures in the American Left after the war. For these veterans biographical documentation, in the form of newspaper clippings and interviews, is readily available and the biographical sketches are substantial. Other Lincoln brigadists simply served loyally in Spain and perhaps died there or, if they returned, lived quiet and unnoted lives in their home communities. For many of these men, nothing is known beyond the fact that a black American with that name was present in Spain with the Lincoln Brigade. Unfortunately, the resources available for the compilation of this sourcebook limited the amount of detective work that was possible for undocumented cases. We hope others will be inspired to take up the search, especially where the hometown of a veteran is known.

To aid future researchers, we have included the passport number for each veteran for whom it was available. The veterans' passport applications will eventually provide an important source of biographical information. Because passport files are kept closed for 75 years after the date of application, however, this information will not be readily accessible until 2012. The files can be opened prior to that date with the permission of the subject or surviving next of kin.

In the sources section at the back of this book is a listing of all the material we at ALBA have discovered on each individual African-American veteran. We hope this list will be used by other scholars and researchers to push ahead with the recovery of this unique and heroic story.

The Veterans

ALEXANDER, FRANK EDWARD

Frank Alexander was born February 8, 1911, on the Omaha Sioux Indian reservation in Nebraska. According to Alexander's interview with the producers of the documentary film *The Good Fight* (Brandeis University Spanish Civil War Collection [BUSCW]), his mother was an Omaha Indian, and his father, a cowboy who had ridden for the Pony Express as a youth, was black. Alexander grew up on the reservation, where he identified himself primarily as an Indian. His father was generally absent. When the family left the reservation and settled in Sioux City, and throughout his life off the reservation, Alexander was treated as a black person.

When Alexander was 15 his mother was stricken with tuberculosis and had to be placed in a sanitarium. At that time Alexander struck out on his own, riding the rails throughout the eastern United States and working as a bellhop in various hotels. After a few years of this life, Alexander briefly returned to Nebraska. He now found reservation life stifling, however. Determined to escape, Alexander says, he and three young male Indian friends stole all of their families' hogs, took the animals across the state line to South Dakota, and sold them for $80. With this seed money, the four friends set out to ride the rails to California.

After arriving in California Alexander joined his brother, Herschel Alexander, who had already become an activist in the Communist party. In Los Angeles, Alexander shared an apartment with his brother and with Alpheus Prowell, Virgil Rhetta, Aaron Johnson, and Norman Lisberg – all black Communists who later fought and died in Spain.

Through the influence of these young men, Alexander became attracted to the activities of the Young Communist League. He recalls that the YCL operated a youth center in the black section of Los Angeles and that the Party and its organizers were very popular in the black community. He recalls meeting various Hollywood personalities, including John Steinbeck and Joan Crawford, who were involved in supporting Party-related activities.

Alexander's introduction to intense political struggle came during the Los Angeles longshoremen's strike of 1934. Black workers were being hired by the big shipping companies as strikebreakers. Alexander and other activists were sent into the black communities to try and persuade blacks to honor the longshoremen's strike. Alexander recalls that this was a difficult task, since at that time there were no blacks in the union.

In the course of his street-speaking activities on behalf of the longshoremen, Alexander recalls, he was beaten by company goon squads and by the police. These experiences hastened the process of his politicization, and he soon joined the YCL. During his early years in Los Angeles, Alexander supported himself by selling chickens from a truck in Beverly Hills and Malibu and working at various construction jobs.

In the spring of 1937 Alexander became the first black from Los Angeles to depart for the war in Spain.

In Spain he was assigned to the Washington Battalion, but he soon contracted pneumonia and was hospitalized. After his recovery he was reassigned to the Mackenzie-Papineau Battalion. Alexander was wounded in the leg at Fuente de Ebro and was hospitalized again. He returned to fight at Teruel and to participate in the retreat across the Ebro. Although he could not swim, he managed to cross the river by supporting himself on stalks of bamboo cane he had cut at the shore.

Alexander recalls experiencing no racial prejudice whatsoever from the Spanish. Of his fellow American volunteers, he says, "I ran into some vets that are racist since Spain. But they weren't racist in Spain."

During World War II Alexander served in the all-black 93rd Division. He was a first sergeant and recalls that as part of his duties he "had to sell the blacks on fighting for the U.S." For this effort he was able to deliver talks to the troops on the union movement in the United States.

After the war Alexander was a full-time Communist party functionary from 1948 to 1955. He served as chairman of the Negro Commission of the Los Angeles Communist party and as a member of the California state committee. He took a highly visible role in the opposition to the Smith Act persecutions of the American Communists and appeared on national television for that purpose.

Frank Alexander left the Communist party in 1956 and entered the construction business. He is now retired and living in Seattle, Washington.

ARCHER, AMOS

Born in 1897, Archer went to Spain at the age of 40. His passport (#483125) was issued on November 2, 1937. At that time his home address was listed as 845 Rosa Street, Youngstown, Ohio. Archer sailed to Spain on November 12, 1937, on the SS *Franconia.* He returned from Spain on December 15, 1938, aboard the SS *Paris.* On March 5, 1939, Archer was killed in Youngstown, Ohio, in an incident related to his relationship with a woman.

BAKER, WILLIAM

On July 24, 1937, in San Franciso, William Baker, age 27, was issued passport #30693. His listed addresses at that time were 2369 Lehar Street, Honolulu, and 190 Embarcadero, San Francisco. Baker sailed to Spain from New York City on August 7, 1937, aboard the SS *Georgic.* He returned on December 20, 1938, on the SS *Ausonia.*

BATTLE, THADDEUS ARRINGTON

A 21-year-old student at Howard University before joining the Lincoln Brigade, Thaddeus Battle was an active member of the American Student Union, an organization of leftist, liberal, and progressive college and university students. After volunteering for Spain, Battle was issued passport #442807 on June 14, 1937. His address at that time was 1401 12th Street, Washington, D.C. Battle sailed to Spain on June 18, 1937, aboard the SS *Alaunia.* In November 1937 Battle participated with other student volunteers in the broadcast of an Armistice Day greeting from Spain to the United States.

On June 7, 1938, Battle's father, W. B. Battle of Nashville, North Carolina, wrote to the U.S. Department of State requesting assistance in finding information on the whereabouts and welfare of his son. Mr. Battle stated that he had not heard from Thaddeus since the news reports of heavy losses in the Lincoln Battalion.

This request was transmitted to the Valencia and Barcelona consulates. On September 10, 1938, the Barcelona consulate reported having learned from "another member of the International Brigades" that Battle had been hospitalized on the Valencia side of Loyalist territory. He had suffered a gunshot wound, but had probably recovered and rejoined his unit by that time.

When Battle returned from Spain on November 9, 1938, he was greeted by a congratulatory telegram from the faculty of Howard University saying, "We are proud that one of our own was a member of the Abraham Lincoln Brigade." Signers of the message included Sterling Brown, Ralph Bunche, Franklin Frazier, Doxey Wilkerson, and B. F. Carruthers.

BEEBE, VERNOLD MASTEN

In August 1938 Vernold Beebe, along with 10 other Americans, arrived at Havre, France, as a stowaway aboard the SS *Normandie*. All 11 were immediately arrested. Beebe and seven of the other stowaways stated that they were en route to Spain to join the Abraham Lincoln Brigade. The spokesman for the group, Henry Ulanoff, stated that several of them had been refused passports and that stowing away was their only remaining way to reach Spain.

On August 31, 1938, the U.S. State Department wrote to inform the elder Beebe that his son was expected to arrive in New York on October 25 aboard the SS *Ile de France*. According to the personal recollections of Lincoln veteran Steve Nelson, Beebe continued on to Spain upon his release. He served there for the remaining weeks of the war and returned to New York when the International Brigades were withdrawn.

BRAXTON, MILTON

Pseudonym for Herndon, Milton (listed below).

BROWN, TOM

According to Lincoln Brigade veteran Robert Steck's report on American prisoners of war in Spain, Brown was born in Wichita Falls, Texas, on February 5, 1910. Before departing for Spain in February 1937, Brown lived in East St. Louis, Illinois. Brown traveled to Spain on March 10, 1937, on the SS *Washington*. His passport (#367927, later lost) was issued on February 18, 1937, and showed his address as 817 North Second Street, East St. Louis, Illinois.

On October 7, 1937, the *Daily Worker* of New York City printed portions of a message on the importance of interracial unity, sent back from Spain by Brown to his "St. Louis CP Comrades."

In 1938, while driving a truck during Franco's drive to the sea, Brown found himself behind enemy lines. He abandoned his truck and tried to walk back to the Republican lines. Thinking that he was a Moor from Franco's North African army, the Italian troops in the area allowed him to pass. He was near the Mediterranean before an enemy patrol, suspicious of his nationality, stopped him. He was imprisoned at San Pedro de Cardenas.

Brown was freed in a postwar prisoner exchange on April 22, 1939, and returned to New York on May 6, 1939. He served in the U.S. Army after Pearl Harbor.

CALLION, WALTER P.

Callion traveled to Spain on May 26, 1937, at the age of 18, aboard the SS *Vollendam*. His passport (#410135, issued on May 12, 1937) listed his address as 2641 Adams Street, St. Louis, Missouri.

Callion was wounded in Spain and sent out of the country via Paris. While in Paris awaiting passage to the United States, Callion encountered Langston Hughes, who mentioned him in his dispatch to the Washington, D.C. *Afro-American* dated September 24, 1938.

Callion returned from Spain on August 27, 1938, on the SS *President Harding*. He served in the U.S. Army in World War II, first at Fort Sill, Oklahoma, and later at Fort Clark, Texas. In the army, Callion attained the rank of sergeant and was assigned to teach machine-gun operation.

CARTER, COUNCIL GIBSON

Carter, a Utah resident, went to Spain in the summer of 1937 at the age of 52 to serve as an ambulance driver with the American Medical Bureau. His passport (#453652, issued on June 29, 1937) listed his address as Carbonville, Utah; Helper, Utah; or New York City. State Department document file 130-, note 138, Spain/311, dated June 18, 1937, contains records and correspondence related to Carter's difficulties in obtaining a passport. These records remain closed. Carter returned from Spain on December 20, 1938, aboard the SS *Ausonia*. In New York City, on December 23, 1938, Carter appeared at a dinner sponsored by the Negro Committee to Aid Spanish Democracy. This dinner was in honor of NAACP leader William Pickens and was also attended by musician-composer W. C. Handy.

In 1933 Carter, then residing in Helper, Utah, corresponded with the legendary Nicaraguan revolutionary leader Augusto C. Sandino, seeking Sandino's views on the current world crisis. A translation of Sandino's reply was collected by the U.S. Embassy in Managua and filed in Washington.

CHISHOLM, ALBERT EDWARD

Albert Chisholm was born in Spokane, Washington, in 1913 while his father was serving in the U.S. Army. When Chisholm was eight his family settled in Roslyn, Washington, where they lived with his mother's parents. His grandfather worked in the mines. Chisholm attended racially integrated schools, but recalls racial conflict as a schoolboy. Later the family moved to Seattle.

Chisholm was attracted to the Communist party by its agitation on behalf of blacks in the trade unions. As a teenager Chisholm became one of the first black members of the Marine Cook's and Steward's Union.

During those years he worked as a bellhop on Pacific cruise ships and joined the Communist party.

In later interviews Chisholm drew a strong connection between Mussolini's invasion of Ethiopia and his own subsequent participation in the antifascist fight in Spain. He told the producers of *The Good Fight:* "I wanted to go [to Ethiopia] to fight against the Fascists. But then shortly after that the Spanish issue surfaced, and I saw there would be my best chance."

Chisholm was issued passport #30673 in San Francisco on July 22, 1937. At that time his address was 314 23rd Avenue, Seattle, Washington. Chisholm traveled to Spain on the SS *Aquitania*, which departed from New York City on August 4, 1937. His group arrived at Cherbourg, France, on August 10, 1937, and from there traveled on to Paris and then over the Pyrenees into Spain. While in Spain, Chisholm recalls meeting Langston Hughes, Paul Robeson, Ernest Hemingway and Tito on their visits to the front. Chisholm returned from Spain on December 20, 1938, aboard the SS *Ausonia*.

Upon his return to Seattle, Chisholm was besieged by local people who thought that he had been fighting as a mercenary and was now wealthy. This, of course, was not the case, and Chisholm shortly returned to his work as a seaman. He continued this work until 1971, when his union membership was revoked for what he says were political reasons. At this writing, Chisholm is retired and still lives in Seattle.

CHOWAN, MICHAEL
No information.

CLEVELAND, ROLAND
Roland Cleveland died in Spain. He went to that country in 1938 at the age of 25. He traveled on passport #33130, issued in San Francisco on January 12, 1938. His address was listed as 3615 Floral Drive, Los Angeles.

COAD, MACK
Mack Coad became involved in labor union activities in North Carolina and joined the Communist party in 1930. He went to Alabama in 1931, worked with steelworkers in the Birmingham area, and then became an important organizer of the Alabama Sharecropper's Union.

Coad went to Spain on October 2, 1937, aboard the SS *Georgic*. He was 43 years old at that time. His passport (#468859, issued on July 10, 1937) showed his address as 514 East 2nd Street, Charlotte, North Carolina. While in Spain, Coad was wounded in the face. He returned from Spain on December 15, 1938, aboard the SS *Paris*. In an interview in the *Daily Worker* of February 11, 1939, Coad recalled that he had volunteered "to help wake the Negro up on the international field."

He later died in the United States while working as a coal miner.

COBBS, WALTER

Walter Cobbs was 23 years old when he traveled to Spain on May 8, 1937, aboard the SS *American Importer.* He was issued passport #3387788 on April 9, 1937. His address was 4227-A Eastern (or Boston) Avenue in St. Louis, Missouri. He returned from Spain on December 15, 1938, on the SS *Paris*.

COLLINS, LEROY

At age 37, on August 18, 1937, Leroy Collins made the passage to Spain on board the SS *President Harding.* His passport (#466818, issued on July 30, 1937) showed his address as 272 Manhattan Avenue, New York City. His passport was lost in Spain. Collins returned to New York on August 4, 1938, on the SS *Manhattan*.

COX, JAMES

James Cox traveled to Spain on the SS *Ile de France,* on March 12, 1937. He was 38 years old in 1939. His passport (#372130, issued on March 5, 1937), which was lost in Spain, showed his residences as 1007 North Garrison and 3421 Delmas, both in St. Louis, Missouri. Cox returned from Spain on the SS *Paris* on December 15, 1938.

CUERIA Y OBRIT, BASILIO

Cueria was one of the more than 2,000 Cubans who joined the fight in defense of the Spanish Republic. Born about 1895 in Marianao, Cuba, to a black mother and an Asturian miner who had emigrated from Spain, he was an outstanding player on his hometown baseball team. He was in the Cuban army from 1917 to 1920 and was the star on an all-army team. Later he joined the Cuban All-Stars and toured Cuba and some of the major cities in the American South.

For a time Basilio stopped playing ball; he moved to Jacksonville, Florida, in 1923 and to New York in 1926, where he got a job in a heating plant in Long Island City. But he soon started playing again. First he joined the Havana Red Sox; then he joined another team and played in several cities in Canada. By 1928 Basilio had ended his playing career, associated himself with the Cuban emigrés and joined the Julio Mella club.

Basilio was in the United States at the time the International Brigades were organized. He traveled to Spain on January 20, 1937, with a U.S. contingent aboard the SS *Berengaria*. He first served with the Lincoln

Brigade, but after five months he transferred to El Campesino's 46th Division. There he commanded a machine-gun outfit connected with division headquarters. At the battle of Jarama he singlehandedly wiped out a machine-gun nest. He assumed the rank of captain and received a personal citation from General Miaja.

Basilio eventually returned to Cuba, where he died in May 1959.

DIAZ COLLADO, TOMAS

Tomas Diaz Collado was a black Cuban living in the United States. He sailed to Spain from New York on January 28, 1937, aboard the SS *Aquitania*. He later returned to Cuba, where he died.

DICKS, WALTER

No information.

DICKSON, NATHANIEL

At the age of 31, Nathan (or Nathaniel) Dickson of 4412 South Arkway, Chicago was issued passport #413175 on May 14, 1937. He sailed to Spain on June 2, 1937, aboard the SS *Aquitania*. To date, no further information is available.

DONOWA, ARNOLD BENNETT

Born in Trinidad in 1896, Dr. Arnold Donowa was educated in the United States and Canada before he established a Harlem practice in dental surgery. He earned his D.D.S. from Howard University and did further work at the Royal College of Dental Surgeons in Toronto and at the renowned Forsyth Clinic in Boston, affiliated with Harvard Medical School, where he also served as chief of x-ray.

Before joining the American Medical Bureau in Spain, Donowa was known in New York for his work in collecting aid for the Spanish people. In 1937 Donowa volunteered to join the Medical Bureau organized by Dr. Edward Barsky. He was issued passport #463381 on July 20, 1937, and sailed to Spain the next day. At the time of his departure, Donowa was 41 years old and maintained addresses at 303 West 154th Street, Apartment 1-A, and 1809 Seventh Avenue, both in New York City.

Donowa served in Spain for almost 18 months and was wounded there. His role in the Spanish war effort was widely covered in the local and national black press and noted in the daily mainstream press as well. He was the subject of articles by Langston Hughes and Edwin Rolfe.

Donowa returned from Spain on December 31, 1938, on the SS *President Harding*. He returned to his work in Harlem and made many appearances on behalf of the Spanish Republic in the days before its final fall. In subsequent years he continued to be active in New York. He gained notice in 1945 at the forefront of a group of African-American dentists protesting against anti-Semitic quotas at dental schools.

Eventually Donowa retired from his practice and returned home to Trinidad, where he died.

DUKES, LARRY STRATFORD

Only 19 years old at the time, Larry Dukes sailed for Spain on February 20, 1937, aboard the SS *Ile de France*. His passport (#366310, issued on February 9, 1937, and lost in Spain) showed addresses at 4500 Fireworks Street, East St. Louis, Illinois, and 3431 Cozens Street, St. Louis, Missouri. Dukes returned from Spain on the SS *Paris* on December 15, 1938.

DUREM, RAMON

Born in 1915 in Seattle, Washington, Ramon Durem in later life gained some notice as the black poet Ray Durem. In a 1962 biographical sketch in his book *Take No Prisoners,* Durem is reported to have left home at 14 and joined the Navy well before reaching legal age. He worked at a wide variety of manual jobs up and down the West Coast and attended the University of California in Berkeley.

Durem traveled to Spain on March 31, 1937, on board the SS *Aquitania.* He traveled on passport #25803, issued in San Francisco on March 20, 1937. His address on that document was 1738 Milvia Street, Berkeley, California. That passport was lost in Spain.

In a manuscript held by the Hoover Institute at Stanford University, noted left-wing journalist Anna Louise Strong reports her surprise at encountering Durem in Spain. She had previously known him as student at Berkeley. At the time of this encounter Durem was hospitalized in Madrid, recovering from wounds received at Brunete. He returned from Spain on December 20, 1937, on the SS *Ausonia.*

In records from the war period, Durem, a light-skinned man, was not identified as black. He later began to publicly identify himself as black, and in much of his later writing he identified strongly with the nationalist stream within the African-American community.

Durem began writing poetry in the late 1940s. His poems were first published in the *Crusader,* a journal edited by Robert Williams, the North Carolina-based black nationalist leader who in the 1960s was forced into exile in Cuba and China. Other poems were published in the literary journals *Phylon* and *Venture* and in the *Herald Dispatch* newspaper.

Durem's early poems attracted the interest of Langston Hughes, and in the mid-1950s Hughes tried to help Durem secure a publisher, but without success. Hughes did include one of Durem's poems in the anthology *New Negro Poets: USA*.

Meanwhile, Durem moved his family to Mexico to avoid the harassments of life in the United States in the 1950s. One of these harrassments, FBI surveillance, is the subject of his poem "Award," which is reproduced in part 4 of this volume. In 1962 Durem and his family returned to reside in Los Angeles. In the early 1960s Durem saw selections of his poetry published in the Heritage anthology *Sixes and Sevens* and in the New York literary magazine *Umbra 2*.

In 1963, at the age of 48, Ray Durem died of cancer in Los Angeles.

DUVALLE, PIERRE

Pierre Duvalle was also known by the pseudonym Gerald Goldwyn (the name on his U.S. passport). According to his videotaped interview in the Manny Harriman Oral History Collection of the Abraham Lincoln Brigade Archives, Duvalle was born in France, near the border of Spain, to a Basque mother and an African father. Duvalle's father served in the French Army.

The family later emigrated to Cuba and from there to New York City, where Duvalle finished high school and attended two years of college. While in school Duvalle was enrolled in the Reserve Officer Training Corps (ROTC) with the 15th Militia. He also worked at a dry-cleaning plant.

During these years in New York, Duvalle encountered the radical political movements of the 1930s and was drawn to the activities of the Communist party. He became friends with communist organizer Milton Herndon, who died in Spain. Eventually, at age 24, Duvalle himself volunteered to serve in Spain.

On September 9, 1937, passport #475431 (lost in Spain) was issued to Duvalle, under the name Gerald Goldwyn. His address was listed as 180 West 135th Street, New York City. He sailed for Spain on September 16, 1937, on the SS *Aquitania*. Duvalle served in the John Brown Artillery Battery, a unit made up of about 80 men, mostly American, charged with the maintenance and operation of two large 155-millimeter guns. The battery saw action throughout 1938 under commander Arthur Timpson.

When asked by Manny Harriman whether he encountered any prejudice or racism among the American volunteers in Spain, Duvalle recalled one incident in which a white volunteer used the phrase "nigger in the woodpile." He also recalled that the offending soldier was reprimanded by his superiors and ordered to apologize.

While at the front in the fall of 1938, Duvalle was accidentally wounded. He was sent to a hospital in Valencia for treatment and recuperation. While Duvalle was hospitalized, the order came for all international volunteers to evacuate from Spain. Duvalle rejoined his unit in Valencia. They traveled by ship to Barcelona, and from there they marched to the French border. After a period of internment in France, Duvalle finally returned to the United States on March 4, 1939.

In New York he returned to his union job at the dry-cleaning plant, but soon moved to California and settled in the San Francisco area. In 1940 the U.S. government ordered resident aliens to come forward for registration. Duvalle registered, and at this time had his first experience with FBI harassment. He was interrogated about his political beliefs and his experiences in Spain and threatened with deportation. As a result of FBI pressures he was fired from his job.

In 1941 Duvalle attempted to volunteer for the U.S. Army but was turned down for medical reasons. He then began working at an aluminum plant. FBI harrassments of Duvalle at his workplace and through his union continued well into the 1950s. At one point Duvalle was imprisoned to await deportation. Finally, deportation proceedings were dropped when Duvalle promised to notify the FBI if he ever left the United States. Duvalle continued to live in San Francisco until his death in the 1980s.

Frankson, Kanute Oliver

Born in Old Harbor, Jamaica, West Indies, circa 1890, Frankson, along with his wife Rachel, were admitted to the United States on April 30, 1917. At that time Frankson stated his occupation as machinist and his destination as Wilkes Barre, Pennsylvania. Frankson eventually took up residence in Detroit, where he worked in the auto industry. According to immigration records, Frankson attempted travel to Cuba in 1928 but was denied entry at the port of Havana.

Frankson sailed to Spain on April 21, 1937, on the SS *Queen Mary*. In Spain he served as head mechanic at the International Garage. He returned from Spain on September 24, 1938, on the SS *President Harding*.

Gamis y Cabrera, Domingo

Domingo Gamis y Cabrera was a black Cuban baseball player living in the United States in 1937. He was a pitcher for the Club Almenares. He sailed to Spain on January 23, 1937, from New York City aboard the SS *Champlain*. In Spain he served as a cook with the Guiteras Company of the Lincoln Battalion. Gamis died in Spain, in the battle of Jarama.

Garland, Walter Benjamin

At 23 years of age Walter Garland sailed to Spain on January 5, 1937, aboard the SS *Champlain*. His passport (#6907), issued in New York, also on January 5, 1937, shows his address as 511 Herkimer Street, Brooklyn.

Because of his previous military experience in the U.S. Army, which was rare among American volunteers, Garland was quickly placed in command of a machine-gun company in Spain. As the clippings listed in the sources section of this volume indicate, he subsequently won wide renown for his military performance. In August 1937 Garland joined Langston Hughes and Harry Haywood in transmitting a radio broadcast back to the United States from Madrid.

Garland served in the U.S. Army again in World War II. He was assigned in 1942 to the 731st Military Police Battalion at Fort Wadsworth, on Staten Island, New York. There he was invited to give a presentation to a class of officers on the Brunete campaign of the Spanish Civil War. Also at Fort Wadsworth, Garland taught mapmaking and scout car classes, mortar school, and machine-gun training. While at Wadsworth, Garland developed a new machine-gun sighting device for use on guns mounted on scout cars. This device was accepted and used by the U.S. Army. Garland made repeated requests for assignment to an arena of combat, all of which were summarily refused.

After the war Garland was cofounder, with fellow Lincoln veteran Burt Jackson, of the United Negro Allied Veterans of America (UNAVA).

GAVIN, EUGENE VICTOR

Eugene Victor Gavin, 27 years of age, sailed to Spain on March 10, 1937, on the SS *Washington*. His passport (#368846, issued on February 23, 1937) showed the address 962 West Federal Street, Youngstown, Ohio. This passport was subsequently reported lost in Spain. In correspondence with the U.S. State Department in the summer of 1937 regarding Gavin's welfare and whereabouts, his mother, of another Youngstown address, stated that he was an American Indian, born and raised in Oklahoma.

The correspondence from Gavin's mother subsequently reports that Gavin was wounded and hospitalized in Spain. The State Department reported to her that Gavin was sent home from Spain on July 10, 1938, due to "total incapacitation" from his wounds.

GAVIN, ROBERT OWEN

In correspondence with the State Department dated May 2, 1938, Robert Gavin (the brother of Eugene Gavin) was reported by his wife to be 29 years of age in May 1938 and a resident of Philadelphia. His wife, whose address was 5852 Haverford Avenue, Philadelphia, sought information on Gavin's welfare and whereabouts.

The State Department confirmed that passport #476728 had been issued to Robert Gavin on February 16, 1937, for "travel to England, France, and Scotland." The Spanish Ministry of Defense subsequently reported that Robert Gavin of the 15th Brigade "disappeared during the month of March of 1938, in combat against the enemy, defending the Republic, in the sector of Belchite-Caspe."

GEORGE, HENRY
Twenty-nine years old, George was issued passport #436583 on June 8, 1937. He gave as addresses 1111 South 24th Street and 2312 Ellsworth Street, both in Philadelphia. George sailed for Spain on June 19, 1937, aboard the SS *Berengeria*. He returned December 15, 1938, on the SS *Paris*. Correspondence of Lincoln Brigade veteran Ben Gardner suggests that Henry George may have been the pseudonym of Benjamin Rice.

GIBBS, THEODORE
Gibbs sailed to Spain on March 24, 1937, aboard the SS *Manhattan*. He traveled on passport #4899, issued in Chicago on March 19, 1937; this passport was lost in Spain. His address at that time was listed as 4224 Greenshaw Street, Chicago. He returned from Spain on December 20, 1938, on the SS *Ausonia*. Gibbs died in Chicago on March 12, 1962.

GOLDWYN, GERALD
Pseudonym for Duvalle, Pierre (listed above).

GRAHAM, MEREDITH SYDNOR
Graham, 25 years old, sailed to Spain on March 10, 1937, aboard the SS *Washington*. He traveled on passport #370943, issued on March 2, 1937. His address was listed as 32 Cornelia Street, New York City.

In September of 1937 Graham's father made inquiry to the State Department regarding his son's welfare and whereabouts. The father, George W. Graham, Jr., of 3650 Bellecrest Avenue, Cincinatti, Ohio, was an agent of the New York Underwriters Insurance Company.

According to a report transmitted by the American Consul at Valencia, Graham was killed in action at Brunete on July 18, 1937. Graham served as an aide to Brigade Commander Robert Merriman, who was reported to have witnessed Graham's death and to have assisted in his burial.

GUTIERREZ DIAS, CENTURIO
No biographical information available. Mentioned in *Toronto Clarion* article on volunteers in Spain (see sources).

HALL, PHILIP E.

According to an unconfirmed source, Hall was a black soldier of fortune, born at Bocas del Toro, Panama. He was captured by Franco's forces in Spain and subsequently sentenced to 12 years of hard labor in San Sebastian, Spain, for assisting Loyalist forces.

HARVEY, GEORGE

No information. May be the same person as Henry George, listed above.

HAYWOOD, HARRY

According to his autobiograpy, *The Black Bolshevik*, Harry Haywood was born Haywood Hall in South Omaha, Nebraska, on February 4, 1898, the youngest of Harriet and Haywood Hall's three children. Both of his parents were born as slaves, the father in West Tennessee and the mother in Missouri. The family moved to Minneapolis in 1913 after the father was beaten by a white gang in South Omaha. Soon thereafter, Harry left school in Minneapolis after incidents of racial harassment. In 1915 the family moved to Chicago, where Harry worked as a waiter.

In early 1917 Harry Haywood joined the Eighth Illinois Black National Guard Regiment. Shortly thereafter, the regiment was federalized for service in World War I. The unit was trained near Houston, Texas and shipped to France in April 1918. Haywood served with the Eighth Regiment for the duration of World War I. Near the end of the war he fell ill, and his return to the United States was delayed by hospitalization. He was finally discharged on April 29, 1919. Back in Chicago, Harry resumed working as a waiter and in 1920 married his first wife Hazel. They parted later that same year.

Haywood's older brother, Otto Hall, was an early member of the U.S. Communist party, joining in 1921, shortly after its formation. In 1922, at his brother's suggestion, Harry Haywood joined the African Blood Brotherhood (a secret organization that included many important black members of the Communist party); six months later he joined the YCL. He joined the Communist party in the spring of 1925. Shortly thereafter Haywood was sent to the Soviet Union to study. Upon his return he worked as a Party organizer in various labor struggles. In 1931 he was appointed to the Communist Central Committee and made head of the Party's National Negro Department. He was placed on the Party politburo in 1934.

Early in 1937 Harry Haywood volunteered to go to Spain, where he served as a political commissar. There he became involved in disputes with other members of the leadership. He was called back to the United States in the fall of 1937. In May 1938 Haywood was removed from the politburo of the Communist party.

Haywood suffered a heart attack in October of 1939. His heart ailment was found to be related to his World War I illness, and he was placed on a veteran's disability pension and exempted from military service in World War II. While recovering from the heart attack, Haywood moved to Los Angeles. There he married Belle Lewis, whom he had known from union activities in the early 1930s. He continued to be active in the Communist party at the local level.

In June of 1943 Haywood joined the Merchant Marine. He remained in the Merchant Marine until after the end of World War II, when he and Belle moved back east to New York City. In New York Haywood continued to work as a seaman and a Party activist. In the fall of 1948 he published a book entitled *Negro Liberation*. In 1955 Haywood ended his marriage to Belle Lewis. Shortly afterward he married Gwen Midlo, who became the mother of his son, Haywood Hall, in 1956.

Throughout the late 1950s Haywood was embroiled in the Communist party's internal conflicts and turmoil. At one point he was involved (along with fellow Lincoln Brigade veteran Admiral Kilpatrick, among others) in the short-lived Provisional Organizing Committee for a Communist Party (POC), a black- and Hispanic-led attempt to found a new left-wing party. Haywood was expelled from the Communist party in 1959.

Before the final expulsion, Haywood, along with his wife and son, had resettled in Mexico City. There his daughter Becky was born in 1963. Haywood remained in Mexico until 1970, when he returned to the United States. His autobiography was published in 1978. He is now deceased.

HERNDON, MILTON

Milton Herndon was the brother of U.S. Communist party leader Angelo Herndon. Angelo Herndon came to national notice in 1932 when he was sentenced to death in Atlanta, Georgia, on a charge of "incitement to insurrection" as a result of his organizing activities there. Herndon's conviction was eventually overturned on appeal.

Milton Herndon was also a Party activist and organizer from Chicago. In 1937, at the age of 28, Herndon traveled to Spain with a passport (#393028, issued on April 19, 1937) bearing the pseudonym Milton Braxton and the address 133 West 140th Street, New York City. He sailed to Spain on May 8, 1937, on the SS *American Importer*.

In Spain, Herndon was section leader of the Frederick Douglass Machine Gun Company. His letter home from Spain to his brother was published in the Communist party press in June of 1937. Herndon was killed in battle on October 13, 1937.

HUNTER, JOHN PORTER

John Porter Hunter sailed to Spain on April 10, 1937, on the SS *Rotter-dam*. In July of the same year he was reported killed in combat. In that same month a Mrs. Bertha Hunter of 82 Schenectady Avenue, Brooklyn, corresponded with the U.S. State Department in an effort to determine if the John Hunter reported dead in Spain might be her missing husband, John Dudley Hunter. A search of State Department passport records and transmissions from Spain discovered no record of a John Hunter under either name.

In an interview in the Abraham Lincoln Brigade Film Project Archives (BUSCW), Vaughn Love recalls Hunter, a husky man who served as a machine gunner, as being from Buffalo, New York. He remembers that during a retreat, Hunter carried his 100-pound gun for over two weeks through forests and hills, eventually constructing a cane raft in order to float the big gun across a river.

HUNTER, OSCAR HENRY

At the age of 28, Oscar Hunter traveled to Spain on January 16, 1937, aboard the SS *Paris*. He used passport #88014, issued on April 12, 1934, and listed his address as 3504 Lake Park Avenue, Chicago.

As recounted in the ALBA oral history interview conducted on May 22, 1980, Oscar Hunter was born in Orange, New Jersey, on May 22, 1908. His mother was "mostly Indian," and his father, from South Carolina, was "mostly French." His father's surname, Lannier, was Hunter's legal name before his mother changed it to Hunter. Hunter's mother died when he was in the fourth grade. At 14 he hitchhiked to Detroit, expecting to get a job in the newly booming auto industry. Along the way, in Cleveland, he was taken in by a local black family who helped him get a job as a window washer in a department store. A supervisor at the department store, also a black man, noticed that Hunter spent his spare time reading and offered to help him get back into school.

Oscar Hunter attended the Hampton Institute in Virginia for five years. It was at Hampton, he says, that he "became a radical." This was due in part, he recalls, to the influence of a Bible teacher named Foster, who had been educated at the Union Theological Seminary. Hunter recalled that he "didn't take the Bible very well because my mother hadn't." When Foster noticed this, he began to give Hunter books on socialism to read instead. While at Hampton Hunter was among the leaders of a student strike. It was during the strike that he met a Hampton faculty member, Louise Thompson, who later became a prominent Harlem activist and married the black Communist party leader William Patterson.

Hunter stayed at Hampton until 1930. Then he went to West Virginia State College on a football scholarship. There he was exposed to the mineworkers' struggles, partly through the influence of a sociology teacher named Ferguson. After college Hunter attended Brookwood Labor College, a school for labor organizers run by the radical Protestant minister A. J. Muste. It was at Brookwood that Hunter encountered the Communist party and Party members for the first time.

He soon joined the Party and worked for it in New York City for a year. He then relocated to Chicago, where the Party was involved in a drive to organize the stockyard workers. During this period in Chicago, Hunter also studied journalism at Northwestern University and joined the Chicago John Reed Club, which at that time included among its members Richard Wright and Nelson Algren.

In 1936 Hunter volunteered to fight in Spain. He obtained his passport by saying that he planned to study at the London School of Economics (this is also what he told his family). He traveled from Chicago to New York in the company of Oliver Law, a third black man, and two young white men. All of them were bound for Spain.

In Spain, Hunter served first with the Tom Mooney Machine Gun Company. There he formed a close comradeship with Douglas Roach, another African-American volunteer, with whom he shared a trench and attempted to operate a World War I-era Russian machine gun. Later Hunter was put in the American-run hospital with Dr. Edward Barsky. He eventually became a political commissar for the hospital. Later he was put in charge of a garage.

As the International Brigades' role in the war wound down, Hunter was sent back to Chicago to arrange hospital space and care for the wounded Americans who would soon be returning home. Upon his reentry to the United States, customs officers confiscated his passport. Shortly thereafter federal investigators began asking questions about Hunter around Chicago, and at the homes of relatives in Cleveland. In Chicago Hunter helped organize the Veterans of the Abraham Lincoln Brigade (VALB) post and continued his previous political activities. Eventually the Party informed him that because of his political activities he was in danger of arrest in Chicago and should leave town. Hunter then relocated to Greenwich Village in New York City, where he remained for the rest of his life. He was given a 4-F exemption during World War II because he had extreme hypertension.

In New York, with the assistance of Joe Gordon, a fellow Lincoln Brigade veteran, Hunter got a job as a furrier. Later he developed his own printmaking process and went into business with it. This eventually led to his establishment of a business producing handpainted wallpaper, which Hunter and his wife, Betty, operated together in his last years.

Hunter reports having been harassed by the FBI during the 1950s. In fact, FBI visits to his workplace helped lead to the establishment of his own business. One of Hunter's brothers would not speak to him for many years because he had been frightened by FBI questioning. Hunter left the Communist party in the early 1950s.

In his later years Hunter was active in anti-Vietnam War protests and in neighborhood issues around his New York City cooperative apartment building. In 1979 he was one of the founders of the Abraham Lincoln Brigade Archives. Hunter died in 1982 in New York.

JACKSON, BURT EDWARD

Burt Jackson traveled to Spain on June 15, 1937, aboard the SS *Georgic* at the age of 22. His passport (#40259, issued on May 1, 1937, and lost in Spain) listed his address as 167-14 109th Avenue, Jamaica, Long Island, New York. He returned from Spain on December 20, 1938, aboard the SS *Ausonia*. In Spain he served as a topographer at the 15th Brigade's headquarters.

Jackson subsequently served in the U.S. Army during World War II as the chief of ordnance for the 99th Division's Air Cobras. After the war Jackson was cofounder, with fellow Lincoln Brigade veteran Walter Garland, of UNAVA. He also attended art school and contributed illustrations to various African-American publications.

JOHNSON, AARON BERNARD

In 1937, at 24 years of age, Aaron Johnson sailed to Spain on April 28, 1937, aboard the SS *President Harding.* His passport (#26291, San Francisco series) was issued on April 6, 1937, and showed his address as 3843 Adair Street, Los Angeles. There is no record of his return from Spain.

JOHNSON, EDWARD

According to Lincoln Brigade veteran Robert Steck's report on American prisoners of war in Spain, Johnson was born in Lynchburg, Virginia, on February 10, 1891. This made him one of the oldest of the American volunteers in Spain. Johnson had served in the U.S. Army in World War I and then settled in London, Kentucky, where he worked on the railroads. Later he moved to Ohio and worked in the steel mills.

Johnson sailed to Spain on February 20, 1937, aboard the SS *Ile de France.* His passport (#367415, issued on February 15, 1937, and lost in Spain) showed the address 135 Hosack Street, Columbus, Ohio. In Spain, Johnson served for a time as head of the general food commissary. He was later captured at Belchite in Spain on March 10, 1938, and held prisoner at San Pedro de Cardenas.

JOHNSON, RICHARD

No information. The State Department name index at the National Archives does show the existence of a 130- passport file dated June 8, 1936 (before the Spanish Civil War), regarding a Richard Johnson accused of an attempted passport fraud. This alleged fraudulent attempt to gain a passport was said by the State Department to have been committed with the assistance of the Chicago office of the Communist party. Since those passport files are still closed, it is not known whether this is the Richard Johnson who served with the Lincoln Brigade.

KEE, SALARIA

Salaria Kee traveled to Spain on March 27, 1937, aboard the SS *Paris*. Her passport (#378164, issued on March 24, 1937) listed her address as Harlem Hospital and 289 Livingston Place, Akron. She sailed in a party of 12 nurses and physicians. She was the only African American in this group and the first black woman to go to Spain. While in Spain she was seriously wounded on three occasions. Finally, she returned to the United States to help rally support for the Spanish cause.

According to the ALBA oral history interview, Kee was born on July 13, 1913, in Akron, Ohio. Her father, a merchant seaman, died in World War I in 1914. Kee's mother also died when she was very young, and she was raised mostly in foster homes.

When she reached high-school age, Kee wanted to become a nurse. Three nursing schools in the Akron area refused to admit her because of her race. Eventually, she was admitted to the Harlem Hospital School of Nursing in New York City. Kee recalls that her move to New York came after a Mrs. Firestone of Akron intervened with Mrs. Franklin Roosevelt, whose husband was then governor of New York.

Upon completion of her training, Kee worked in the Seaview Hospital in New York City. Here, she recalls, black nurses were sent to work in the tuberculosis wards, where supervisors refused even to enter. Kee recalls that many nurses she worked with contracted the disease. In 1936 Kee attempted to volunteer to work as a nurse with the Red Cross in the wake of disastrous floods in the Midwest, but her services were refused on account of her race. Shortly thereafter she learned of an American medical mission preparing to serve in Spain. Being a Catholic, she had often read about the nuns who worked among the poor and the sick, and she wanted to serve in that way.

Kee departed for Spain by ship with others of the American medical unit. Upon arrival in Spain she was assigned to the International Medical Unit at Villa Paz, in one of King Alfonso's former summer homes. At the hospital in Villa Paz, Kee met her husband, Pat O'Reilly, who had been wounded while serving with a British International unit. They were married at the hospital and subsequently made a life together in the United States.

During her time in Spain, Kee says, she experienced no anti-Catholic feelings at all on the Loyalist side. The Loyalists "wasn't just Communists," she said, noting that at the time she "didn't even know what a Communist was. I thought it was for white people only, like the Mafia."

In late 1938 Kee returned to the United States on board the SS *Queen Mary*. She resettled in New York and for a time made many speeches on the Spanish cause before a variety of groups, including "churches, schools, and the NAACP." Later she taught training classes for practical nurses and nurses' aides.

Kee served in the Army Nurse Corps in the last months of World War II. She recalls that her Spanish Civil War experience was highly valued by her superiors. She and Pat O'Reilly lived out their working years in New York City and returned to Akron in the early 1970s.

Salaria Kee O'Reilly died in Akron in 1991.

KILPATRICK, ADMIRAL

Admiral Kilpatrick traveled to Spain on February 20, 1937, on the SS *Ile de France*. His passport (#367543, issued on February 16, 1937) showed the addresses 5810 and 6003 Thackery Avenue, Cleveland, Ohio. He returned to the United States on December 20, 1938, on the SS *Ausonia*.

According to the ALBA oral history interview conducted on June 8, 1980, Kilpatrick's father was born in Oklahoma to an Indian father and black mother. Kilpatrick's mother was from Kentucky. Kilpatrick's father worked first as a cowboy in Oklahoma and then in the mines in Colorado. Admiral Kilpatrick was born in Colorado on February 20, 1898. In Colorado, Kilpatrick's father got a job with the company that eventually became Republic Steel. He ended up moving the family to Cleveland, Ohio, to work for Republic Steel there when Admiral was six years old.

Kilpatrick states that his father was a Debs Socialist, and he recalls going to political meetings with him as early as 1910 or 1911. Kilpatrick eventually joined the Socialist party himself, and later the Industrial Workers of the World (IWW) as well. He finished high school in Cleveland and worked in "mills, foundries, electrical shops, lumber camps," changing jobs frequently.

Kilpatrick worked with the union in the 1919 Cleveland steel strike, in which the companies brought in thousands of blacks to serve as strikebreakers. Due to his union activities and Socialist party connections, Kilpatrick recalls he was in contact with the Communist party from its inception in this country. He finally joined the Party in 1927. In 1931 he was selected by the Party to work and study in the Soviet Union. He also traveled in Eastern Europe. He returned to the United States in 1935 and worked in organizing the Congress of Industrial Organizations (CIO) and the unemployed movement.

Kilpatrick then volunteered to go to Spain. He states that in Spain he worked with an international intelligence unit to stop the sabotage of Loyalist trucks. He was wounded by shrapnel from an aerial bombardment.

Upon his return from Spain Kilpatrick resumed his union work and continued it throughout World War II. He eventually became president of Local 735 of the Mine, Mill, and Smelter Workers; then he became an international representative. After the war that union was expelled from the CIO as Communist-influenced. Kilpatrick left the union because of political disputes during the early 1950s and went to work at Westinghouse.

During the Red scare of the 1950s Kilpatrick was called before congressional investigators. He refused to talk but did not take the Fifth Amendment. In the 1950s Kilpatrick started a small independent trucking business. He was expelled from the Communist party around 1960. In 1961 he was convicted of larceny (wrongfully, he states) in Cleveland and served a brief term in prison.

Kilpatrick was the father of three daughters and one son. At the time of the interview he was living in Cleveland in a senior citizens' housing project, where he served as chairman of the tenants' committee. He is now deceased.

LAW, OLIVER

Oliver Law was the first African American ever to command an integrated American fighting force. Law served for six years in the U.S. Army as a private. He later worked in the building trades in Chicago and as an organizer of the unemployed councils. As a result of his organizing work he had frequent run-ins with the Chicago Police Red Squad and was once seriously injured by a police beating. Shortly before departing for Spain, Law was arrested while leading a protest march against the Italian Fascist invasion of Ethiopia.

Law sailed to Spain on January 16, 1937, on the SS *Paris*. His passport (#360284, issued on January 7, 1937) showed the address 4608 Calumet Avenue, Chicago. He was approximately 37 years of age.

In Spain, Law's leadership qualities and previous military experience were highly valued. He first served as commander of a machine-gun company. When the previous Lincoln Battalion commander, Martin Hourihan, was promoted to another assignment, Law was chosen to replace him and given the rank of captain. He led the battalion for three months until he was killed in combat during the Brunete offensive on July 10, 1937.

Law's historic achievement was finally recognized in his hometown 50 years later when Chicago Mayor Harold Washington declared November 21, 1987, to be Oliver Law and the Abraham Lincoln Brigade Day in Chicago. Washington's declaration recognized Oliver Law as "a leader of movements for the relief of the poor and for political rights for blacks and working people in Chicago in the early 1930s" and as "the first black American to lead an integrated military force in the history of the United States."

Lewis, Abraham

Abraham Lewis, age 32, sailed to Spain on March 27, 1937, aboard the SS *Paris*. He traveled on passport #6397 (New York series, issued on March 19, 1937), which listed his address as 1524 Prospect Avenue, Cleveland. This passport was lost in Spain. Lewis returned from Spain on February 4, 1939, on the SS *President Harding*.

According to the booklet *Black Americans in the Spanish People's War against Fascism*, Lewis was born into a sharecropper family in Alabama and later migrated to Cleveland, Ohio. There he became a laundry worker.

In Cleveland, Lewis eventually joined the Communist party and became a leader in the Future Outlook League, a local African-American community organization. He contributed articles to the black community newspaper and was active in the Scottsboro Defense Campaign, the NAACP, and other causes and organizations. He was credited with being the first black to force Cleveland's previously discriminatory St. Luke's Hospital to perform surgery on him. Upon returning from Spain, Lewis resumed his community activities in Cleveland until his death in 1949.

Lewis, Charles Howard

Charles Lewis, aged 24, sailed to Spain on June 12, 1937, aboard the SS *Georgic*. His passport (#431965, issued on June 2, 1937) showed his address as 871 Home Street, Bronx, New York. Lewis was killed in Spain.

Lisberg, Norman

Norman Lisberg, born in Abita Springs, Louisiana on February 19, 1911, to Camille and Emmanuel Lisberg, sailed to Spain on June 12, 1937, on board the SS *Georgic*. His address was 919½ East Jefferson Street, Los Angeles. He carried a passport (#28772, San Francisco series) issued May 28, 1937.

Lisberg was reported wounded in the fall of 1937. He recovered from that incident and returned to action. He was killed at Teruel on January 25, 1938.

In April 1939 the Metropolitan Life Insurance Company initiated correspondence with the U.S. State Department (cited in the sources section of this volume) seeking confirmation of Lisberg's death in Spain.

In his interview with the BUSCW, Vaughn Love recalls Lisberg as a very poor young man who had been raised in New York and had later moved to Los Angeles.

LOVE, VAUGHN

Vaughn Love sailed to Spain on February 20, 1937, on the SS *Ile de France*. His passport (#6325, New York series) was issued on February 10, 1937, and listed his address as 742 St. Nicholas Avenue, New York City. He was 29 years old. Love returned from Spain on December 20, 1938, on the SS *Ausonia*.

According to a lengthy audiotaped interview conducted for the Abraham Lincoln Brigade Film Project, Love was born and raised in Eastern Tennessee in the town of Dayton, near the city of Chattanooga. He left Tennessee for West Virginia at about 14 or 15 years of age. There he finished high school and attended Bluefield College. He played football at Bluefield with considerable success. After two years at Bluefield, Love transferred to West Virginia State College to study and play football. An injury ended his football career, however, and he left West Virginia for New York, hoping to attend Columbia University.

Love states that he arrived in New York in 1929, "just in time for the Depression." In New York he became involved with the Federal Theater Project. This led to connections with the League of Struggle for Negro Rights and the Southern Labor Committee and eventually to service in Spain. In another interview Love recalls that when the war in Spain broke out, "We didn't know too much about the Spaniards, but we knew that they were fighting against fascism, and that fascism was the enemy of all black aspirations."

Love recalls entering Barcelona, Spain, by boat from Marseilles under an anarchist ship captain. He also recalls one of his first encounters with Spanish peasants, who, unfamiliar with black people, came over and attempted to wipe the dirt from his face. When he explained that he was a Negro from North America, he says they hugged him and exclaimed, "Oh, los esclavos! Si! Si!" Love says, "they knew there was black slavery in America, 'los esclavos,' and that they were only one little step away from us los esclavos."

In later life Love worked in communications. He lived in New York until his death in 1990.

McDaniels, Eluard Luchell

McDaniels was born in Mississippi in 1912. He left home at an early age and made his way to California. There he was eventually taken in by a family in San Francisco, where he finished high school and studied art at San Francisco State College.

Also in San Francisco, through involvement with the early battles of the longshoreman's union, McDaniels developed ties to the labor movement and the Communist party. He states that in the early 1930s he traveled back East and South to participate in various labor-organizing campaigns, including that of the Alabama Sharecroppers' Union. McDaniels was also involved in the Federal Writers Project of the WPA in the 1930s.

McDaniels volunteered for the Abraham Lincoln Brigade and traveled to Spain on June 25, 1937, aboard the SS *Ausonia*. His passport (#29525, San Francisco series, issued on June 12, 1937) showed his address as either 1116 Stockton Street or 2833 Sacramento Street, both in San Francisco. During the war Spanish Loyalist troops, awed by his prowess at grenade pitching, gave McDaniels the nickname "El Fantastico."

McDaniels returned from Spain on December 31, 1938, on the SS *President Harding*. In the years during and after World War II McDaniels worked as a seaman. He lived in the San Francisco area until his death.

Mitchell, Andrew

Andrew Mitchell volunteered to fight in Spain at the age of 34. He traveled to Spain on July 21, 1937, on the SS *Berengeria*. His passport (#459723, issued on July 12, 1937) showed the address 17 Elmore Street, Pittsburgh. In Spain, according to the personal recollection of Lincoln Brigade veteran George Watt, Mitchell attended officer training school at Tarazona in the winter of 1937-38. He then assumed command of a recruit company in training. He later led a company to the front. Mitchell disappeared in the retreats of April 1938 and was presumed dead. In his book *Men in Battle*, Lincoln Brigade veteran Alvah Bessie writes of Mitchell as "a handsome Negro who commanded our recruit company for a time and wore lieutenant's stripes. He walked like a king or like a panther; he had one of the most beautiful speaking voices I have ever heard, and a sense of humor about his job that was beyond cavil. He went to the front later as a soldier, I have never seen him since."

MORGAN, CRAWFORD

Crawford Morgan was born circa 1911 in North Carolina and later lived in Norfolk, Virginia. During the Depression he became involved in organizations of the unemployed in New York City and was on one occasion arrested in a demonstration at the Home Relief Bureau.

Morgan volunteered to go to Spain at the age of 26 and traveled to Spain on March 10, 1937, on the SS *Washington*. He used passport #369937, issued on February 26, 1937, which showed his address as 419 West 53rd Street, New York City. This passport was lost in Spain.

In Spain Morgan first served at brigade headquarters as a runner. He was wounded in the leg at the battle of Quinto and hospitalized. After recovering he served as a truck driver with the brigade motor pool. Morgan returned from Spain on December 15, 1938, on the SS *Paris*.

Morgan served in the U.S. Army, in all-black units, from August 1942 to May 1946 (serial number 32423315). He was stationed briefly at Camp Pickett, Virginia, and then for over a year at Camp Shelby, Mississippi. The rest of his army service was in the European theater with a heavy transportation battalion. After leaving the army Morgan took up residence in Norfolk, Virginia, and worked as a truck driver until 1949. He later returned to New York City and became an offset printer.

On September 15 and 16, 1954, Morgan testified at length on behalf of the VALB in hearings before the Subversive Activities Control Board (SACB) of the U.S. Department of Justice. The SACB was in the process of declaring the VALB to be a subversive organization. Morgan was called by the VALB's attorney as a defense witness. He testified that "being a Negro, and all of the stuff that I have had to take in this country, I had a pretty good idea of what fascism was. I got a chance there [in Spain] to fight it with bullets, and I went there and fought it with bullets. If I get a chance to fight it with bullets again, I will fight it with bullets again."

Morgan died in New York City in 1976.

PAGE, THOMAS

Thomas Page was born in New York City on September 29, 1909. The family lived in Manhattan, near 10th Avenue on 59th Street, and Page went through two years of high school before dropping out. In an interview conducted for the Abraham Lincoln Brigade Film Project, Page recalls that his political education began during the Depression as a member of the Unemployed Council, when he began to discover the reasons he was unable to find work. Earlier in the Depression years, Page reports, he circumvented the shortage of legitimate employment by engaging in the illegal manufacture and sale of liquor.

Through his involvement in the Unemployed Council, Page eventually joined the Communist party. He said, "As I understood events in that particular era, it was the Communist party who did anything. Everybody else just talked."

As a result of these involvements, Page also became aware of the spread of fascism in Europe and the growth of far Right groups in the U.S. In order to counter the fascist threat, Page volunteered to join the fighting in Spain. He left for Spain on March 10, 1937, on the SS *Washington*. His passport (#368136, issued on February 18, 1937) showed the address 14 Randall Court, Rockville Centre, New York.

Page entered Spain by boat from Marseilles. Along with a number of other Americans, he was first assigned to the Spanish 86th Brigade and was later moved to join the bulk of the Americans in the Lincoln Brigade. As a third company sergeant in the Lincoln Brigade, he was seriously wounded in the chest during the Ebro offensive and received a citation for bravery. He returned from Spain on December 20, 1938 on the SS *Ausonia*.

Upon returning from Spain, Page worked for a period as a guard at the Soviet Pavilion at the New York World's Fair and then in the New York fur market. He served in the U.S. Army during World War II in North Africa, Italy, and France. He was assigned to the 376th Engineering Brigade, Company C (serial number 32541380).

After the war Page took up photography and learned camera repair. During the 1950s, Page recalls, he had several visits from the FBI. These eventually stopped because he persistently refused to talk to them. Later Page worked for the Bell Telephone Company until his retirement. He is featured prominently in the film *The Good Fight*.

PARKER, CHARLES AUGUSTUS

Charles A. Parker traveled to Spain using passport #577021, issued on August 16, 1938. He gave his address as 292 Lexington Avenue, New York City, or 1610 Dear Street, Brooklyn. He was killed in the fighting in Spain.

PECK, JAMES LINCOLN HOLT

Peck was an African-American aviator who served as a pilot in the air force of Republican Spain. In the United States before the war, Peck had obtained a commercial pilot's license and had studied at the University of Pittsburgh for two years. As of 1930 there were only five black pilots in the United States. Despite his education and flying experience, Peck's applications to the U.S. Air Corps and Navy flying schools were rejected out of hand. Unable to support himself as a pilot, Peck worked for a time as a professional musician. Eventually, he volunteered to become one of the 31 American fliers who served in Spain.

Peck traveled to Europe early in 1937 aboard the *Queen Mary*, along with Paul Williams, another black pilot bound for Spain. Once in Spain, they were integrated into the Spanish Air Ministry rather than being organized into a separate international unit. Peck was commissioned as a lieutenant in the Republican Army Air Force of Spain. In 1941 Peck told the *People's World* "that what we were fighting in Spain was a species of that thing which at home had kept me, a trained pilot, grounded, while keeping hundreds of thousands of other Negro youths from being what they wanted to be."

Peck flew for the Republic until the fall of 1938, when he was sent home along with the other international volunteers. Upon his return Peck wrote stories about his adventures in Spain for *Harper's, Popular Aviation, Scientific American,* and other magazines. He authored the book *Armies with Wings,* which was published by Dodd, Mead & Co. Most of his readers were unaware that the author was an African American.

PRINGLE, CLAUDE

According to the Lincoln Brigade veteran Robert Steck's report on American prisoners of war in Spain, Claude Pringle was born on January 22, 1894, in the town of Holston, Halifax County, Virginia. He grew up in Logan City, West Virginia, and served in the U.S. Army during World War I. After the war he became a coal miner in Bellaire, Ohio, where he was involved in the mineworkers' strike of 1922.

At 43 years of age, Pringle was among the oldest of the U.S. volunteers. He sailed for Spain on May 1, 1937, on the SS *Britannic* (passport #392813, issued on April 19, 1937). The passport listed his address as 637 L Street, Washington, D.C., or Bellaire, Ohio.

Pringle was one of the 300 volunteers being transported from France to Spain aboard the *Ciudad de Barcelona* when the ship was sunk by a fascist torpedo. Many Americans drowned, but Pringle and the other survivors made their way to the Spanish shore. Once in Spain, Pringle served with the predominantly Canadian Mackenzie-Papineau Battalion and was wounded in the shoulder at Teruel. In a report to the United States from Spain, John P. Davis, Executive Secretary of the National Negro Congress, wrote, "This morning I saw two Negro kids walk down Glory Road: Claude Pringle and Otto Reeves were decorated as loyal, well-disciplined soldiers of the Spanish People's Army."

Pringle was still fighting with the "Mac-Paps" when he was taken prisoner during the retreat from Gandesa. He was interned at San Pedro de

Cardenas and released in a postwar exchange of prisoners on April 22, 1939.

PROWELL, ALPHEUS DANFORTH

Prowell sailed for Spain on August 14, 1937, aboard the SS *Champlain*. His passport (#30845, San Francisco series, issued on August 2, 1937) showed his address at the time to be 1001 East 47th Street, Los Angeles. Prowell died in Spain.

RANSOM, MARCUS

Marcus Ransom was 28 years old when he sailed for Spain (passport #33208, San Francisco series, issued on January 17, 1938). His address at the time was 1265 41st Street, Los Angeles.

According to the recollections of fellow Lincoln Brigade veteran James Yates, as recorded in the booklet *Black Americans in the Spanish People's War against Fascism,* Ransom, who was severely wounded while fighting in Spain, was evacuated to a French hospital and died there from his wounds.

REEVES, OTTO COLEMAN

According to a manuscript by Lincoln Brigade veteran Morris Brier ("Three Friends," BUSCW), Otto Reeves was born in Cleveland, Ohio. His father was the minister of a storefront church and a construction worker. When his father became unemployed during the Depression, Reeves left home in order to lessen the burden on his family. He eventually made his way to Los Angeles, California. There Reeves, who had graduated high school in Cleveland, was able to get a live-in job as a cook and house-keeper in a fraternity house at the University of Southern California.

Reeves's political activities began when one of the young white students in the fraternity invited him to go to a rally for the Scottsboro case. This same white student also took Reeves to Communist party meetings and demonstrations. Reeves subsequently became independently interested in political affairs and began to educate himself. Nevertheless, he did not join the Communist party or any other organization before going to Spain.

Reeves sailed for Spain on May 15, 1937, aboard the SS *Georgic* carrying passport #27636 (San Francisco series, issued on May 7, 1937). His passport carried the address 844 34th Street, Oakland, California. In Spain, Reeves served with the Mackenzie-Papineau Battalion as a machine gunner. Morris Brier, who served with him there, recalls that Reeves said he had come to Spain for two reasons: "One, to prove to myself that I am capable of risking my life for something I thought was correct, and two, I was testing the Communist party and its white members; whether they really meant they were our friends." Brier reports that Reeves did join the Communist party in Spain.

During the retreat after the defeat at the Ebro, when his company was virtually surrounded and ammunition was low, Reeves volunteered to go out for more. He never returned and was presumed to be killed.

RHETTA, VIRGIL

Born on July 1, 1909, Virgil Rhetta was a schoolteacher in California before serving in the Lincoln Brigade. He traveled to Spain ·(passport #33285, San Francisco series, issued on January 21, 1938). His address was listed as 9233 Fifth Street, Los Angeles. Virgil Rhetta was killed in Spain.

ROACH, DOUGLAS BRYAN

Roach, a native of Provincetown, Massachusetts, on Cape Cod, was a graduate of the Massachusetts Agricultural College at Amherst. There, although barely five feet tall, he achieved notice as a star wrestler. He joined the Communist party in 1932.

Roach sailed for Spain on January 6, 1937, on the SS *Paris*. At that time his address was 24 Conwell Street, Provincetown. At Brunete, Roach was seriously wounded by shrapnel in his shoulder. Unable to continue fighting, he was sent back to the United States, where he went to work organizing for the seamen's union.

Roach died of pneumonia at New York's Mount Sinai Hospital on July 13, 1938, at the age of 29. His funeral was held at the Mother A. M. E. Zion Church in New York, with the Reverend Benjamin Robeson (Paul Robeson's brother) presiding. His body was sent home to Provincetown, accompanied by fellow Lincoln Brigade veterans Paul Burns and Walter Garland.

ROBERSON, JAMES

Roberson is remembered in the memoir of Lincoln Brigade veteran James Yates as a black Chicagoan who fought in Spain. Unfortunately, no other record of his participation has yet been found.

ROCHESTER, STERLING TAYLOR

Born in Barclay, Maryland, on October 15, 1901, Sterling Rochester was visiting the Soviet Union when the Spanish Civil War began. He left from the U.S.S.R. and met up with the American contingent in Spain. He traveled on passport #234264, which had been issued to him on August 6, 1935. His address at that time was 108 Olive Street, Philadelphia.

In Spain, Rochester served as a machine gunner until he was so seriously wounded that in June 1937 he was sent back to the United States to recover. There Rochester undertook an extensive speaking tour to rally support for the Spanish struggle.

Having resettled in Philadelphia, Rochester was cited in a memo dated November 21, 1939, from FBI Director J. Edgar Hoover to Assistant Secretary of State Adolph Berle, as one of a number of "members of the Communist party" who "during the recent elections in Philadelphia, Pennsylvania . . . sought election on the Democratic and Fusion tickets." Rochester continued as an activist in the Communist party until he died in Philadelphia.

RODRIGUEZ, JULIUS
Rodriguez sailed for Spain on March 10, 1937, on the SS *Queen Mary*. He was 28 years old. His passport (#371416, issued on March 3, 1937) showed his address to be 701 West 117th Street, New York City, or 2800 Bronx Park, East Bronx, New York. Rodriguez served as an ambulance driver in Spain. No information is available regarding how, or whether, he returned.

ROOSEVELT, PATRICK
According to an interview with him in the archives of the Abraham Lincoln Brigade Film Project, Patrick Roosevelt was born in Washington State on December 1, 1905. He grew up in Washington and in California, the second-youngest of eight children. He stated that his mother was a schoolteacher and his father a doctor. Roosevelt finished high school in California and attended the California Institute of Technology before he became interested in aviation. He obtained training as a pilot and barnstormed around the country in the late 1920s and early 1930s. In those days, however, opportunities were severely limited for a black man in aviation.

Roosevelt recalls encountering IWW organizers as a young man and reading their literature and the writings of Marx on his own. He states that his desire to volunteer in Spain was fueled mostly by his anger at the Italian invasion of Ethiopia. On January 17, 1938, Roosevelt was issued a passport that showed his address as 1121 East Washington Boulevard, Los Angeles. He sailed for Spain that same day.

In Spain, Roosevelt was wounded in August 1938 during heavy shelling on Hill 666, Sierra Cabals. Roosevelt lost a leg as a result of his wounds. He recuperated for a time in France before he returned to the United States and settled in New York City. Because of his technical and mechanical background, Roosevelt was able to get work as a machinist and electronics worker and joined the United Electrical Workers CIO Union. He lived in New York until his death.

ROSARIO, CONRADO FIGUEROS
Conrado Rosario, age 25, sailed for Spain on March 10, 1937, aboard the SS *Queen Mary*. His passport (#369591, issued on February 25, 1937) carried the address 65 East 99th Street, New York City. Rosario was killed in Spain in September of 1937.

ROSE, OLIVER CHARLES
Oliver Rose sailed for Spain to join the Lincoln Brigade on October 23, 1937, aboard the SS *Champlain*. No further information has been found on his participation.

RUCKER, JAMES BERNARD
At the age of 25, Rucker sailed for Spain on February 17, 1937, on the SS *President Roosevelt*. His passport (#366607, issued on February 11, 1937) showed his address to be 1617 Harvard Avenue, Columbus, Ohio. No information can be located regarding Rucker's time in Spain.

SWANSON, WEST
No information is available regarding West Swanson, except that he was a black American with the Loyalist forces in Spain.

TAYLOR, DANIEL BEDE
Daniel Bede Taylor, 26 years of age, traveled to Spain on passport #499323, issued on February 23, 1938. His address at that time was 2519 West Lake Street, Chicago. He returned from Spain on December 15, 1939, on the SS *Paris*.

TAYLOR, JOSEPH
Joseph Taylor, at 29 years of age, sailed for Spain on June 5, 1937, aboard the SS *Lancastria*. His passport (#429934, issued on June 1, 1937) showed the address 82 East 10th Street, New York City. His passport was lost in Spain.

As a sergeant in the Loyalist army, Taylor was reported in July 1938 to have participated in the capture of 340 Italian prisoners on the Ebro River front. Taylor was also wounded in the shoulder during the fighting in Spain. He returned from Spain on December 20, 1938, aboard the SS *Ausonia*.

During World War II, Taylor served in the U.S. Army, assigned to a Medical Sanitary Company in North Carolina. He later resettled in New York City, where he lived until his death.

THORNTON, RALPH

At 34 years of age, Thornton sailed for Spain on April 10, 1937, on the SS *Rotterdam*. He carried passport #378849, issued on March 26, 1937. His address at that time was 2406 Bertrand Street, Pittsburgh. He returned from Spain on December 20, 1938, aboard the SS *Ausonia*.

VERDIER, HERBERT

According to correspondence with the U.S. State Department from Mrs. Martha M. J. Major of Savannah, Georgia, Herbert Verdier's mother, Fiebie Verdier, died when Herbert was about two years old. His father, William Verdier, died when Herbert was about six. Verdier was then raised by Mrs. Major and her husband in Savannah. In the correspondence included in the State Department file, the adult Verdier addressed Mrs. Major as "Mother."

Herbert Verdier left home at the age of 17, worked as a seaman, and lived in New York City at 81 West 132nd Street, Apartment 11. On February 18, 1937, Verdier was issued passport #368137. He sailed for Spain on March 10, 1937, on the SS *Washington*.

On June 11, 1939, Mrs. Major wrote to the State Department, seeking information on the whereabouts of her adopted son; she had not heard from him since he went to Spain. State Department officials in the United States and France found no record of Verdier among the Americans evacuated from Spain. He may have been killed while fighting in Spain.

WARFIELD, FRANK

Warfield, age 35, sailed for Spain on May 8, 1937, on the SS *American Importer*. His passport (#382127, issued April 1, 1937) carried the address 3721 Cook Avenue, St. Louis, Missouri. Langston Hughes reported encountering Warfield in Paris in September of 1938 where he was among the wounded soldiers from Spain awaiting repatriation to the United States.

WATERS, GEORGE WALTER

George Waters, only 18 years of age, sailed for Spain on May 15, 1937, on the SS *Georgic*. His passport (#27638, San Francisco series) was issued on May 7, 1937, and showed his address to be 510 Cedar Street, San Francisco. This passport was lost in Spain.

According to a notation in the State Department RG59 name index, there exists in Waters's 130- passport file a letter from his father to the San Francisco passport office. In that letter the elder Waters is said to state that he believes his son intends to join the Loyalist forces in Spain. He requests that his son therefore be denied a passport. Passport files remain closed for 75 years after date of issue.

In Spain, Waters served as an ambulance driver. He returned to the United States on December 31, 1938, aboard the SS *President Harding*.

WATSON, ALONZO

Alonzo Watson was the first African American to die in the Spanish Civil War. He was killed on February 25, 1937, at Jarama. He was 45 years old.

As an obituary in the *Daily Worker* stated, Watson was a member of the Communist party's Harlem Divsion and a personal friend of the prominent black communist leader James Ford. Originally from Chicago, Watson served in World War I with the 365th Illinois Infantry. Watson worked as a painter and was a member of the International Workers Order (IWO).

According to the *Worker,* Watson had lived at 772 St. Nicholas Avenue in New York City along with his sister, Hazel Coney. He was also survived by his wife, Anne, and his children Alonzo, Jr., 13; Harold, 11; and Jewel, 10.

Watson had traveled to Spain with the first group of volunteers who left New York on December 26, 1936, on the SS *Normandie*. His passport (#6227, New York series) was issued on December 23, 1936, and carried the address 47 East 12th Street, New York City.

WHITE, WILLIAM EDWARD

William Edward White was born on June 28, 1892, in Morton, Pennsylvania. He sailed for Spain on December 26, 1936, on the SS *Normandie*. His passport (#6898, New York series, issued on December 23, 1936) listed as addresses 800 Home Street, Bronx, New York, and 1912 Westmoreland Street, Philadelphia. This passport was lost in Spain.

White was sent home from Spain on November 23, 1937. The State Department files record a request by the International Brigades in Barcelona for new documentation to replace his lost passport. A new passport was issued to White in Paris and confiscated from him upon his arrival in New York aboard the SS *Berengeria.*

WICKMAN, MORRIS HENRY

Wickman traveled to Spain on March 10, 1937, on the SS *Washington*. His passport (#370524, issued March 1, 1937) showed the address 321 St. Nicholas Avenue, New York City.

In an interview published in *Black Americans in the Spanish People's War against Fascism*, James Yates recalls that Morris Wickman was a Communist party organizer from Philadelphia who served in Spain as a political commissar. He was killed in combat in Spain at the age of 36.

WIDEMAN, JEFFERSON

Wideman also appears in sources as Jefferson Weiderman. He sailed for Spain on March 18, 1937, on the SS *Normandie*. He was 27 years of age. According to his passport (#373577, issued on March 11, 1937), his address at the time was 1443 North Thirteenth Street, Philadelphia.

Wideman returned from Spain on December 15, 1938, on the SS *Paris*. At ceremonies marking the return of the Lincoln Brigade to New York City, Wideman joined battalion commander Milton Wolf in laying a wreath at the Eternal Light in Madison Square for those who had died in Spain.

WILLIAMS, FRED

According to the correspondence of his sister Tassie Smith (4348 Page Boulevard, St. Louis, Missouri) with the U.S. State Department in May 1938, Williams was born in Lexington, Mississippi, to Asa and Lizzie Williams and was 21 years old at the date of writing. His home address, when he left for Spain, was 2912 Madison Avenue, St. Louis. According to Mrs. Smith, Williams received his passport (#479613) in St. Louis on October 7, 1937.

Williams sailed for Spain on October 23, 1937, on the SS *Champlain*. On July 19, 1938, in response to his sister's inquiry, the U.S. consulate in Barcelona relayed word that Williams was alive and well and serving with the 15th Brigade. Mrs. Smith inquired again on June 28, 1939, when her brother did not appear after the war. The State Department could not locate him on any of the lists of Americans evacuated from Spain. Williams may have died in the Spanish Civil War.

WILLIAMS, PAUL ELISHA

Paul Williams was an African-American pilot in the Spanish Air Force during the Spanish Civil War. Williams was born in Youngstown, Ohio, in 1909. His family had migrated to Ohio from New England and Pennsylvania. In a *Daily Worker* interview published on March 6, 1938, Williams stated that his family were "Navy people." He said that his great-great-grandfather had been with the Union Naval Forces during the Civil War.

Williams graduated from high school in Youngstown and attended Carnegie Tech in Pittsburgh. As a student he worked at the Pittsburgh railroad yards. He later transferred to the Ohio School of Aeronautical Engineering and subsequently obtained work as a pilot flying for the Ohio Aero Company. Williams was the only black pilot working in the Ohio area at that time. Later, with three partners, he formed a company to design and manufacture a light bomber plane to sell to the government. The venture failed, however, because they were unable to compete with the larger companies.

During this period Williams also worked as a test pilot before finally entering the U.S. Navy, in which he was the first African American to attain the rank of lieutenant, junior grade. After leaving the navy Williams taught aeronautics to Civilian Conservation Corps (CCC) workers at Patterson Field in Dayton. The CCC workers rebuilt army planes that would ordinarily have been scrapped. In September 1936 Williams began to build another plane of his own design, the WX21.

Williams sailed to Spain on August 11, 1937, on the SS *Queen Mary*. On the voyage he met up with another black pilot, James Peck, a friend from his Pittsburgh days, who was also headed to Spain to fly for the Republic. Williams served for several months as a pilot in the Spanish Air Force. After returning to the United States he participated in the activities of the Friends of the Abraham Lincoln Brigade.

WILLIS, SAMUEL CONWAY

Samuel C. Willis, age 24, sailed to Spain on June 5, 1937, aboard the SS *Lancastria*. His passport (#424420, issued on May 20, 1937) showed his address as 2033 North Carnac Street, Philadelphia. Willis was killed in Spain.

YATES, JAMES

Yates's life story is told in some detail in his book *From Mississippi to Madrid*. He was born in 1906 in Brown Settlement, Mississippi. He moved to Chicago, where he became active in the unemployed councils and the fights to free the Scottsboro youths and Angelo Herndon.

Yates sailed to Spain on February 20, 1937, on the SS *Ile de France*. He recalls that he was ready to leave with the first group on December 26, 1936, but was unable to get a passport in time because there was no record of his birth in rural Mississippi. He was finally issued passport #365628 on February 5, 1937. It showed his address to be 239 West 111th

Street, New York City. Yates returned from Spain on February 16, 1938, on the SS *Lafayette*.

Yates served in the U.S. Army during World War II. He trained at Fort McClellan in Alabama and then served the rest of his time in the Signal Corps at Davis Monthan Field, near Tucson, Arizona. In February 1943 Yates was transferred from his original unit just before the unit was to ship overseas. In a letter to the VALB office he reported having "learned from good sources it was because I fought in Spain."

Following the war Yates became an active member of the International Brotherhood of Railroad Porters and head of the Chelsea-Village NAACP branch in New York City. At this writing he still lives in New York City.

YOUNGBLOOD, CHARLES

Charles Youngblood, age 24, sailed to Spain on April 21, 1937, on the SS *Queen Mary*. He carried passport #384454, issued on April 5, 1937. His address at the time was 2064 Seventh Avenue, New York City. Youngblood was killed in the fighting in Spain.

PART 3

Reports from the War Years

Introduction

The 1930s were a unique time of soaring political passions. The crushing impact of the Great Depression forced countless people from every walk of life to question the very foundations of American economic and political culture. Then, as the threat of fascism in Europe grew, thousands of artists, professionals, workers, students, and others throughout the world found themselves drawn out of ordinary life and into extraordinary commitments on behalf of justice and democracy. For three years Spain became the focal point for these political passions. It is only in hearing voices from the 1930s that we can begin to fathom the idealism and sense of impending danger that caused so many to give so much. For this reason we have reproduced the following selection of documents from the years of the Spanish Civil War (1936-1939).

By the 1930s Langston Hughes was already being called the American Negro poet laureate. Hughes was born in Topeka, Kansas, in 1902 and grew up in various cities of the American Midwest. He graduated from high school in Cleveland, Ohio, and attended Columbia University in New York for one year. Hughes then dropped out of the Ivy League to gain his artistic education in the streets and tenements of Harlem. In 1926 he published his first book of poetry, *The Weary Blues*. From that time until his death in 1967, Hughes brought forth a steady stream of verse, fiction, theatrical works, and occasional journalism. His work in these many forms was usually strongly rooted in the concerns and traditions of the African-American community.

In 1937 Langston Hughes traveled to Spain as a correspondent for the *Baltimore Afro-American* newspaper. His article "Negroes in Spain," reprinted in this volume, was written during this trip and published in the *Volunteer for Liberty*, the battlefield newsletter of the International Brigades in Spain, as were the other Hughes selections included here. In this report Hughes addresses the participation in the Spanish Civil War of black people from Africa and all points of the African diaspora. He also discusses the use, by Franco, of African Moors as troops for the fascist cause.

The speech "Too Much of Race" was given by Hughes at the Second International Writers Congress in Paris in July 1937. In this address Hughes details the special stake that peoples of African descent had in the fight against fascism.

Hughes's poem "October 16th" was reprinted in the *Volunteer for Liberty* to commemorate the anniversary of abolitionist John Brown's raid on the U.S. Army arsenal at Harper's Ferry, Virginia. By addressing this event in the International Brigade newsletter, Hughes was explicitly linking the antifascist cause with the cause of African-American freedom. The figure of John Brown, a white man who fought alongside blacks against slavery, also represented a model for the international volunteers of every race who made common cause for Spanish democracy.

William Pickens was a national officer of the National Association for the Advancement of Colored People (NAACP) at that organization's New York headquarters. He traveled to Spain in 1938 on a fact-finding mission. The article "What I Saw in Spain" was published in *Crisis,* the official journal of the NAACP. Pickens gives a picture of the situation in Barcelona at the time of his visit. He also describes the bombardment of that city by Italian planes. Pickens gives special attention to the role of the black volunteers he encountered. His report echoes the sentiments often heard from the blacks who went to Spain, saying, "There is no color question in Spain. People are just people."

Richard Wright was one of black America's foremost novelists. The author of *Native Son* and *Black Boy* was also, through much of the 1930s, an activist in the U.S. Communist party and a frequent contributor to the Party's paper, the *Daily Worker.* Here we present Wright's *Daily Worker* interview with Louise Thompson, a black communist leader in Harlem, upon her return from a trip to Spain. This article, "American Negroes in Key Posts of Spain's Loyalist Forces," details the leadership positions taken in Spain by soldiers Walter Garland, Oliver (Canute) Frankson, and Oscar Hunter.

Salaria Kee was the only African-American woman to serve in the Spanish Civil War. She was attached to the medical bureau as a nurse at the Villa Paz hospital. Kee's path to Spain and her experiences there are described in a booklet produced during the war by the Negro Committee to Aid Spain. That booklet, *A Negro Nurse in Republican Spain,* is reprinted here.

Negroes in Spain

LANGSTON HUGHES

In July, on the boat with me coming from New York, there was a Negro from the far West on his way to Spain as a member of the 9th Ambulance Corps of the American Medical Bureau. He was one of a dozen in his unit of American doctors, nurses, and ambulance drivers offering their services to Spanish democracy.

When I reached Barcelona a few weeks later, in time for my first air-raid and the sound of bombs falling on a big city, one of the first people I met was a young Puerto Rican of color acting as interpreter for the Loyalist troops.

A few days later in Valencia, I came across two intelligent young colored men from the West Indies, aviators, who had come to give their services to the fight against fascism.

ALL FIGHT FASCISM

And now, in Madrid, Spain's besieged capital, I've met wide-awake Negroes from various parts of the world – New York, our Middle West, the French West Indies, Cuba, Africa – some stationed here, others on leave from their battalions – all of them here because they know that if fascism creeps across Spain, across Europe, and then across the world, there will be no place left for intelligent young Negroes at all. In fact, no decent place for any Negroes – because fascism preaches the creed of Nordic supremacy and a world for whites alone.

In Spain, there is no color prejudice. Here in Madrid, heroic and bravest of cities, Madrid where the shells of Franco plow through the roof-

Reprinted from *Volunteer for Liberty* 1, no. 14 (September 13, 1937).

tops at night, Madrid where you can take a street car to the trenches, this Madrid to whose defense lovers of freedom and democracy all over the world have sent food and money and men – here to this Madrid have come Negroes from all the world to offer their help.

"Deluded Moors"

On the opposite side of the trenches with Franco, in the company of the professional soldiers of Germany, and the illiterate troops of Italy, are the deluded and driven Moors of North Africa. An oppressed colonial people of color being used by fascism to make a colony of Spain. And they are being used ruthlessly, without pity. Young boys, men from the desert, old men, and even women, compose the Moorish hordes brought by the reactionaries from Africa to Europe in their attempt to crush the Spanish people.

I did not know about the Moorish women until, a few days ago, I went to visit a prison hospital here in Madrid filled with wounded prisoners. There were German aviators that bombarded the peaceful village of Colmenar Viejo and machined-gunned helpless women as they fled along the road. One of these aviators spoke English. I asked him why he fired on women and children. He said he was a professional soldier who did what he was told. In another ward, there were Italians who joined the invasion of Spain because they had no jobs at home.

What They Said

But of all the prisoners, I was most interested in the Moors, who are my own color. Some them, convalescent, in their white wrappings and their bandages, moved silently like dark shadows down the hall. Others lay quietly suffering in their beds. It was difficult to carry on any sort of conversation with them because they spoke little or no Spanish. But finally, we came across a small boy who had been wounded at the battle of Brunete – he looked to be a child of ten or eleven, a bright smiling child who spoke some Spanish.

"Where did you come from?" I said.

He named a town I could not understand in Morocco.

"And how old are you?"

"Thirteen," he said.

"And how did you happen to be fighting in Spain?"

Bring Moorish Women

Then I learned from this child that Franco had brought Moorish women into Spain as well as men – women to wash and cook for the troops.

"What happened to your mother," I said.

The child closed his eyes. "She was killed at Brunete," he answered slowly.

Thus the Moors die in Spain, men, women, and children, victims of fascism, fighting not for freedom – but against freedom – under a banner that holds only terror and segregation for all the darker peoples of the earth.

A great many Negroes know better. Someday the Moors will know better, too. All the Francos in the world cannot blow out the light of human freedom.

Too Much of Race

LANGSTON HUGHES

The following address was made by Langston Hughes, outstanding American poet and novelist, at the Second International Writers Congress in Paris a month ago.

Members of the Second International Writers Congress and people of Paris: I come from a land called America, a democratic land, a rich land – and yet a land whose democracy from the very beginning has been tainted with race prejudice born of slavery, and whose richness has been poured through the narrow channels of greed into the hands of the few. I come to the Second International Writers Congress representing my country, America, but most especially representing the Negro peoples of America, and the poor peoples of America – because I am both a Negro and poor. And that combination of color and of poverty gives me the right then to speak for the most oppressed group in America – that group that has known so little of democracy – the fifteen million Negroes who dwell within our borders.

We are the people who have long known in actual practice the meaning of the word fascism – for the American attitude toward us has always been one of economic and social discrimination: In many states of our country Negroes are not permitted to vote or to hold political office. In some sections freedom of movement is greatly hindered, especially if we happen to be sharecroppers on the cotton plantations of the South. All over America we know what it is to be refused admittance to schools and colleges, to theatres and concert halls, to hotels and restaurants. We Negro writers know what it is to be unable to work in editorial offices or

Reprinted from *Volunteer for Liberty* 1, no. 11 (August 23, 1937).

write for the motion pictures. We know Jim Crow [railroad] cars, race riots, lynchings, the sorrows of the Scottsboro boys. In America, Negroes do not have to be told what fascism is in action. We know. Its theories of Nordic supremacy and economic suppression have long been realities to us.

FASCISM ON WORLD SCALE

And now we view fascism on a world scale: Hitler in Germany with the abolition of labor unions, his tyranny over the Jews, and the sterilization of the Negro children of Cologne; Mussolini in Italy with his banning of Negroes on the theatrical stages, and his expeditions of slaughter in Ethiopia; the Military Party in Japan with their little maps of how they'll conquer the whole world, and their savage treatment of the Koreans and Chinese; Batista and Vincent, the little American-made tyrants of Cuba and Haiti; and now Spain, and Franco with his absurd cry of "Viva España" in the hands of Italians, Moors, and Germans invited to help him achieve "Spanish unity." Absurd, but true!

We Negroes of America are tired of a world divided superficially on the basis of race and color – but in reality on the basis of poverty and power – the rich over the poor, no matter what their color. We Negroes of America are tired of a world in which it is possible for any one group of people to say to another, "you have no right to happiness, or freedom, or the joy of life." We are tired of a world where forever we work for someone else and the profits are not ours. We are tired of a world where, when we raise our voices against oppression, we are immediately jailed, intimidated, beaten, sometimes lynched. Nicolas Guillen has been in prison in Cuba, Jacques Roumain in Haiti, Angelo Herndon in the United States. The great Indian writer, Raj Anand, cannot come to the Writers Congress in Paris because the British police have taken his passport from him.

"MURDER IS NOTHING"

I say, we darker peoples of the earth are tired of a world in which things like that can happen. And we see in the tragedy of Spain how far the world-oppressors will go to retain their power. To them, now, the murder of women and children is nothing. Those who have already practiced bombing the little villages of Ethiopia, now bomb Guernica and Madrid. The same fascists who forced Italian peasants to fight in Africa now force African Moors to fight in Europe. They do not care about color when they can use you for profits or for war. Japan attempts to force the Chinese of Manchuria to work and fight for the glory and wealth of the Tokyo bourgeoisie – one colored people dominating another at the point of guns. Race means nothing when it can be turned to fascist use. And yet race means everything when fascists of the world use it as a bugaboo and a terror to keep the working masses from getting together.

Just as in America, they tell the whites that Negroes are dangerous brutes and rapists, so in Germany they lie about the Jews and in Italy they cast their verbal spit upon the Ethiopians. And the old myths of race are kept alive to hurt and impede the rising power of the working class. But in America, where race prejudice is so strong, already we have learned that the lies of race mean continued oppression and poverty and fear – and now Negroes and white sharecroppers in the cotton fields of the South are beginning to get together; and Negro and white workers in the great industrial cities of the North under John L. Lewis and the CIO have begun to create a great labor force that refuses to recognize the color line. Negro and white stevedores on the docks of the West Coast of America have formed one of the most powerful labor unions in America. Formerly, the unorganized Negro dockworkers – unorganized because the white workers themselves with their backward ideology didn't want Negroes in their unions – formerly these Negro workers could break a strike. And they did. But now, together, both Negroes and whites are strong. We are learning.

They Fear Us

Why is it that the British police seize Raj Anand's passport? Why is it that the State Department in Washington delays unduly in granting me permission to go to Spain as a representative of the Negro press? Why is it that the young Negro leader, Angelo Herndon, was finding it most difficult to secure a passport this spring in New York? Why? We know why!

It is because the reactionary and fascist forces of the world know that writers like Anand and myself, leaders like Herndon, and poets like Guillen and Roumain represent the great longing that is in the hearts of the darker peoples of the world to reach out their hands in friendship and brotherhood to all the races of the earth. The fascists know that we long to be rid of hatred and terror and oppression, to be rid of conquering and of being conquered, to be rid of all the ugliness of poverty and imperialism that eats away the heart of civilization today. We represent the end of race. And the fascists know that when there is no more race, there will be no more capitalism, and no more war, and no more money for the munitions makers – because the workers of the world will have triumphed.

October 16th

LANGSTON HUGHES

Perhaps today
You will remember John Brown

John Brown
Who took his gun,
Took twenty-one companions
White and black,
Went to shoot your way to freedom
Where two rivers meet
And the hills of the
North
And the hills of the
South
Look slow at one another –
and died
For your sake.

Now that you are
Many years free,
And the echo of the Civil War
Has passed away,
And Brown himself
Has long been tried at law,
Hung by the neck,
And buried in the ground –

Reprinted from *Volunteer for Liberty* 1, no. 18 (October 11, 1937).

Since Harpers Ferry
Is alive with ghosts today,
Immortal raiders
Come again to town –

Perhaps
You will recall
John Brown.

Walter Garland, machine-gun company commander, ca. 1938.

Burt Jackson, Tom Page, and Joe Taylor (left to right), Batea, Spain, March 1938.

Larry Dukes,
Mackenzie-Papineau
Battalion,
May 1938.

Joe Taylor, brigade scout, with unidentified scouts, Ambite, Spain,
December 1937.

James Cox,
Lincoln-Washington
Battalion,
October 1937.

Claude Pringle, Mackenzie-Papineau
Battalion, with unidentified
volunteers, January 1938.

George Waters, ambulance driver,
ca. 1938.

*Langston Hughes (left) and Crawford Morgan, Fuente de Ebro, Spain,
October 1937.*

*Crawford Morgan, Mirko Marković, [?] Parker, and Langston Hughes (left
to right), October 1937.*

Salaria Kee,
probably just before
leaving for Spain, 1937.

Sam Willis, runner, Mackenzie-Papineau Battalion, ca. 1937.

Vaughn Love,
Lincoln-Washington
Battalion,
December 1937.

Eluard Luchell McDaniels, with unidentified volunteers, Gandesa, Spain,
ca. 1938.

Albert Chisholm,
November 1937.

Otto Reeves (left) and Frank Alexander, both with the Mackenzie-Papineau
Battalion, December 1937.

*Patrick Roosevelt, New York,
shortly after the war.*

IN MEMORIAM
OLIVER LAW
Commander of the Lincoln
Battalion in the July
offensive

Died on the Field of Battle
July 10, 1937

*Memorial tribute to Oliver Law
in the* Volunteer for Liberty,
October 11, 1937.

*Douglas Roach (right), marching in parade during
the first convention of the Veterans of the Abraham
Lincoln Brigade, Washington, D.C., February 12, 1938.*

What I Saw in Spain

WILLIAM PICKENS

When some one in a group of New Yorkers asked me in the summer what I intended to do in my month of vacation, "Perhaps go to Europe," I replied. "What for?" they asked. – "Just to see how many democrats are still left running loose there." – "Well," said Jimmie Harris, one of the group, "you better hurry, or you'll be able to call a mass meeting of them in a 'phone booth."

"Will you visit Germany?" some one challenged. – "No, sirree, for my opinions are so strong against dictators that they may stick out of my pores, be discovered, – and I could be framed." Think of that, – when only ten years ago, even six years ago, I had more friends in Germany than in any other nation outside of the United States, and when traveling about Europe I always felt "at home" when I got into Germany. But today there is no law in Germany, only will and whim, and there is no health for a democrat. I am going to die a democrat, – and I do not want that end to be forced upon me by fascist dictators. The last time I was in Germany was just a few months before Hitler; the next time I go to Germany will be at least a few months after Hitler.

So this time I planned definitely to got to France and England, two countries that might still be listed in the democratic column, and I left the matter pending as to whether I should go to Switzerland and Prague or to Belgium and Denmark also. This question was settled when we had a dinner for the Medical Bureau of New York, which is supplying medical aid and ambulances to the Spanish Government, and they asked me to visit Spain. Well, visit Spain I would. Friends in Paris had already been suggesting Spain. It was difficult, for in all American passports there is a red

Reprinted from *Crisis*, October 1938.

stamp now, indicating that they are not good for Spain. This is not to keep Americans free from Franco and Italian bombs. It has no relation to the safety of Americans; it seems part of the unconscious "plot" of the democracies to run out on all the democracy that is left in Spain, and to aid what they ought to hate: Fascism in Spain. For, note, these same passports do not forbid Americans to go to China, where bombs are thicker, nor to other places almost as dangerous to the individual. But Spain is cut out. That had to be overcome. I would go legally, although many Americans, French and English go illegally, or rather without the consent of their own governments. When I went into Spain an English woman went in, in spite of her government, and an American woman came in the same evening, without American o.k., and after two months of trying to get in from southern France.

Perhaps I could never have got in illegally: it would have taken too much time or too much pain or both, and I had only a short time. Accordingly, we got in touch with Secretary Hull's office, the American state department, with the straight request that I get permission to enter Spain. In the few days before I left on the Queen Mary, the reply could not be received, and the Medical Bureau was to cable me in Paris and the State Department was to cable the American ambassador there. When I reached Paris, I soon received a cable from Mr. Reissig of the New York Bureau office, saying that the matter was "pending" in Washington and suggesting certain Paris contacts. Thinking that the American government had not yet made up its mind, I went to the international organization in Paris that aids the Spanish Government and began to get ideas. The second day, I suggested that we call up the American ambassador and ask if he had heard from our state department. Surprisingly he had; perhaps he had the cable when I arrived in Paris.

Now to the American embassy with my passport, to get the necessary notations made in it. It did not take the Americans as long as it takes Europeans: the Americans used only one hour and fifteen minutes, doing what could have been done in fifteen minutes. They cancelled the prohibition against entering Spain and entered a note from the embassy that I was permitted to enter.

THE FRENCH ARE LEISURELY

But, not yet. The fight has just begun: the French authorities have to give their permission, since I am to enter Spain from France and over a closed French border. So next to the Prefect of Police. Now there is where it takes time. Not a gendarme nor a functionary in the place knew who the Prefect was. At least they would not say, but only referred one to the information window, before which a long line was already formed, waiting to ask the clerk perhaps similar questions, many of which could have been answered by the elevator boy, but for the official notion that all information must be secured from the information clerk. So there!

After entering this line and at long last getting up to the clerk and putting in my inquiry and stating briefly what I needed, the information clerk went away to find a personage for me, leaving me at the window and a long line behind me. This personage was finally secured and came out, learned my request, and told me of another line which I must enter in order to leave my passport (for two days!). One always has a reluctance at leaving his passport in European offices, outside of English offices. Once in Moscow I left my passport and when I went back it took the girl clerks what seemed like hours to find it. I actually waited painfully looking on while the embarrassed clerks went through baskets of jumbled passports, examining first one and then another, trying to find my precious American one. At that time, too, we did not have any official relations with Russian, and it was looking as if I were to be there for months, while the long red tape was being unwound, measured and cut and re-wound in America to "prove" my American citizenship. But at last the thing was found.

But I was determined to get into Spain, so I left my passport with the French. Two days later I went, got on the end of [queue], and when I reached the window my passport was not ready, had not been sent back yet from some high-and-mighty place. I was asked by the very kindly girls to come back in two hours. So I walked for miles along the Seine, looking at the book stalls that are erected against the river wall, such as vegetable stands in America. In practically all of the stalls I saw many copies of Hitler's "Mein Kampf." The French are reading that book. They are learning Hitler's intentions, and his opinion of the French. Almost to the Louvre in my walking, I hailed a cab and went to a restaurant near the Madeleine, where I had an appointment; left a note and took a cab back to the Prefecture. This time, after I negotiated another line, I was asked to wait "a few minutes," and was many minutes later called to the window and given my passport, with authority of France to cross the French border into Spain.

About "Neutrality"

No, that is not all, – not yet. There is still the Spanish ambassador's office, the long train ride to southern France, to Perpignan, the last French town, the seeing of the authorities and the Spanish consul there, the arrangements about money (very queer and uncertain in time of war), and then the tackling of the actual border, where the French military must pass you on one side and on the other the Spanish must receive you, both looking you over carefully. What a pain to enter Spain! But it is not the fault of the Spaniard; it is due to the false idea about "neutrality," a word I shall not respect so much in the future as I have respected it in the past. When there is a human fight going on, other humans cannot be neutral. They may act neutral, if they be afraid, but they cannot be neutral, ever. When a thug attacks the innocent, when a brute attacks the helpless, when a grown-up is beating a child, one certainly then is far from neutral. But in an effort to keep the peace with Italy and Germany, France has endeavored to follow England and act neutral. Those people of France and England do not want war, are afraid of a great war. What sane government heads are not afraid of war? Hitler is the only kind that does not fear it. But is war being avoided or its ultimate horrors lessened or increased by yielding to the bullying type of state heads?

From Perpignan to Barcelona we travel by road, auto and bus, for 125 miles, or a longer distance, into Spain. Trains are too dangerous, too visible to the eyes of war planes. Cars can take cover on the lovely highways that are canopied by the branches of the plane trees. In a Spanish town we stop for a bite of lunch and refreshments. What a monstrosity is war! In southern France are fruits, the best in the world, food in abundance, bread, sweets, vegetables, all begging to be sold. The shops and stalls are full of food. Just a few miles away is Spain, where this food would be worth its weight in gold, where people are smoking weeds for cigarette tobacco, where food is reduced to bare necessity even in the best hotels. That is "neutrality": the nations have closed their borders to these people who are on the defensive; they could not for a long time buy even anti-aircraft guns from France and England for the defense of Barcelona, which is open to frequent attacks from the Italian airmen from the Balearic Islands.

And this town in Spain in which we stopped was, unlike Barcelona, situated back from the coast, and yet it had been horribly bombed. Houses looked like skeletons, like ruins. These houses are not of wood. There is no wood for buildings in most of Europe, especially southern Europe. The houses are of rock and brick and earth, and that is why the whole city is not reduced to ashes when it is bombed and individual blocks set on fire. It is impossible to describe the wreckage from these powerful explosives that fall from the sky. Jupiter had no thunderbolt as terrific as these bombs.

We arrived in Barcelona, capital of Catalunya, great city on the Costa Brava, with more than a million inhabitants in normal times, but now with over two million, including the refugees from Franco areas, city of great Paseos and Boulevards, and of artistic buildings with their stone and iron fronts carved or moulded into the flowing lines of sea waves or the foliage of trees. Life was not just something to go through in Spain: it was evidently something for the Catalonians to enjoy, "before the war."

It was just before night when we arrived, and were put out at the Majestic Hotel on Paseo de Gracias, a great avenue with four walkways for pedestrians and three for vehicles, the central vehicular way being a two-way passage. The Majestic is (was) the leading hotel of the city. When we registered we were told: "The elevator is not running; you must walk up." Fortunately buildings are not skyscrapers in Europe. The top floor here was the seventh. I had a room on the sixth floor up. No elevators; all energy being saved for the prosecution of war and defense.

Catalunya was evidently a very prosperous part of the world, and the most prosperous part of Spain. Why did we not go there when there was peace and when the travelers by foot on the highways went playing stringed instruments and singing? One Boston woman who came in the next morning told me that she was in Barcelona seven years before and that it was so prosperous that it was really wicked, and that she could hardly walk a block along the great Paseo Ramblas without "being insulted" every few hundred feet. But now in imminent danger of hellish attack at any hour, and more especially on any moonlit night, the men of Barcelona have no time to tease foreign women. And yet life goes on in Barcelona: hating, loving, having babies and planning futures. The air bombs have driven the people together against the enemy and force them to construct underground refuges. These refuges are being built in many streets and under whole squares. Republican Square has one that can take in at least one thousand humans. All refuges have two exits or entrances so that in case one is blown in by a bomb, the other may be open. But that is not all, for they have air vents in addition and picks and shovels stored inside for digging out.

The first day in Barcelona I set out to find the Internationale pour l'Enfance. It was not at the address given me in Paris, so I had a walk which was not wasted, for it carried me through much of the city that was being bombed about the time I set off from Paris, two days before I arrived: six-story buildings, ripped from top to cellar by a single bomb, and in some cases demolished altogether; the Old Cathedral hit and blown to ruins, with its stark facade standing there like Kenilworth Castle remains. They call this cathedral "Old," because, before the present war started they were building on a new Cathedral, which they had got only so far with, that it too now stands there like a ruin. Windows blown out of the old and not yet put into the new. A German young man in his early twenties accosted me and made himself known, German in race but anti-German in sympathies. He said: "I would like to show you some of the ruined work of some of my fellow countrymen here." Some of those planes were German. In one bombing earlier in the year, the planes had killed 800 and wounded 1,500 people. The bombs hit where life was crowded, at the market and on the boulevards or Paseos. Later I found the International for Children on the same street as the Hotel Majestic, and a young Swiss doctor in charge, Dr. Jaeggy. The American young woman who had been in charge had left for home the same day on which I arrived.

AMERICAN NEGRO FIGHTERS

Yes, there are American Negro boys in Spain, fighting with the Loyalist troops. All honor to those boys! They are making history. Among them are some of the greatest heroes of the war. There was McDaniels, of San Francisco, who drove back a whole company of Franco's troops by the use of hand grenades, when the Loyalists were re-crossing the Ebro. He is now a black god in Spain, with one explosive bullet in his left thigh. The bullet hit into the thigh then exploded and moved in three pieces downward. But he is all right, and will be up soon and at 'em again, unless they send him to the States for propaganda purposes as they are thinking of doing.

There is Oscar Hunter, once a student at West Virginia State, and one of the first group to go to Spain when the war opened. He is now Political Commissar of Hospitals, a very high officer. "How long do you think," he asked me, "it might take me to get up to such a position in the United States."

"Well, not in the next hundred years," I replied sincerely. He has made it within a year in Spain.

There is no color question in Spain. People are just people. One of the tests for that: the Spanish girls and women who are interested in any colored man, do not sneak, as they often do in the United States, but they go along openly, naturally, and apparently without even any consciousness of being out of any conventions. They laugh and play and joke, and smack each other with their hands in public and in offices, and on the Paseos.

And there is also Abe Lewis; and there is Joe Taylor; also black boys like Luchell McDaniels. McDaniels is as black all over his body as a well-shined pair of black shoes. When I saw him, he was undressed and his wound was being swabbed by an American nurse in Mataro Hospital, about 30 kilometers out of Barcelona. This is a great military hospital.

These boys, although they are risking their lives for the ideal of popular government, are rather happy in what must seem to them like a normal world. "It's not like the States here," said Joe Taylor, "for here I get some breaks perhaps just because I am colored." When I met Joe, it was first through his voice: going through the Mataro Hospital, which is located in a monastery, I heard singing before I came to the door of one ward, group singing, – Negro singing. "There must be the Negro boys," I thought, and felt that it was odd to find them segregated in Spain. But when we opened the ward door, there was but one Negro, Joe Taylor, and there were all the white patients and the nurses, and they were all singing, Negro songs under Joe's leadership. "Come on, mule!" was the refrain of the song which I had heard. Spanish and French, and American and German and Italian, – all were singing this song. Other songs followed, always led by Joe Taylor. It was not just a remark, but something that I meant and still mean, when I told the hospital authorities: "Joe Taylor is worth more to your patients than any surgeon in the place." They admitted it.

Strange how much we learn in a short period of contact: how cordial were these beleaguered people. It was a high privilege to visit this great military hospital, a privilege which they are reluctant to grant to those whom they know, let alone to a stranger. But they gave me this permit, and wanted to send me to other parts of Spain, if only I had had the time. French and English and American correspondents were being denied hospital permits at the same time my permit was being granted.

I shall long remember some of the Spanish leaders: people like Constancia de la Mora, a stateswoman, if ever there was one. She is head of the Foreign Propaganda Service, and is in charge of foreign correspondents in Spain. From here they must get their permits to write articles, and must submit to her censorship. Then there is San Marti, splendid Spaniard, dark and rather handsome. He it was who issued me a permit for visiting military hospitals, and he seemed to understand as soon as we had talked a few minutes. Immediately afterwards an American correspondent and hospital worker from France was denied any permit, even to go with me to Mataro. They took me in a state car, with guide and chauffeur. They made my short stay profitable.

OUR FIGHT, TOO

One night the Italians from Mallorca, largest of the Balearic Islands, attempted to raid us, but were driven off by the defense planes. It was just after dinner, and we were seated in one of the hotel salons, conversing. Suddenly a whistle went by, a policeman whistling as he rode his motor-cycle. All lights of the city went out. It must be done by master switches at the power plant.

Were you ever in a dark hotel, in a great dark city, with all streets dark, and even auto lights out, not a spark of fire or light to be seen, except the great search lights playing on the scattered cloud and the sky, seeking out the enemy? "Were you afraid?" people ask. There seems to be no thought of fear in such a circumstance. There is a feeling of defiance. We, men and women, went out on the Paseo to watch the sights, with no more fear of being hit in the momentarily expected raid than we have hope of winning first prize in the sweepstakes. Of course, it was possible. Those search-lights are a beautiful sight, on a dark sky, – and the music of those planes! It was hours before the attempted raid was over. I actually got tired, and went in and felt my way up the stairs, six flights, in pitch-dark, and undressed and bathed and went to bed without so much as the light of a match.

Today these Spanish people, in their old, old home, antedating the Caesars there, are fighting on the front for popular government, – for self-government. It is our fight.

American Negroes in Key Posts of Spain's Loyalist Forces

RICHARD WRIGHT

LOUISE THOMPSON, RETURNING FROM FRONT LINES, TELLS 'DAILY' WON THEM SIGNAL HONORS

Because of distinguished records of bravery and heroism, Negro members of the Abraham Lincoln Brigade in Spain have been promoted to leading military positions in the Loyalist armies, Louise Thompson, Negro secretary of the English Division of the International Workers Order, declared yesterday after a three weeks tour of war-torn Spain.

Miss Thompson, who is also a leading figure in the National Negro Congress, arrived in New York Saturday aboard the S.S. Paris. In addition to her trip to Spain, she spent five weeks in France as a representative of her organization which has collected $30,000 to aid Loyalist Spain. She was enthusiastically greeted throughout Spain by American volunteers and the Spanish people.

"But my greatest interest was in the American Negro volunteers fighting in the International Brigades and in the Moors fighting with the fascist Franco. I wanted to see with my own eyes the difference between these two dark-skinned people fighting on opposite sides of the struggle," said Miss Thompson.

BROADCAST FROM MADRID

On August 27, Miss Thompson, together with Harry Haywood, Langston Hughes, and Walter Garland, made a special radio broadcast in Madrid for the benefit of American Negro fighters.

Reprinted from *NYC Daily Worker*, September 20, 1937.

"These Negro soldiers are not in the work battalions as was the case of the Negroes who fought in France during the World War. They occupy any military position for which they are qualified."

Do any of these Negro volunteers regret having gone to lay down their lives for Spain? Miss Thompson answers by giving the exact words of Walter Garland, Negro volunteer from New York, who said, "You know, in a measure we Negroes who have been in Spain are a great deal luckier than those back in America. Here we have been able to strike back in a way that hits at those who for years have pushed us from pillar to post. I mean this – actually strike back at the counterparts of those who have been grinding us down back home."

This 23-year-old Walter Garland, Miss Thompson informed us, now has a rank of lieutenant and has been stationed for the past five months at the American Military Training School. He was wounded three times in action, and spent 130 days of unrelieved hell in the trenches when he went into action for the first time in his life.

Another Negro fighter in Spain from whom Miss Thompson brought greetings to his Negro and white comrades in America was Harry Haywood, who has the rank of captain and is the political commissar in the George Washington Brigade.

FRANKSON PRAISED

Miss Thompson also told a story of an African lad who had come to Spain to study and got caught in the mesh of war. She told of how he gladly laid aside his books and took up arms against fascism.

"He said that he could not afford to lose the opportunity to do his bit toward defeating fascism so that not only he but the millions of his fellow countrymen in Africa would have a chance at an education," said Miss Thompson.

Still another heroic Negro figure from whom Miss Thompson brought greetings is Vaughn Love of Harlem who is now in an officer's training school. Love saw his first action at Brunete, a 21-day stretch of fighting in which he distinguished himself for conspicuous bravery.

Then she told the story of a Negro machinist over whom numerous Loyalist brigades have been in competition to get his services. This is [Kanute] Oliver Frankson, chief of mechanics at Auto Park, the transport base of the International Brigade. It is claimed, Miss Thompson reports, that Frankson was largely responsible for the continuous flow of food and goods into Madrid even after many lines of communication had been cut off by the fascists. He formed brigades of mechanics to work upon trucks and autos partially destroyed by fascist shells.

Then she told of Oscar Hunter, a guy from the stockyards of Chicago who is now political commissar at Murcia. Oscar Hunter studied at Hampton Institute in the South and is known among the Loyalist peoples as the "man who can get things done."

She gave accounts of many others, all playing vital roles in defense of Spanish liberty.

DISCUSSES MOORS

One of the most interesting parts of Miss Thompson's interview with the *Daily Worker* was her remarks regarding the Moors fighting with France. It was reported that there were some 30,000 of them in Franco's lines.

Those whom Miss Thompson saw in hospitals in Madrid could not tell their story for they could not speak Spanish. But enough is known of them to know that the story of their fighting against the Loyalists is a story of how the fascists have duped and defrauded a terribly exploited people.

The most remarkable spirit Miss Thompson encountered among the Spanish people was the deep understanding of why Moors, Germans and Italians were fighting against them. So high has become the political consciousness of the civil population that when Italian, German, or Moorish prisoners are brought into towns they are greeted by, "Long Live the Italian Peoples!" or "Long Live the German Peoples!" or "Long Live the Moorish Peoples!"

"They know," said Miss Thompson, "that these people have been misled. They bear toward them no ill-will."

To help settle the problem of the Moors, there has been formed the Hispano Moroccan Anti-Fascist Association. This organization spreads posters throughout Loyalist territory informing the people of the true state of affairs. Its appeal is two-fold: one of its purposes is to convince the Moors that the government of Loyalist Spain is their friend; the other purpose is to combat the antagonism of the Spanish people toward the Moors who have been tricked into the ranks of the fascists by Franco.

On the question of the unity and morale of the Spanish masses, Miss Thompson said the following:

"Loyalist Spain is truly united. Everywhere I went was a feeling of deep confidence that they could defeat the fascists. This was true of young and old, and those whose sons and husbands were at the front, or those who had lost their sons and husbands in battle.

"The military equipment of the Loyalists may not be what the military equipment of fascist countries are, but the Loyalists have something which no fascist university can give; and that's the courage that they are fighting to free a great and beautiful land which is their home."

Congress Delegate

During her five-week stay in Paris Miss Thompson was, along with Max Bedacht and William Weiner of the International Workers Order, a delegate to the World Congress Against Racism and Anti-Semitism.

At this congress there were 327 delegates representing 93 organizations from 26 different countries. It is estimated that these delegates represented some 40,000,000 people.

The manifesto issued by the congress reads in part: "This world assembly urges you to reject the bloody lie of racism, that of theoreticians as well as that of dictators."

At its closing sessions the congress established an International Coordinating Committee with headquarters in Paris. The task of this committee is to keep in contact with all national committees in other countries and to call world congresses.

Miss Thompson will make a public report on her trip Saturday at the Royal Windsor Palace (formerly St. Nicholas Arena), 66th St. near Columbus Ave., when a memorial meeting for IWO members who have fallen in Spain will be held.

A Negro Nurse in Republican Spain

THE NEGRO COMMITTEE TO AID SPAIN

[*In 1938 the Negro Committee to Aid Spain, with the Medical Bureau and the North American Committee to Aid Spanish Democracy, issued a 14-page biographical booklet about Salaria Kee under the title* A Negro Nurse in Republican Spain. *The anonymous booklet sold for 5 cents and was designed to promote American, and especially African-American, political and financial support for the Spanish war effort. The text of that booklet follows.*]

What have Negroes to do with Spain? What has Spain for us? What about Ethiopia? Why should Negro men be fighting in Spain? What do they expect out of it? These are the questions Negroes are constantly asking. It is their immediate response to any appeal for Spain. Quite apart from the broad question of humanitarianism the answers are simple.

Fascist Italy invaded and overpowered Ethiopia. This was a terrible blow to Negroes throughout the world. Ethiopia represented the last outpost of Negro authority, of Negro self-government. Hundreds of Negroes in this country attempted to join the Ethiopian forces. But Ethiopia at that time was so remote that few succeeded. I say "at that time" advisedly. Since then the rapid move of world events has brought Europe and the Orient much closer to local thinking and knowledge.

Even at that time thousands of dollars were collected from peoples in all the liberty loving countries of the world. Sweden and Denmark sent ambulances and medical supplies. Negroes from New York sent a 75-bed

---

Reprinted from the Negro Committee to Aid Spain, with the Medical Bureau and North American Committee to Aid Spanish Democracy, *A Negro Nurse in Republican Spain* (New York, 1938).

field hospital and 2 tons of medical supplies. They sent two delegations to the Emperor Haile Selassie. They brought two Ethiopian delegations to this country to win supporters for Ethiopia. A young white physician from Evanston, Illinois was the first foreign casualty. He was killed in an Italian-fascist airplane raid on the Ethiopian field hospitals. Germany and Italy and Japan conspicuously sent nothing – except poison gas with which to slaughter the Ethiopians.

Italy moved on from the invasion of Ethiopia. She advanced her troops into Spain. Here was a second small nation, feudal and undeveloped. Bitter resentment against Italy still rankled. The hundreds of Negro boys who had been prevented from going to Ethiopia understood the issues more clearly now. To them Spain was now the battlefield on which Italian fascism might be defeated. And perhaps Italy defeated in Spain would be forced to withdraw from Ethiopia. Ethiopia's only hope for recovery lies in Italy's defeat. The place to defeat Italy just now is in Spain.

The lynching of Negroes in America, discrimination in education and on jobs, lack of hospital facilities for Negroes in most cities and very poor ones in others, all this appeared to them as part of the picture of fascism: of a dominant group impoverishing and degrading a less powerful group. The open pronouncements of Germany and Italy against all non-Aryans is convincing evidence. Thinking thus, hundreds of Negro men went to Spain. Here in the International Brigade of Volunteers they found other Negroes. From Djibouti, Emperor Haile Selassie's chief mechanic came "to strike a blow for a free Ethiopia." From South Africa, from Cuba, from French Senegal, from Haiti, from the Cameroons, Negroes came, stayed and fought.

Negro physicians came to man hospitals and serve the wounded. Negro ambulance drivers and stretcher bearers. And one young Negro nurse.

This is the story of the experiences that shaped this nurse's thinking and brought her finally to the trenches in Republican Spain, and in field hospitals on the front, and base hospitals behind the lines. Here she met and nursed Spanish, English and Czechs, and Irish and Scotch, and poor whites from Georgia, and Ethiopians from Djibouti and Negroes from Haiti and Africa and America. Finally, blown out of a trench by a bomb explosion, she came home to recover and to continue work for medical aid for Spain's women and children.

CHILDHOOD

Salaria Kee's life began much as the life of millions of other Negro girls in this country. Her father was a working man. His job as attendant at the State Hospital for the Insane paid a small wage. His family was constantly increasing. There were all the usual elements of tragedy and frustration. There were the sacrifices of the older children that a younger one might have the education which economic circumstances and the lack of adequate provisions on the part of Government made otherwise impossible. There were all the conflicts of racial prejudice and the limitation it imposes on every Negro child in this country.

When Salaria was six months old her father was stabbed to death by a patient at the State Hospital for the Insane. The hospital was understaffed. Difficult patients could easily overpower a lone attendant. His meager wages permitted no margin for saving. Compensation was negligible. His widow took their four small children to Akron, Ohio. There they lived with friends of Mr. Kee's youth. Two years later Mrs. Kee returned to Georgia. Here she married a farmer. She had known him from childhood there in Millageville. The children stayed on with friends in Akron, Ohio.

Mrs. Jackson took them to her home. Mrs. Jackson's husband was a bellhop at the Country Club at Akron. Her husband therefore had only uncertain tips as earnings. Besides they had five children of their own. Public provision for the care of dependent Negro children, even in the North, has always lagged far behind that provided for white children. And provision for white children, except in isolated instances, is far behind the standard of normal decency that an advanced country like ours should sustain. Twenty-six years ago conditions were worse.

Mr. Jackson's "tips" could not stretch very well over a family of eleven. When Salaria's brother Andrew was nine years old he left school. Grocer's delivery boy was the best job he could find. The wage was $1.50 a week. Shortly afterward George and Arthur left school and went to work.

They carefully kept Salaria in school. She was bright in her studies and active in athletics. At Akron's Central High School she was told that she could not play on the basketball team because "no Negro had ever been admitted on the team."

In speaking of this Salaria says, "I was very despondent, naturally. But, my brothers told me to keep going, not to let this stop me."

The brothers then took the case to the school board and finally secured her transfer to West High School. The right to enter athletic activities there without restriction, was specified. That was her first realization that one does not accept and submit to unfair practices. One resists and fights.

TRAINING AND WORK AT HARLEM HOSPITAL

During the summer vacations Salaria worked in the office of Dr. Bedford Riddle, successful Negro physician of Akron, Ohio. She had graduated from high school when Dr. Riddle persuaded her to take up the profession of nursing. Upon his advice she entered Harlem Hospital Training School.

Harlem Hospital has a mixed staff, Negro and white, in most departments. Yet within the institution there were sharp practices of racial discrimination. In the dining room this was quite noticeable. Certain tables were reserved for white workers. Ranking white staff members ate in private dining rooms while Negro members of the same rank ate in the common dining room. Older Negro nurses cautioned that this had always been so and nothing could be done about it. One day Salaria entered the dining room with a group of her fellow students. They found only one vacant table so seated themselves there. The waitress refused to serve them saying that this table was reserved for white social workers. The dietician confirmed this. At once the five students rose, gathered up the ends of the cloth and dumped the table over.

Conditions at Harlem Hospital had been "smelly" for a long time. When news of this story leaked out the Mayor sent a committee to investigate the conditions. By that time the students had organized themselves and were ready with certain basic demands. These were:

1. Discontinue racial discrimination in the dining room.
2. Appoint one Negro dietician to the staff now composed of five white.
3. Grant more authority to the charge nurses who now function merely as straw bosses and petty foremen.

All these demands were met at once.

That was Salaria's first experience in group action, in organized, programmatic resistance to injustice. Previously her brothers had assisted her in each situation. Usually she was the only Negro involved. When one place did not concede they moved her on to another. Now she was learning to resist, to organize and change conditions. She emerged with a strong new feeling of group identity. This was 1933.

In 1934 Salaria was graduated at Harlem Hospital Training School. After a brief service at Sea View Hospital she returned as a regular member of the Harlem Hospital staff. She was assigned to service in the obstetrical division. For some time there had been rumblings of the desperate conditions at Harlem Hospital. Now as a nurse with responsibility Salaria began to feel the force and meaning of these things. The ward was overcrowded and understaffed. One nurse in charge of a maternity ward and a nursery of fifty babies. Fifty babies to be fed and cleaned three times each night – one-hundred and fifty feedings and one-hundred and fifty changes, and one nurse to do it. In addition there was the ward for abnormals. this usually contained about twelve babies and as many infected or abnormal mothers, many infected with communicable diseases. These, of course, should have been isolated and cared for by one nurse exclusively. Sometimes these diseased mothers wandered off into the ward of healthy babies. Once Salaria found one of these women feeding a healthy baby with milk left by her own diseased child.

She wrote a report calling attention to these conditions. Immediately she was transferred to the delivery room and warned to "mind her own work." Ordinarily two nurses assist each physician in a delivery case. Here Salaria found herself alone with three deliveries in three separate rooms and of course three different doctors.

That summer infantile diarrhea spread through the hospital. Daily from three to five babies died. People in the street began to grumble among themselves referring to the hospital as the "Death House." The hospital continued admitting new patients. No extra measures were undertaken to curb the epidemic. Discontent finally crystalized in organized protest. A picket line was thrown around the hospital demanding an investigation into the deaths of so many babies, and that the maternity ward be closed during this investigation. These demands were met. Analysis of the doctors' monthly report stating the true cause of death of patients was compared with the final report sent monthly to the department of hospitals. It became apparent that the department of hospitals was not being accurately informed of the conditions. A public investigation followed, serious conditions were exposed and Salaria learned that the individual is only as secure as the group.

REPUBLICAN SPAIN

Salaria's activities centered with the more progressive nurses. Together they attended lectures and discussions on civic affairs, local, national, international. These discussions helped her to understand what was happening in Harlem and its relationship to events in Europe and Africa. German fascism and its attack on Races, Italy's raid on Ethiopia. Now Spain. When Italy invaded Ethiopia she was ready. With groups of Harlem nurses and physicians she assisted in gathering the first two tons of medical supplies and dressings sent from this country to Ethiopia. She was active in the drive Harlem physicians initiated and which resulted in a 75-bed field hospital being sent to Ethiopia.

When Mussolini advanced his Italian troops from Ethiopia into Spain she understood that this was the same fight. She had developed enough to understand it. On March 27, 1937 she sailed from New York with the second American Medical Unit to Republican Spain. A party of twelve nurses and physicians. Salaria was the only Negro in this group. Hundreds of Negro boys had preceded her. They had gone as soldiers, physicians, ambulance drivers. She was the first Negro woman to go.

It was April third when the party reached Port Bou, Spain. A huge delegation of Spanish men, women and children came down to welcome them. A small boy left the crowd and came over to Salaria. Taking her hand he complained softly, "Why didn't you come yesterday?"

"Why yesterday?" Salaria asked him.

"Because yesterday the fascists came in their planes and dropped bombs. My mother and my father and my small brothers died. We had no doctors and nurses to care for them after the bombs struck. Stay here. If the fascists return with bombs maybe all of us would be killed if you don't stay here."

Official instructions directed that they set up their hospital at Villa Paz near Madrid. Villa Paz had been the summer home of King Alfonso XIII, deserted since his abdication in 1931. It was a beautiful, low, white palace set in a lovely garden. There was a brilliantly tiled swimming pool screened by tall cypress trees. The palace was now occupied by cows and goats. The peasants still lived in the cramped, damp hovels. The floors were dirt. For heat they burned dry cow dung on top of a tile stove built in the corner. The peasants were so accustomed to poverty and hardship that even now they did not dare move into the King's abandoned palace. Instead they turned it over to the cattle.

This was Salaria's first concrete example of discrimination where race was not a factor. Here it was peasantry versus nobility. The peasants had previously accepted the belief that nothing could be done about it just as Harlem nurses had earlier accepted racial discrimination in the hospital dining room. Like the Harlem nurses the peasants were now learning that something could be done about it. One resisted, one fought, liberty could be a reality. There was nothing inviolable about the old prejudices. They could be changed and justice established.

The American Medical Unit, with the authorization of the Republican Government of Spain, turned the cows out at once. They cleaned the building and set up the first American base hospital in Spain. The cows went back to live in the mud floored huts of the peasants.

The palace was exquisite. There was plumbing throughout. Only water seldom ran in the pipes. The nurses and patients collected enough money among themselves to install a gasoline pump – which ran sometimes. There were four bathrooms. The peasants had never known until now just what they were for.

The palace was electrified. But the wiring system was obsolete. Often in the midst of a critical operation doctors and nurses found themselves suddenly in darkness. Many patients died as a result. Again the nurses and doctors and patients contributed – this time 1800 pesetas. With this they installed a reliable, modern power service.

It had never occurred to the King to screen his lavish palace. Palaces are feudal in their splendor. Often they entirely overlook simple sanitation. Flies and mosquitoes were a constant menace to wounded men. Again the medical staff pooled limited personal funds. They bought screening, built frames, cut out new windows, built doors. The former stables were converted into a long dining room, with an ample kitchen opening onto it. All the work was done by the patients, assisted and directed by the nursing staff and personnel. Busy days. So much to do, so little with which to do! Fuel was scarce, water uncertain and food poor, mostly beans and rancid olive oil. They were often hungry.

The young Spanish women who helped them were between 15 and 30 years of age. None could read and write. The new Government was making every effort to liquidate illiteracy. (Forty-five percent of the people were illiterate when the war broke in 1936. This number has been reduced by twenty percent now.) Two wounded Spanish-American soldiers volunteered to teach as they convalesced. In six months Villa Paz had liquidated its illiteracy. Everybody could read and write.

The American Base Hospital at Villa Paz

The hospital beds were soon filled with soldiers of every degree of injury and ailment, of almost every known race and tongue and from every corners of the earth. Czechs from Prague, and from Bohemian villages, Hungars, French, Finns. Peoples from democratic countries who recognized Italy and Germany's invasion in Spain as a threat to the peace and security of all small countries. Germans and Italians, exiled or escaped from concentration camps and fighting for their freedom here on Spain's battle line. Ethiopians from Djibouti, seeking to recoup Ethiopia's freedom by strangling Mussolini's forces here in Spain. Cubans, Mexicans, Russians, Japanese, unsympathetic with Japan's invasion of China and the Rome-Berlin-Tokyo axis. There were poor whites and Negroes from the Southern States of the United States. These divisions of race and creed and religion and nationality lost significance when they met in Spain in a united effort to make Spain the tomb of fascism. The outcome of the struggle in Spain implies the death or the realization of the hopes of the minorities of the world.

Salaria saw that her fate, the fate of the Negro Race, was inseparably tied up with their fate; that the Negro's efforts must be allied with those of other minorities as the only insurance against an uncertain future. And in Spain she worked with freedom. Her services were recognized. For the first time she worked free of racial discrimination or limitations.

There were not too many skilled hands to make the wounded comfortable. Everybody's services were conscripted. Nurses taught carpenters to make hospital supplies – shock blocks, back rests, Balkan frames for fractured arms. Fire and fuel they needed desperately.

Fascists have captured Spain's coal mines and they are now being worked by German industrialists. Two years of war and all Spain's trees have been burned for fuel. One morning in a cold rain they brought in a young French soldier. A leg had to be amputated immediately. There was no time to warm him – and no fuel even, had there been time. Instead of rallying the patient collapsed with shock and chill. The building was clammy cold.

"Pack his bed with hot water bottles," the doctor ordered. Collectively the nurses puffed at oil stoves which refused to take fire with dilute kerosene. It seemed horrible to watch this young chap die when so simple a thing as hot water could save him. They were all young nurses. Helplessly they looked at each other.

Salaria glanced at the clock, noted it was approaching lunch time and soup should be boiling. Nimbly she gathered up hot water bottles, ran down the stairs and, unnoticed, into the kitchen. With a big pitcher she filled the three hot water bottles with steaming soup. The patient recovered.

Another time the fires were going but the pump had broken down so there was no hot water. A special diet patient needed soft boiled eggs at careful intervals. Wine is on every Spanish table. A pitcher of wine was soon boiling on the stove and the patient had his eggs on schedule.

The days passed. Long hours of work with night indistinguishable from day. Monday was quite the same as Saturday. But Sunday was different. They could always tell Sunday. As early as seven o'clock in the morning the peasants arrived. Tiny burros drew little canvas-covered carts loaded with their women folks and children. They came to the Hospital Americano for help. Infants a month old, blind children, children covered with ulcers – usually the result of no medical care or health education. (The Loyalists are fighting for education and social service.) Sometimes they brought a chicken or a young goat in their arms as a thanks offering. Often fresh eggs, a real service to special diet cases. The milk and medical supplies sent from America were shared with these undernourished children. Cod Liver Oil to rickitic [sic] babies and warm clothing, often from the limited personal supply of the nurses. So much need everywhere. The nurses and medical staff gave away their personal belongings when supplies were slow coming from America.

NEGRO SOLDIERS IN SPAIN

When Salaria went to Spain hundreds of Negro men had already recognized Spain's fight for liberty and freedom as part of their own struggle.

Oliver Law, Walter Garland, Douglas Roach, Milton Herndon were on the Jarama front. The brigade had been one-hundred and twenty days in the trenches. Oliver Law was commanding. They say it was his turn for a leave. He had come over with the first American volunteers to Spain and had not had a day's leave. He was delighted at the thought of a Negro nurse coming, and prepared to welcome her. But, the story goes, from months in the trenches his cloths were in rags. He had no shoes and his underwear showed through the rents in his trousers.

He was in excellent spirits. He called the Negro chaps together and suggested that they draw straws, the one drawing the shortest should go in his stead. Douglas Roach drew that one. The others watched him eagerly as he dressed himself for the occasion. Doug's wardrobe was in good shape despite months in the trenches. He had an amazing technique for successful foraging. He would have loaned the outfit to Law but Doug was short, and Law inches taller.

Later Salaria had Doug as a patient. He came to Villa Paz with a deep shrapnel wound in his shoulder. Recovery was never complete. He was furloughed home and died some months later. She nursed Lieutenant Garland when he was wounded a second time. This was in the same battle in which Oliver Law was killed. Garland was twice a patient at Villa Paz. Salaria describes him:

"Garland could never be convinced that he was wounded and not fit for the front lines. Every morning he would ask, 'Will the doctor send me back to my brigade. Those boys need me.' One day planes flew low over the hospital continuously. At supper check up Garland was missing. About ten o'clock next morning the Brigade headquarters telephoned our Commandant to know if we were missing any patients. Two Americans, an Englishman and a Frenchman had reported for duty. It was Garland and his companions. Anti-fascist fighters never felt they were unfit for action as long as they could walk."

AT THE FRONT

Early in April (1938) the order came to move to the front. Every nurse as well as every fighting man who goes to Spain looks forward impatiently to the day when he can be in the thick of the fighting instead of serving "behind the lines." Three doctors, six nurses, a corps of carpenters, mechanics, orderlies and a convoy of three ambulances, two trucks and equipment to set up a field hospital. They set up their unit outside a small town near Teruel. The first two days were quiet. From the village each morning the women and children and old men went out to work in their fields. At sunset they returned to their small houses. At evening the third day fascist planes flew low, dropping bombs. Next day no one went to the field. Most of them were dead. The wounded were brought to the American field hospital for first aid. From there they were evacuated to the base hospital at Pueblo De Canada. That night the field hospital convoy moved farther setting up their unit near Pueblo De.

Salaria describes those days at Pueblo De.

"That evening about seven o'clock patients began to pour in by hundreds. All that night we worked to treat well as many as possible and start them on the way further behind the front lines. When morning came we had nineteen patients left. These were wounded so badly that it did not seem safe to move them. By eight o'clock that morning we were visited by five fascist planes. These flew very low and slowly over our unit. For about twenty minutes they circled close above us then flew away. Within an hour they were back. This time they were ten. They turned their machine guns on us and began firing – terrifically, continuously. No one was injured and they flew away after a while. At 11:15 fifteen planes returned. This time they were confronted by seven Government planes and together they battled just over our hospital unit. We could hear the stray bullets as they fell through the olive trees."

"In about thirty minutes the seven Government planes had driven back the fifteen fascist planes. During all this we had plenty of work to do and so we continued. At 1:25 about twenty-five planes came over in formations of one, two, and three. Long before they reached our camp they began dropping bombs. We could hear them falling and also see them. I was sitting under a tree eating dinner with the American Dr. Pike. The bombs were falling close and closer, even closer than I realized until Dr. Pike suggested that we move into a trench nearby. We did. When I settled myself in the trench I recall seeing Dr. Barsky. After that I heard one explosion, then I went to sleep. I was waked by Dr. Barsky shouting to know if I was hurt. I told him, "no." I heard screams. Helen Freeman, an American nurse, had been badly wounded. A Spanish nurse, and later we learned, an English nurse were also seriously injured. Many of the patients had been killed. Already newly wounded were being brought in. We began at once to work on them. Suddenly we ran out of sterile supplies. Just up the hill our mobile operating officer was parked in charge of an American ambulance driver. Two of us rushed up the hill to get more supplies. When we reached the ambulance the driver was lying outside with his head blown away."

The next morning the hospital contingent was ordered to evacuate. The fascists had broken through the lines. They journeyed all that night. The roads had been ploughed up by fascist bombs. Once they picked up empty shells exploded from Franco's guns. Marks on the shells indicated they were made by an American firm. (The American embargo is on arms to the legal, republican government of Spain. Germany and Italy are free to buy arms from any country and send them to Franco. So there is really no restriction against arms to the fascists.)

Next morning they set up the field hospital. It was thirty-six hours since they had eaten. Hundreds of wounded had been served in the interval. The journey over shelled roads had been difficult. Before completing the hospital they built a fire in the field, in preparation for a meal. The fire was hardly kindled when enemy planes began strafing the field. The hospital was cut off from the lines by enemy fire. Two ambulances were captured, four doctors lost. Many of the staff swam the Ebro River to safety.

Salaria was lost from her unit. She hitchhiked and by slow stages rejoined the American medical unit near Barcelona. Here they set up a 4000-bed hospital. They were pitifully short of the most commonplace supplies. Many seriously wounded patients had to go with bandages unchanged for days because there were no surgical dressings. Patients who were able to sit up washed their soiled dressings in the early morning and had them waiting for the doctors and nurses when they came to redress them.

Barcelona was under continual bombardment at this time. Children's colonies became the special target of fascist bombardment. After bombardments the nurses accompanied the ambulance to the scene. They carried small spades. First with their hands they gathered up the broken fragments of human bodies – brains, limbs, a section of a head. After that they felt with their hands under the soft loose earth. They saved the spade for last. There might be danger of striking some body not dead and who have a chance of recovery. At second depth they used the spade.

One morning the ambulance and nurses [were] sent to one of the children's colonies. A bomb had torn the building in half. One-hundred and fifty children had been killed. Salaria was digging at the third level. A tiny hand protruded. A bright calico sleeve covered the arm. She put aside the shovel and began gently disengaging the earth about, so that no further injury would be done the child to whom the arm must belong. With all the earth aside she lifted carefully. There was only the little arm. A distracted Mother rushed across the street and hugged the arm to her breast moaning, "My baby, my baby."

So many tragedies she shared with the Spanish people! Her face became a familiar one in Spanish papers and movie houses. (She appeared in two movies in this country – "Heart of Spain," and "Return to Life.") Several times the Republican Government dispatches cited her for courage and efficiency.

More and more Spain's cause seemed to her the cause of minority groups throughout the world.

[Later Salaria Kee's] hospital unit suffered a particularly heavy bombardment. The group was eating dinner under the trees and counting the bullets that splattered about the field from the low flying enemy planes. Suddenly the signal was given "Cover! In the trenches!" Lying flat, face buried in the earth floor of the trench she heard a tremendous explosion. Some time later she was uncovered and dug out from under six feet of rock, shell, and earth. A bomb had exploded at the end of the trench.

The resulting injury left her unfit for further hospital service. She was furloughed home. She reported at once for service with the Medical Bureau in New York. She has given particular attention to securing medical supplies – so desperately needed – for the people in Spain. Her experience with them gives her first hand knowledge of the great need. It is difficult, she says to see so much goods everywhere and to recall how many times a patient's life was lost from infection just because there was no surgical dressing or the simplest of antiseptics. And so during these months of convalescing Salaria Kee is traveling through the country urging aid to the people of Spain, medical aid, food.

"Negro men have given up their lives there," she says, "as courageously as any heroes of any age. Surely Negro people will just as willingly give of their means to relieve the suffering of a people attacked by the enemy of all racial minorities – fascism – and it's most aggressive exponents – Italy and Germany."

PART 4

Testimonies

Introduction

The following pages provide the opportunity for a firsthand encounter with the voices of the African-American veterans of the Spanish Civil War. In these documents the veterans reflect on their experiences in Spain, the influences and circumstances that led them there, and the ways in which the experience of being black in America shaped their political commitments and life choices.

These testimonies are arranged in alphabetical order, but by coincidence the first two veterans from whom we hear, Frank Alexander and Albert Chisholm, are also at this writing the only ones still living. Both reside in Seattle, Washington.

Problems with the government, especially during the Red scare years of the 1950s, are a common theme. The testimony of Crawford Morgan is extracted from his 1954 appearance before the Subversive Activities Control Board (SACB). The SACB was a U.S. Justice Department agency established to identify "subversive" (i.e., socialist or communist) organizations deemed harmful to national security. Once an organization was identified as subversive and placed on SACB lists, it had to register with the government and submit its financial records and membership lists. This process was established as a means of controlling and suppressing left-wing organizations without technically outlawing them. In 1953 the SACB accused the Veterans of the Abraham Lincoln Brigade of being a subversive organization, and in September 1954 hearings were held to decide the VALB's status.

Ray Durem addresses the issue of Cold War harassment in the poem "Award [A Gold Watch to the FBI Man Who Has Followed Me for 25 Years]." His poetry dates from the 1950s and early 1960s. It reflects his experience as a black radical in a time of repression and reawakening struggle. As such it is an extension of the black radical tradition enacted by

Durem and the others in Spain. Apparently recalling the battlefields of Spain in "To Mack Parker," Durem vents his rage at southern racism with the wish "to die carrying a ninety pound gun up a southern slope . . ."

The other testimonies in this section are from oral history interviews with Lincoln Brigade veterans. In the early 1980s ALBA conducted an oral history program, collecting and transcribing lengthy audiocassette interviews. The tapes and transcripts are in the ALBA collection at Brandeis University. During this same period Manny Harriman collected several dozen videotaped oral histories of his fellow veterans. Extensive interviews were also conducted by the Abraham Lincoln Brigade Film Project as background research for the documentary film *The Good Fight*. All of these are available in the ALBA collection. The interview with Albert Chisholm was prepared by Jeremy Egolf, a writer with an interest in the Lincoln Brigade.

By the time these interviews were conducted events in Spain were five decades distant and the participants were of advanced years. While some particulars may thus be faded by the passage of time, the testimonies do capture the flavor and feel of life in the Depression-era United States. They also provide an invaluable picture of how the subjects saw their earlier activities in light of subsequent decades of experience.

In the testimonies of these black veterans at least two themes recur. One is the early experience of racism, and another is an encounter with the radical social, communist, and labor movements of the 1930s as an avenue for fighting racism and exploitation. All of the veterans quoted here came to see the struggle against racism as being inextricably linked with the struggle for a just and democratic economic order. Some of them later reevaluated, and ended, their relationship with the Communist party, but all of them remained loyal to their initial vision.

Many of the veterans also cite the influence of their childhood upbringing on the course of their lives. Admiral Kilpatrick's father was a Socialist party activist. Vaughn Love speaks of the antiracist tradition in his native eastern Tennessee mountains. Frank Alexander recalls his American Indian mother as especially inspiring him to fight for his rights.

The economic suffering brought by the Depression is also a consistent theme. Most of these veterans tell stories of hitting the road, hopping freight cars or hitchhiking, in search of work. They also speak repeatedly of a special animus toward the racist doctrines of Nazism and fascism. They cite the impact of Mussolini's invasion of Ethiopia in inspiring them to fight fascism in Spain.

The veterans interviewed also address contemporary issues. From the Cold War to the arms race to civil rights and the Vietnam War, these men became tireless activists who remained engaged in the life of their local and national community for as long as their strength allowed.

Frank Alexander

> "I just knew that I wanted to go to Spain . . . I'm the kind of person who wants to fight back, and I thought this was a way of really getting to the source. I thought the American people would learn much faster when America became involved in that struggle, that they would wise up to the problems that were here. . . . I figured that was the best way to show my support for what I believed in. So when they began to talk about sending guys over there, I said, 'Put me on the list.' "

[The following text is an excerpt from the Abraham Lincoln Brigade Film Project interview.]

Tell us about your early life, where you were born and so on.

I was born on February 8, 1911. I was born and raised in Nebraska on the Omaha Indian Reservation. That's a Sioux tribe. My mother was Indian and my father was a black man that rode horses for the Pony Express back in the old days. In those days, it was blacks and Mexicans mainly that were cowboys. Our whole history, in the movies, talks about white cowboys. But in the main there were black cowboys and Mexican cowboys from Texas on up to Wyoming. And that's what he did.

So you grew up on the reservation.

Yes. I left the reservation when I was 14 years old.

Did you grow up speaking Sioux or English or what?

I grew up speaking both languages. It's been a long time since I spoke the Indian language, but I remember a lot of it and could probably rehash it. But I grew up speaking both languages.

Did your mother raise you with a sense of Indian history? Did she talk to you about that kind of thing?

Yeah. My mother was not full Indian. She was half white and half Indian. Her father was a Scotch-Irishman. But I always admired her Indian background, and I think that I got that whole feeling to fight for something through her and from the way she raised us. She taught us not to accept second rate from anybody. And it went on through life. I was a real ornery person most of my life, in many ways. I wanted my full rights in every situation.

Your mother, even though she was half white, she identified more with the Indian than the white?

Yes. I would say so, once we left the reservation and we moved to Sioux City, Iowa. We went to the public schools in Sioux City, Iowa, and there was an awful lot of prejudice there. I don't look Indian, you know. I may have the color, but I don't have anything else. My hair is different and all. And we were treated differently in town than we had ever been treated out on the reservation. It was something wholly different. Black people in the city were totally segregated and had a whole separate part of town. We didn't live in that area because my mother had gotten a place in a part of town that was primarily white. And we ran into an awful lot of problems with the other people when they saw us kids because we didn't have the same straight hair that she did.

Then, when I was about 15, my mother got tuberculosis and she finally had to go into a sanitarium. And after that I just went off and traveled all over the Eastern states. I begged food, begged for clothing, begged for everything. I rode the rails and lived in the hobo jungles and stuff like that.

Eventually I went back to the reservation, and I stayed there for about six months, until my mother finally died. Then I had to leave again. The reservation was just too small-time for me now. Some of the Indians, you know, they had never been off the reservation. Some of them had never been to Sioux City, only 36 miles away. And so young men brag, what it's like to be in the big city with girls and shows. So three of these young Indian guys decided to come with me and leave. So all of us stole all of the hogs and stuff from our families and loaded them up on a wagon. We took 22 hogs in and got $80 for them. Then we left the wagons and the horses right there and caught the next freight train.

We started out for California–because I had heard so much about California and the fact that you could sleep outside and get all sorts of jobs. We road the rails together out to Phoenix, but eventually the three Indians decided to go back to the reservation.

They were just miserable. We didn't have no place to go, and every block we would go the police would stop us.

Because you were vagrants? Is that why?

Well, I think because I was black and they were Indian.

So I picked on up and headed out to California, to Los Angeles. My brother was already out there, and he was also already active in the Communist party. He was not a paid functionary in the Communist party, but he was active. He was working with the Young Communist League in Los Angeles. And naturally, as soon as I found him, he started taking me to different functions and meetings and so forth.

He explained all these things to me. And also, we were living among a lot of the blacks that later died in Spain–Alpheus Prowell, Virgil Rhetta, Aaron Johnson, and my brother and I all lived in the same one-bedroom apartment. I was the only one that wasn't politically conscious of what was going on. All the rest of them were very articulate and all.

What's your brother's name?

Herschel Alexander. He died in 1976.

See, in those days, the Communist party, and the YCL, was a very popular body, especially in the black communities. And so these guys had the respect of . . . the community as a whole . . . because of the struggles that they carried on.

I want to know what some of those struggles are. What do you remember yourself? Were you involved in any of them?

Well, the first one that I was involved in was the Longshoremen's strike in 1934. They were hiring blacks to replace the Longshoremen to break the strike. And our idea was to discourage blacks from going there as scabs and strikebreakers, despite the fact that at that time no blacks were in the Longshoremen's Union at all, you see.

You must have had mixed emotions about this.

Yeah, it was a problem. But they explained how it was the efforts of the bosses to separate people and in that way keep the wages down and use one group against the other. Eventually they were going to let the blacks go, and they would hire the whites back, and you knew that the white workers wouldn't want you in the shop if you had worked as a scab. So it was just a temporary thing, and the best thing you could do was to work with the white workers and try to educate them and fight for the rights of blacks to get into the union.

So I went out on the speakers' trucks, and we'd go through the crowds of blacks and talk to them on the avenue and tell them about the threats and what was happening, and about what the police had done to our trucks to discourage us from going into the black community.

What did they do to your trucks?

Oh, they tore them up. Chopped the tires with axes and stuff like this, so we had to get another truck and another truck and another truck. And the big shipping companies could pay for the police to do anything in those days. They did anything they got paid for. That was my first encounter with real struggle. I got beat up three or four times by the goons and by the police, mainly by the police. And I just made up my mind then that I was no longer going to sit back. It just stirred something in me that said you've got to fight, you got to do something. And I started from that day on. I've been doing it ever since.

Were there other major things that affected you politically, that made you more committed or changed your view of the world during this period?

Only what I could read as to what was happening in Germany and was happening in the world in general. And that's about it. And I just knew that I wanted to go to Spain when I heard about Spain.

Why did you want to go?

Because I told you that I'm the kind of person who wants to fight back, and I thought this was a way of really getting to the source. I thought the American people would learn much faster when America became involved in that struggle, that they would wise up to the problems that were here. So I figured that was the best way to show my support for what I believed in. So when they began to talk about sending guys over there, I said put me on the list.

Did you have any friends that wanted to go too?

They came afterwards. I was the first black, the first black from L.A. Alpheus Prowell, Aaron Johnson, Norman Lisberg, they all came later. I was the first one. I went early. I left in February of 1937.

Was it important when you were in Spain to stay near the other black soldiers, or did you just mix in wherever they sent you?

No. I think there was a conscious effort of the Brigade to separate the blacks out and make sure there was one in each of the units, you know. Squads and stuff.

Why was that?

I would assume to show sincerity and equality of everything, you know. There wasn't any encouragement for us to stick together. We got together on occasions. There wasn't the need for it like you find in the society that we live in today. You could pour out your grievances or your problems with anybody and everybody. Whereas living under this system you always try to more or less get off to the corner because this poor white guy doesn't understand this problem. But you didn't get that feeling there, you see.

You didn't run into Americans there who still had racism in them?

No. I ran into some vets that are racist since Spain, but they weren't racist in Spain. 'Course, I didn't find too many racist whites on the front lines of Guadalcanal in the U.S. Army, either. There were racists off the front lines. But you don't find no racists when you go to war and you're on the front lines. You're going to be buddy-buddy with everybody. I know they were racists.

I take it that you were still very active in communist activities after Spain?

Yeah. Even while I was in World War II. I was in the 93rd Division, which is an all-black division, and I spoke on several occasions within the division on the American trade union movement, democracy, and all these things, because they wanted to convince the black soldiers that they were fighting for something better. So they permitted me and others to do things like this. I couldn't go in there and promote the Communist party, but I could go in there and promote the right to unionize. We had sessions on unions and on what blacks should do and work toward to get into unions.

So you had a generally positive experience during World War II? You weren't discriminated against because of your political background?

No. I was discriminated against in the sense that I was put into a Jim Crow division with all blacks and all white officers.

Was that a shock to you, having been in an integrated war before?

Yeah. It was not easy to take. In one army I was completely equal; in the other army I was subordinate, I was not equal.

When did you start getting harassed about your political beliefs?

Oh, as soon as I came back from World War II. I became very active in the Communist party, and I began to get the pressures. I came back and became an organizer on the south side of L.A. We had a membership of 10,000 people in California, and I was responsible [for] at least 3,000 of them. I organized programs and I worked picket lines. We were the first, as far as my knowledge goes, to set up picket lines in front of the Bank of America to get a black hired as a teller or secretarial worker . . .

When did the FBI start knocking on your door?

That was during the McCarthy period. I was the chief liaison for all of the Smith Act defendants in Los Angeles. I was the only person outside of the lawyer that could see them.

So after the war you were involved pretty exclusively with Communists?

Totally, totally. I married, I devoted my entire life for nine years to the Communist party. Everything that I had and everything that I could. Up through 1955.

What happened then?

It was the Hungarian situation. It was a terribly hard thing. It's even worse now with Poland. Because, maybe I'm wrong, but it is just hard for me to see certain things. I can't see how all that many million people can be wrong. But I'll never be able to leave my philosophy. And I'll never be able to renege on the working class and whatever struggles they have. But I got to the point where I said, "What the hell. I'm denying my family, I'm denying my kids, and we're not going anyplace. We're going in a circle."

I still support the movement in every way that I possibly can since the late fifties. But I dropped out as far as my own full-time activity. At this point my primary support was through giving money, you know, because I began to make a lot of money. At least, a lot as far as I was concerned.

Were you involved in antiwar demonstrations about Korea or things like that?

Oh God, yes, I was in every damn picket line about Korea or Vietnam that there was.

Albert Chisholm

"I signed up to go to Spain because in that era, fascism was on the march. Italy attacked the country of Ethiopia . . . It was sort of a primitive society, but nevertheless it was something that black people throughout the world could look up to because it was governed by a black administration. . . . I was asked if I would like to go to Spain and fight against fascism. I told them, 'Sure, I'd be glad to go.' I wouldn't be in Ethiopia, but I'd be fighting the Italians in Spain, striking a blow against fascism."

[*The following text is an excerpt from an oral history interview conducted by Jeremy Egolf of Redondo Beach, California.*]

I was born at Spokane, Washington, in 1913. I was mostly raised by my mother, who was separated. We were poor and had a hard time surviving. We moved from one place to another. At that time, dark people generally took whatever work they could find. We were a closely knitted family, so if we didn't have any work, we shared with each other what we could find.

When I was about eight, we moved with my grandparents to Roslyn, where my grandfather got a job in the mines. It was a beautiful place because it was forested. I could go hunting and fishing with the kids. I went to an integrated school, but the black kids had a tough time going there. The black and white kids didn't get along very well, so mostly black kids had to stick together.

Two years later, the whole family moved to Seattle, to 21st and Denny. At that time, most of the black people lived around Madison and 24th. I went to Longfellow School. It's a park now. Miss Gifford was the principal, and she hated blacks. I was a talented kid. I could draw, I could write good, and I loved history. But I never got the chance to do anything with it. From Longfellow, I went to Minor. Going to that school was even worse. It was like going back to the South. It was racist as hell. The teacher was named Miss Smith. She couldn't stand her own shadow, so you know she ain't going to stand for mine. Anything I did was wrong. She would ridicule me in front of the whole class. I went to high school but couldn't finish because I had to go to work at about age 15.

My family didn't give me a lot of encouragement and support against dealing with the racism. Nobody taught me anything in relation to life in America. I know how phony it is. Racism makes money. My parents had the attitude of, "This is the situation, just do the best you can. Take what they give you, go to church, and so on." But that never rubbed off on me.

In the meantime the Communists were fighting like hell in the unions to permit black people to join. They fought until I had a chance to join the Marine Cooks and Stewards Union and to get a job. My first job was on the *President Harrison,* a passenger liner going to the Far East, early in the 1930s.

The Communist party coached me better than my parents did. They were the ones that had an understanding. If the majority of the ethnic, nonwhite people, particularly the black people, understood the society we live in, they wouldn't live in it. I overcame my parents' attitude because of my hatred of the way I was treated. I knew people treated me the way they did because they didn't like the color of my skin. When you got on the street car or something like that, little white children would look at you like you were some kind of zoot-suit character or a little animal. Black people conditioned themselves to accept all that. Instead of loving themselves, we'd rather love the white people.

The big problem in this capitalist world today is Russia. If they didn't have Russia as a problem, there'd be the blacks next on their list. But blacks don't want to learn that, they don't want to understand that. If they could organize and love themselves, they could create their own jobs.

The Communists told me I couldn't fight the battle alone. When you're a Communist, that's the greatest type the human race can have. You think of the best interest of the human race. If you can't do that, you're no Communist. You don't have to have a degree and all that stuff, because your mind is conditioned to want to know what's best for the interest of the human race. You don't give a damn about anything else. That's what makes communism so potent. I joined the Communist party when I was a kid, when I was on the ship and the Communists were out picketing for better conditions. I grew up with the Party.

I signed up to go to Spain because in that era, fascism was on the march. Italy attacked the country of Ethiopia, which was a black country. The leader of Ethiopia was Haile Selassie, "the Lion of Judah, King of Kings." It was sort of a primitive society, but nevertheless it was something that black people throughout the world could look up to because it was governed by a black administration. It wasn't a colony of anybody. Black people as a whole had no more contacts with Ethiopia than I did, but they were proud of it. In the meantime, in the United States, black people were catching hell all over the country. So when Italy attacked Ethiopia, the majority of the black people wanted to assist the Ethiopians. But the administration of the United States said no. It was out of jurisdiction, out of bounds for America. We did things like collect money for Ethiopia, but the money couldn't even be sent over. The white Fascists here were shocked that black people would have any kind of unity with black people anywhere else.

I was asked if I would like to go to Spain and fight against fascism. I told them, "Sure, I'd be glad to go." I wouldn't be in Ethiopia, but I'd be fighting the Italians in Spain, striking a blow against fascism. This was about the spring of 1937. Other guys, from New York and the East Coast, had been there a year or so before I arrived.

About two weeks after I volunteered, a group of us from Seattle caught the Greyhound [bus] and went to New York. They had it all arranged, hotels and everything. They had our passports fixed up. We were there about three days. We wanted to get over as soon as possible, so we all took the British ship *Manhattan,* which was the first to sail. It took about five days to get to Brest, France. There were no harbor facilities, so we had to get on jitney boats to go ashore. We told the immigration people that we were all tourists.

It was my first time in France. Like they say, you'll love Paris. The people were so human; they acted like they were used to black people. You could go meet a white girl and just walk down the street. There was nothing to it. Here, you'd get lynched. We stayed in Paris for two weeks; then they put us on a train for Toulouse, where we stayed in an old castle. About three days later, we got on a bus and went down to the base of the Pyrenees Mountains, where we discarded things we didn't need to take. It took us 11 hours to cross the mountains. Some of the French border guards were pro, and some were against us. We were lucky; there were a lot of border guards who saw us, and they just turned their heads away. We went over the border at night, and timed it so we would be across at daybreak. Anyway, we got over the border.

We were in España, in a little town called Figueras. We had exercise and training , but we didn't have rifles at the time. We stayed at an 800-year-old castle. It had everything you would read about in a storybook, like a drawbridge and some creepy stone stairs going down to the dungeon. There were five prisoners they were going to execute the next morning. We could witness the execution if we wanted to, but I was young and wanted to go out and see what the girls looked like.

The people talked so fast that I thought, "Gee, I'll never learn this language." But as the weeks went by, I seemed to get the tone of the language, and then it seemed they didn't speak so fast. Then I'd pick up a word here and there, and as soon as I learned to point my finger and ask, I was OK. They were glad to tell me anything I wanted to learn.

We stayed in Figueras about a month; then they put us on a train for Barcelona. That's where I got my first air-raid bombardment. That was something that really scared me. We came in at night. About half an hour later – just long enough to get a sandwich – the spotlights and siren went on. I didn't know what to do. We were supposed to put all the lights out. Then you could hear the drone of the planes. When they started dropping bombs on the outskirts of Barcelona, which is a large city, it was just like an earthquake. Everything was shaking. The bombs started dropping around the train station, and I was wondering where I could run. The civilians were supposed to have some kind of bomb shelters, but we didn't know anything about them. I got under the train. The bombing lasted about half an hour. We stayed in the station the rest of the night. You could just hear all those poor people screaming and hollering. Even though I was frightened I was madder than hell. I was mad and scared that something would happen to me and I wouldn't be able to do what I'd come to do.

Then, around daybreak, we left there to go down the coast. We could hear explosions in the distance – thump, thump, thump. We were trained at Albacete, the headquarters of the International Brigades. We were all grumbling because we wanted to go and fight fascism, but we had to be trained. Finally our chance came. Early one morning we were called out and told that the men whose names were called were to step forward. Finally, I heard my name, Albert Chisholm. About 500 of us were told to get our stuff packed. A convoy of trucks left for Belchite that afternoon.

When we got to Belchite there was nothing standing except for a bell tower. It was a bloody battle – bodies all over the place. We had to go and help bury the bodies. They were bloated, swelling up. We put them in bags. Anyway, that's where I joined the Abraham Lincoln Brigade. At the time it was called the Abraham Lincoln-George Washington, but they dropped the George Washington. I almost got it on the first evening because we were standing behind a parapet. One of the officers wanted to write our names into the company. An expansion shell came across the parapet and exploded among us. All it did to me was just tear the shoulder off my tunic. I fell into a big bomb hole behind where I had been standing. Several other guys were wounded.

I was on the front line until we were repatriated a year later. Capitalism was able to do what we couldn't. Our main problem was not having enough ammunition. The Soviet Union sent us as many men as they could to train us. They sent us their planes, with the star on the tail; they were damn good planes. They sent us their artillery, machine guns, and rifles; of course, they weren't modern, but they were adequate.

While in Spain, I met Paul Robeson, Langston Hughes, Tito, and Hemingway. They all came down to wish us well and gave us encouragement. You bet it helped our morale. They were fighting just as hard as we were. And the Lincolns were fighting just as hard as anyone else who was in Spain at the time.

Our last battle was the July 1938 offensive across the Ebro. If we could cross the Ebro and attack the fascist forces in that area (northeastern Spain), we would give relief to the southern front. One night we started building pontoons. We attached them together to form a bridge across the river. I helped on that. The river was about two hundred yards wide, so it took a lot of time, but we worked on it all night. Finally, we got it constructed. We had to get across there as fast as we could. Our company was miles down the line. No sooner did day break than our men started across. We had to get the whole damn thing across before the enemy knew what was happening. The forces that got over ran down the line and captured or killed any resistance. They got 15 miles, but then it started getting light.

Our company was still waiting to get across. It was getting too damn light for me. I told this guy, "I bet we'll have visitors." And sure enough, here came an observation plane. It flew around and circled around, and then he came down. We tried to shoot it down, and the damn bullets were going through the fuselage. We were shooting rifles and machine guns at that bastard, and the pilot didn't give a damn, he acted like he didn't care if he lived or not. We couldn't hit a vital spot or the engine. I knew when he got away that that was it.

I said, "I don't know about you, but I'm going to look for a safe place here. They'll be back in force." I started backing off. What the hell could you do when you're dead? About half an hour later you could hear the planes. I must say that the Fascists, they were scientific bombers; they dropped those bombs just where they wanted them and leveled everything. In a few minutes, you couldn't see anything because of the clouds of dust. They got the bridge and everything. I never got a chance to get across.

When we were repatriated in the autumn of 1938, our train to France had to stop once or twice because there was bombing all around us. When we finally got back to the United States, I went home to Seattle and tried to get some rest. People thought I was a soldier of fortune who had made millions of dollars, and they came over to the house. My aunt asked me if I knew who all the people were. I was lying in bed, and I looked at all the faces in the room – white, black, everybody. We finally had to call the police to get them out.

I went back to sea the rest of my working life, until 1971. In the 1960s I gave morale to the Viet Cong. When we sailed to Vietnam, I was the only one who could travel at night. A lot of taxis and restaurants and places were being blown up. I was able to get into the Viet Cong restaurants. They would send someone down with a motorcycle to the docks at night to get me, and we'd go all over the city. They're wonderful people. They didn't want capitalism; they wanted socialism.

The union was given the word to keep an eye on me because I was a radical. They withdrew my dues book in 1971. At that time there was a little depression here in Seattle. Jobs were scarce, including seamen's jobs. Seamen couldn't pay their dues. I was one of them. They made an extension for some of the seamen and said they'd have to recheck some of the books. That's when they got mine. When I asked for my dues book back, the man at the union hall said, "What book?" They could do that because they had connections with the Coast Guard, so there was nothing I could do.

I left the Communist party a few years ago because of some differences. But I still believe the Soviet Union is a great country, and I still believe in socialism. If I could give some advice to the young people of today, I'd tell them they have to learn about the power machine in relation to the economic structures they have to live under. Don't accept anything if you don't know what you're accepting. If they're poor and they accept what we have, then all right, as long as they know what they're accepting. Here we have no health security. If that's what you want, then go for it. The only ones I know who oppose health security are the rich people.

If you say smoking too much cigarettes is against the interest of the people, then bring about exposing the doggone thing and prove it. And that's what capitalism can't stand. It can't stand to be exposed. To bring about a better way of life, you've got to fight the enemy any which way you can.

Ray Durem

[The following poems by Ray Durem date from the mid-1950s. All are included in the out-of-print collection Take No Prisoners, *published in 1971 by Paul Breman of London.]*

AWARD
[A GOLD WATCH TO THE FBI MAN
WHO HAS FOLLOWED ME FOR 25 YEARS.]
Well, old spy
looks like I
led you down some pretty blind alleys,
took you on several trips to Mexico,
fishing in the high Sierras,
jazz at the Philharmonic.
You've watched me all your life,
I've clothed your wife,
put your two sons through college.
what good has it done?
sun keeps rising every morning.
Ever see me buy an Assistant President?
or close a school?
or lend money to Somoza?
I bought some after-hours whiskey in L.A.
but the Chief got his pay.
I ain't killed no Koreans,
or fourteen-year-old boys in Mississippi
neither did I bomb Guatemala,
or lend guns to shoot Algerians.
I admit I took a Negro child

to a white restroom in Texas,
but she was my daughter, only three,
and she had to pee,
and I just didn't know what to do,
would you?
see, I'm so light, it don't seem right
to go to the colored rest room;
my daughter's brown, and folks frown on that in Texas,
I just don't know how to go to the bathroom in the free
        world!

Now, old FBI man,
you've done the best you can,
you lost me a few jobs,
scared a couple of landlords.
You got me struggling for that bread,
but I ain't dead.
and before it's all through.
I may be following you!

PRISONS, PRISONS
I been in prison all my life.
Different kinds of jailers, that's all.
Some with bars,
some with stars,
some with pretty bare shoulders
and soft brown arms.
One use a time clock to keep me straight,
another uses a thirty-eight –
but the weapon keeps me on this rock pile
is the twist of a hip and a faithless smile.

LOVE AT THE BOOKER T
The midnight music madly swirling
starts out the bowels of Africa,
dips in Haiti,
rests a frenzied moment deep in Cuba,
emerges, torn and jangled,
from the shadows of New Orleans –
higher, higher in the heavens –
comes down through Moody's horn,

fills this love-warm room with joy,
reminds us of our tragedy.

STAN GETZ PLAYS IN SAN FRANCISCO
Bleak is the word for the world!
On this high plateau of solitude
the dawn frost chills the blood
under a sunless, loveless sky.

Through walls, the murmur of tongues,
the half-tender touch of the female,
kisses carefully parcelled out, caresses budgeted,
those I love self-slaughtered in the darkness,
mean, misled, and miserable –
        Emmett's corpse for sale in Chicago
Kenya waiting for the sun.

Where is the one who will comfort me?
Where is she who will warm the dark hours?
Where the love, the passion, and the play,
the mind and the body,
the soul and the sex and the smile,
Intermingled, interweaving, breathless!

Wine is no friend to man – merely
a substitute for miracles –
but heaven is far away, and I am here,
and the wine is near.
Sometimes it softens
the long dread reaches of the night hours
seals up the consciousness,
shuts out the fiercer noises of the world.

TO MACK PARKER
Let me die in a tiny skiff on an angry bay, sky grey,
tide going one way, wind the other, afraid to row, motor won't start,
waves hungry, fear freezing the oarlocks,
panic lapping at the gunwales.

I want to die carrying a ninety pound gun
up a southern slope, magnolia trees,
hot July day, dust on mouth,
hungry, agony of thirst, never get to the top,

bullet stop me.
I will be dead but not tortured.

Let it be the fast knife of a jealous man,
the wayward hand of a woman,
a drunk at the wheel,
steel from a thermo-jet,
hand grenade:
there death hides his hate and in that cold kiss
there is surprise but not betrayal.

Don't let me stand on the third tier
of a county jail and hear the feet of my oppressors,
see the fear turn ashen the dark faces of my brothers,
see the black hand point my way,
setting me up for a white murderer.

When a man dies betrayed
he died afraid
and very lonely.

TO THE PALE POETS
I know I'm not sufficiently obscure
to please the critics, nor devious enough.
Imagery escapes me.
I cannot find those mild and precious words
to clothe the carnage.
Blood is blood and murder's murder.
What's a lavender word for lynch?

Come you pale poets, wan, refined, and dreamy –
here is a black woman working out her guts
in a white man's kitchen
for little money and no glory.
How should I tell that story?
There is a black boy, blacker still from death,
face down in the cold Korean mud.
Come on with your effervescent jive,
explain to him why he ain't alive.

Reword our specific discontent
into some plaintive melody,
a little whine, a little whimper,
not too much – and no rebellion,

God, no! Rebellion's much too corny.
You deal with finer feelings,
very subtle – an autumn leaf
hanging from a tree –

                I see a body.

TAKE NO PRISONERS
Dark little mother mistress
brown and round and supple,
coarse as clay
yet fine as a shaft of moonlight –
how could a princess be my wife?

It took an African king, a black Judas,
a white and mercenary sadist,
a ship,
three hundred years
and many tears
to make my wife –
and I lost her.

The blues beat us,
the sun threatened us,
the white man sickened at our vision
and tortured us –

        one more victory for the paddy,
        taste it! not too many more are scheduled.

Anyway, I lost her,
with her little sweet sexed self.
Lost her smile. Lost her soul.
Lost her fine, fine body.

Well, love is a luxury –
and luxuries are for pale people.
I can wait.
All these chalk-faced evil peasants
live in daily dreadful terror –
three centuries of guilt
unnerves them.
I'll wait.

In this savage American jungle
we blacks must always walk catlike.

Sleep with a friend to guard you,
and a friend to guard the friend.
And wait!

This game is for keeps.

Oscar Hunter

"They said that they wanted volunteers to go and start developing the trenches. So Doug [Roach] and I volunteered. I remember our running through a set of olive trees, and we got to a point and we started to dig. Doug and I were both of us workers, not high school kids, not college boys, but workers, and we really dug, see. And we did it as long as we were at the front together. They'd always say when you'd get to the part of the trenches where Douglas and Oscar are, be sure and have a ladder, 'cause you're going to have to climb down. It was funny as hell. But we survived and they didn't."

[*The following text is excerpted from the ALBA oral history interview conducted May 22, 1980.*]

Could you tell me about your background and early life?

I was born in Orange, New Jersey, to a woman who was mostly Indian and to a father who was a South Carolinian and mostly French. I was born on May 22, 1908. I was born into an atmosphere of militancy because my mother was a woman who didn't feel she wanted people to bring up her children, not even fathers, and so we lived in an atmosphere of independence. Everyone in school knew that you couldn't touch Lily Hunter's children.

She went to work every day until she dropped dead. She worked for the rich people. She worked for the Colgates who later on became the great soap and toothpaste company. They would give my mother stuff. She would bring home food at night and, one fortunate thing for me, . . . books. These kids would graduate from prep schools and give up their books, so my mother would bring home sacks of books. So I had a huge library, which I learned to savor very much. It was a terrific thing as I look back over the years.

It's very difficult for me to talk about how did I ever get to where I am. People say, "Well, how did you ever become a Communist? How did you ever go to Spain?" And it was a very simple thing for me to understand because, for instance, my mother didn't believe in the First World War at all. She made that known to us very graphically. She used to say that before she'd let my oldest brother enlist or go to war, she'd cut his throat. So I grew up in that atmosphere until one day I came home from grammar school and she was dead. That's all – she had gone too hard trying to support us, and she stopped.

By that time I was in about the fourth grade in school. My oldest brother Charlie decided to keep the house going, and I had an older sister who found a man and left. So I had a very young sister who had just been born when my mother died, and me and my brother, and we took up with a woman who was from the South. Then I began to grow up and I got into trouble with her, you know. So I got an idea through a man I'd been friendly with. He left town and went to Detroit because the automobile industry was just starting. It was just after the First World War. He wrote me a little note and said if you come here, I can get you a job. So I quit school and took off.

I started off toward Detroit hitchhiking. On the way I thought I'd stop and see my mother's sister in Cleveland. When I got there, I guess I was about 14, but I'm passing for 21, so she put me to work. I went to work in this department store as a window washer. And, you know, I was still a kid who liked to read. So there was a guy there who watched me. I worked my ass off, but he used to watch me, and he came up to me and said, "What the hell are you doing working here? You're reading all the time, why don't you got to school? I'm going to put you in school," he says. "You're going to have to save money and it'll take a year, but I'll get you into one of the best schools down South, my school." So I say, "Where's that?" He said, "Virginia." "OK, what's the name of the school?" "Hampton Institute."

And sure enough, it worked. I went to Hampton, spent five years, changed my life. Became a radical, carried on my mother's tradition, and that's how I got involved in the whole Marxist thing.

When I left Hampton I went North, and the Depression had come by that time. I said, "The hell with this, boy." I could see what was going on. "I've got to get back to some school." The man who had given the talk at our graduation was president of West Virginia State College, so I wrote him a letter and said that I was a right tackle and wanted to go to college. So he wrote me a letter and said you get here, you'll stay.

So I hitchhiked down to West Virginia, and that started it too, because I saw the coal mines for the first time. And I met a man named Ferguson in the Department of Sociology. He was one hell of a teacher. Never mentioned Marx. Didn't need it. In West Virginia? Just look around you. Then one summer back in Cleveland I met some folks who said I ought to go to Brookwood Labor College. You ever heard of A. J. Muste? Well, A. J. was a very famous labor educator at Brookwood. So I went there about a year and there I heard about the Party. I met Communists. They were trying to organize a revolt against the leadership of Brookwood Labor College.

Then after Brookwood I lived in New York; I joined the Party and worked for the Party. But I decided I didn't want to stay. I thought I'd go to Chicago, and I did. When I went to Chicago a movement was on foot to organize the stockyards, and I got a job in the stockyards. And that's where I was when the Spain thing happened.

Was there much trouble trying to organize the stockyards there?

Oh yes. You know, people bullshit me, how much they organized. But what is now a union, I was one of the first people to fight for it, to work for it. I was one of the training people because after all, I'd been to Brookwood. But I found out something. I found I was having trouble with Party people. Very bad trouble. You know, people are very strange to me. For instance, why should someone who's a member of the Communist party in Chicago know more about blacks and the history of blacks than I did? And I'd spent all those years, almost seven years, in the South and been trained by all those marvelous people. You know, they couldn't stand me. I was always in trouble. I didn't have the correct line. I didn't have the correct approach. I didn't have this, I didn't have that. I kept right on anyhow. I didn't give a damn. One thing I did have, I know how to get on the floor to work with individual guys.

I was by that time going to journalism school besides working in the yards. I went to the Northwestern School of Journalism at night. I joined the John Reed Club. Dick Wright was a very dear friend of mine. He belonged to the John Reed Club then, [and] Nelson Algren – these are all names that came up in the '30s.

Then things began to pop in Europe, the fascist thing. And then a guy came in from New York, and he was recruiting, telling us how many people they wanted by Christmas to send to Spain. I walked into the Party headquarters. I knew the district organizer Morris Chiles, so I said, "Morris, I'm interested in going to Spain." And it was all settled. I wrote to my brother and got a passport. And by Christmas I was all ready. Then I took five guys to New York with me from Chicago. You know who one of them was? Oliver Law. Eventually, Law became one of the big shots up there, but he got killed.

Later, at Jarama, I was teamed up with a guy named Doug Roach, who's a black who died very early when he came back from Spain. Doug and I worked together and stuck close together. Then they began to move us up, and I knew it was coming. You could hear the artillery. So Doug and I got together, and he said, "Look, we're in the Tom Mooney Machine Gun Company." That was what it was called. And they gave us a gorki. It was a 1914 machine gun used by the czar's army. Just pure nonsense.

They said that they wanted volunteers to go and start developing the trenches. So Doug and I volunteered. I remember our running through a set of olive trees, and we got to a point and we started to dig. Doug and I were both of us workers, not high school kids, not college boys, but workers, and we really dug, see. And we did it as long as we were at the front together. They'd always say when you'd get to the part of the trenches where Douglas and Oscar are, be sure and have a ladder, 'cause you're going to have to climb down. It was funny as hell. But we survived and they didn't.

Then one night they decided it was time for us to move up. We hadn't seen an enemy by then. Nothing, just this gun in our hands, this machine gun. And I swear, Doug and I never got that thing to fire. It was older than most of the guys were. Anyhow, Doug and I moved up that night together, and the commander told us to move up to the front and start digging and set up a machine-gun nest. Absurd. But the way Doug and I solved our problem was, as people died, we took their rifles, and we didn't have a machine gun, but we had about 10 guns in our hole, and we just kept loading them and firing them.

After a while it was decided that I would go to training school. Well, I needed some minor surgery anyhow, and I thought, this will be a good chance to get it; if I stay up here I'll never get it. So they took me to Albacete for more training. I got out of Albacete and went down to the hospital for some surgery. All the wounded from Jarama were in this hospital, and you should have heard the roar from these guys. That started my career as the hospital commissar. And that's what I did until the very end of the war.

Then the Spanish Communist party sent for me, and they said through a black interpreter, "You are going home. We know it's not long now, and we have been told that in Chicago, where you come from, they have not made enough preparations to receive the wounded and ill people who are going to be coming there. It's your job to go and do that work." So I came back to this country, and I worked in Chicago with the doctors and organizing Cook County Hospital and getting beds in there and places for our people. I also helped set up the post of the Veterans of the Abraham Lincoln Brigade in Chicago. But the heat from the government was on me all the time. They kicked me off of the WPA.

Then one day the Party called me in and said, "Look, we want you to get out of town." And so I just packed. I was living with an artist by that time, and we just came to New York. That was in 1941, and I've been living in this neighborhood ever since.

Did you get called up in the Second World War?

No, as a matter of fact, I was 4F. I was very dangerously hypertensive. They used to have a worker's insurance plan run by the Party, and in Chicago I went to sign up for it. But they took my blood pressure and they wouldn't insure me. But when it was time to go to Spain there were no difficulties. I found that out much later. So they didn't want me in the U.S. Army. A doctor took my blood pressure and made me 4F. I almost died from it too, a couple of years later, until I met a doctor here in New York who worked on me and cured me. I was a heavy drinker by then. Not a heavy drinker, but I'd drink a lot, a jazz buff. I'd hang around with musicians.

What did you do when you came back to New York?

There was a guy I'd known in Spain named Joe Gordon, and I ran into him at a May Day. I told him I was broke, and he said, "I'm going to take you to the Furriers' Union." Son of a bitch. So the next day we go to the Furriers' Union, and sure enough he got me a job.

So I stayed in the Furriers' for years until I developed this process. I've been a good student, you see, and I discovered a way of making printing screens that were different from what they do in the ordinary commercial screens. So I went in with a guy on this printmaking process, and he cheated me. Well, what else can I tell you? I ended up in wallpaper.

When did you actually leave the Party?

Oh, I had a very interesting experience about the Party. When I came back from Spain, they just took it for granted I was a member, so they gave me an assignment. Also, when I first got back to Chicago, they needed to raise money. Everything was "peace" then, the peace movement. So I had myself a loft on the near North Side, and it was a huge place, so I used to raise money for the Party and for the peace movement. And I was an old jazz buff, so I introduced jazz to the goddamned fools.

The gangsters down the street didn't know what the hell I was up to, but that there was a lot of good music and a lot of beautiful broads, and a lot of people came there. And they used to run gambling games for me to raise money. But that didn't satisfy the Party. So I was called in, and I say, "Before I sit down, I want to ask you a question. Is this a trial of some kind?" And they say, "Oh no Oscar, we just want to talk to you." So I sit down and a guy takes out a book and starts to read from Stalin. So I get up and say good night. I say, "When you read Stalin, you know what you're getting ready to do. You're getting ready to have a trial, and I'm the one that's going to be on trial. You're not going to do that to me, baby." So I walked out.

It was miserable. Imagine the Party saying to me, "You get out of town." I had a good life going there. Some guy was even talking about putting me up in a cabaret you understand, on account of I know so much about jazz. And they told me to get out of town. And they did it in a very interesting way. They called me on the telephone, a lot of secret shit, you know, and said go to such and such a place on such and such a street in the loop and order coffee and see that there's an empty chair in the cafeteria behind you and . . . all this cloak and dagger. Finally, the message was, "Oscar, they decided that you ought to break up that apartment that you have and get out of Chicago." But I was never really expelled from the Party. I just sort of dried out, you know, just sort of stopped.

Would you go back and do it all again?

Yeah, every bit. I'll tell you why. I don't think anyone can really do your reading for you. That's my way out. I didn't let anybody read for me. See, and another thing, I've got too much humor in me to be bitter. I don't think I was the best Communist in the world. I know I wasn't. I think that I had certain corruptions. I liked women. I liked a drink now and then. And I liked to have fun.

Admiral Kilpatrick

"I don't have to have no damn praise or be remembered by anybody about going to Spain. I'd go today. I'd go any other day, as old as I am. . . . But I wasn't doing it just for Spain alone. I was doing it for Kilpatrick. I was doing it because I was a member of the movement that believes in that type of struggle. . . . I was a Communist. A Communist fights oppression, and they fight tyranny everywhere. So that's the reason I went to Spain."

[The following text is excerpted from the ALBA oral history interview conducted June 8, 1980.]

What was your parents' background?

My father was born about 60 miles from Tulsa, Oklahoma. At that time it was more or less nothing but Indians and blacks. My grandfather was head Indian, and he married a black woman that was taken out of slavery by the Indian people. My mother was born in Kentucky, and she come from a slave background.

My father worked as a cowboy, rode the range, worked in mines. He worked in a mine in Colorado, and we moved there. He worked for a steel company called McCorrigan McKenney Steel; that's part of Republic Steel now. I was born in Colorado on February 20, 1898.

When we moved to Cleveland, Ohio, I was about six years of age. During the period of about 1910-11 – I was around 13 years old – I became active in certain politics. I would put out fliers and go to meetings with my dad and listen to speeches. My father was an old Socialist. He was with the Eugene Debs section. So from this point of view, I became acquainted with many of the old-line socialist people in the movement. And I was able to meet many of the people that went on to build the communist movement in this country, coming from both the socialist and the communist side. I went through that period. I joined the Socialists, the IWW – you know, the Industrial Workers of the World, they were called the Wobblies. I saw the Palmer raids and the struggles around the Sacco and Vanzetti case.

As far as I was concerned, this was the only way that the common man was to have anything, was to carry out these types of actions. I still think the same way. My understanding of the world and its problems is based on Karl Marx's *Communist Manifesto* and *Das Kapital*.

I went to school in Cleveland through high school, then I went to work in mills and foundries, electrical shops and things like that, lumber camps.

Were you always active politically every time you went to a different job?

Yes. There's the question of organization. If I went to a place where there was no union, I would try to organize a union. What would happen, they would kick me the hell out. I'd go somewhere else where there was a union, I would get in the union. My father always told me that anyplace you go, where you are working, if anybody is organizing a union – a gutter union or even a dog union – join the union. That was his philosophy for me.

When I was growing into a man, I could understand what he was talking about. It wasn't, it isn't even today, a question of whether a union is bad or good. The question is that every working man and every working woman should be in some type of union organization. I don't give a damn who is at the head of it. They should be in it.

In those days blacks were often not accepted into some unions. I even had to organize auxiliary workers because they were black. They couldn't join the union.

How could you explain that to somebody who is black?

I can say from personal experience, it's pretty hard to convince black workers about the unions if we are going to take it from the point of view that they are treated the same as whites, because they are not. Even at this late date. But it wasn't hard to show that even under an auxiliary capacity, it is better to have somebody to speak for you than being out there alone.

One of the earliest things where I played any kind of personal role was during the 1919 steel strike. I carried on organization work at that time. I carried on picketing. I was able to carry on agitation against the strikebreaking and things like that. You know what happened there? They got thousands of blacks to work during the strike, and they kept them inside of these compounds in the steel mills until the strike was over, and then they dispersed them. We determined that it was a form of forcing people into slavery, and also of scabbing on the working class.

It was no easy task, organizing the American workers. The whole AFL [American Federation of Labor], which was the head organization of the American workers at that time, didn't even want to organize workers. They wanted craft unions. It was just craftsmen, and they didn't want to over-crowd the unions at that time. It wasn't just a question of black workers. Other workers had to become apprenticed before they could get in.

It's just like a kid coming out of high school today. He goes to ask for a job. The first thing that is thrown at him: "What experience have you had?" How the hell can you have any experience if you've just come out of school and you never worked before?

It's just a vicious circle when it comes to these kinds of questions. It's a foolish thing to ask a young worker today. The young kids today, I don't care what they say about them, they are the future leaders of this country. And if not for them, this country is going to go strictly to hell. These old goofuses sitting around here, they aren't going to save a damn thing.

I go to the colleges. I go to the high schools and things. Sometimes I participate with the kids in the curriculum that they take. Some people think that kids mostly are dancing and singing and using dope. That may be true with some kids, but the majority of the kids in this country are very serious about their lives, and that is the truth. And those people who are sitting back, trying to degrade the young people, they actually don't know what they are talking about.

When did you first come into contact with the Communist party?

From the inception. I was a pretty grown person when the Party was orga-nized. I worked with a lot of those men, especially Foster. Foster used to be my idol at one time.

But I didn't join the Party until around 1927. I was in the Wobblies. I could have become a charter member of the Party, but I didn't, because I wasn't developed that politically to understand what the hell difference it was. I was in the Wobblies as a good organization. I was in the Socialists and that was a good organization.

Then Eugene V. Debs, he says if he had to pledge loyalty to his gov-ernment, it would be the Soviet government. I remember the time that he said that. I was in a lumber camp in Bangor, Maine, and a Russian White Guard was going to cut my head off with an axe. We had a crew of three cutting cordwood, and we got to talking about the Russians, and I said to this guy, "You don't have to worry about that no more when you go back. The Bolsheviks have got the country now, and they are different. They are doing a damn good job."

That's what I said! So he goes on to try and whack my head off with the axe. He went to speaking Russian. After a while this guy quieted down, and he told me that he was not only a member of the White Guard, he was up in the class where he was next to the forces of the czar. I didn't know nothing about that. The funniest part of it is that us three people kept on working together. I didn't say nothing else to him. But we did cut wood. We done what we had to do to live, because you had to work to live.

Then I joined the Party, and later I was picked to go to school in the Soviet Union. I was able to travel to some other countries. I met with sessions of the Comintern. I met all kinds of people there. You had Party people from China and Germany and France and Czechoslovakia and Africa. Anywhere you mentioned, it was there. And we had a chance to meet every once in a while.

When did you get back to the United States?

[In] 1935. Then from 1935 to 1937 I worked in the trade union movement, to organize the CIO. I helped to organize the unemployed movement, things of that type, in Cleveland.

In those struggles you get into jail a lot of times. I've been in jail so goddamn many times, I thought I was living in jail. You get in jail for demonstrations, you get in jail for standing up in strikes, violating strike regulations about how many pickets you can have . . . So I've been in jail a lot of times.

When did you go to Spain?

I went to Spain in 1937. It was in the summer, because I know we went across the mountains at that time. We went across the Pyrenees Mountains into Spain, then to Albacete.

Were you wounded in Spain?

Yes, I was. I come to almost dying even before I knew I was wounded. I got hit here [under the armpit] with a piece of shrapnel. It went in here, and I kept on going. Then later on I began to get dizzy, and then the thing begins to swell up and so forth. I happened to be in a place where a lot of people were wounded, and I happened to be one of the ones in charge to see that they got to hospitals, and so they had the transportation for me. When I got to the hospital I almost fell out, so the doctor checked, and he found the shrapnel under the armpit. He said that if I had been maybe five or six hours more, it would have given me some kind of lockjaw and I would have been dead. But I didn't give a damn, because I didn't even know I was wounded until that time. I just thought it was my arm getting stiff like that. What did it was [that] the planes came over and dropped terror bombs, the bombs that blow up. When they hit those stones, they fragment and fly all over the hill. And that's when I got it.

What did you do after Spain and during World War II?

I was working during the war period. Sometimes I was a member of a shop committee and so on. Then I become president of a union, the Mine Mill and Smelter Workers' Local 735. I stayed in that for a long time until I was an international representative. Then I couldn't get along with some of my colleagues, because I thought they were backing off on a lot of things where they shouldn't, and I expressed myself. They worked out a way to see that I wasn't around there too much longer.

So I became delegate to the CIO. Then I went back to work again at Westinghouse. I was working on constructing transformers for PT boats, things like that. Then the union I was with got thrown out of the CIO during the convention in Cleveland in 1948.

We had some people to give up the struggle at that time. But in the class struggle you can't stay in it when it's good and jump out and leave it when it's bad. You go all the way. They send you to jail, what difference does it make? People have died for causes and things. You go back to the Haymarket days, people was murdered and killed.

Were you bothered in the McCarthy era?

Sure. They had me before committees and things like that.

Which did you take, the First Amendment or the Fifth?

I never took no damn one. I just told them to go to hell. I told them my own opinion was my own, and you go jump in the goddamn lake. They said, "You'll find yourself in jail." I said, "I don't give a damn. You put me in jail." So they never put me in jail for that. But I didn't take no Fifth Amendment. Why the hell am I going to take the Fifth? They knew who I was, I didn't give a damn. I had already stated it in open meetings and in delegated bodies to the unions. So why should I talk like that? The committee should take the Fifth, I don't want no Fifth. I've been trying to take the Thirteenth, Fourteenth, and Fifteenth amendments all my damn life and got nowhere, so why should I take the Fifth? It don't mean nothing.

Did you have a family?

I have three daughters and a son. Two of them are in Connecticut, and one of them's here in Cleveland now.

How did they relate to your political position?

They don't have nothing against it. The fact is, they are old now. My only young kid is the boy, and he's about 29, 30. The girls, one of them is in commercial art, and the other one teaches anthropology in a little school in Merton, Connecticut. But they live their own life and I live mine. We see each other once in a while. The boy has a couple of babies, and I play with them, and it's just one of those things.

They are good kids. But I can't expect for them to live a certain life I lived. They are not reactionary, if that's what you mean. They was taught like I was taught – you look at yourself from a class point of view. So I would say that they have the right attitude towards other people, because they do participate in the movements. The girls participate in the women's lib, and I know they participate in many other things that is kosher as far as the majority of the people is concerned. So I don't even worry about them.

Do you have much involvement with the other Lincoln Brigade veterans or with the VALB, the veterans' organization?

I guess I get letters from them and things like that. I don't have nothing against what we did in Spain being remembered. These people, including myself, went to Spain for a good cause, to fight against fascism. We know that. Now that that has happened, I'm not even against remembering that we was in the Spanish Civil War. But I would like to remember it as one of the entities in the whole international struggle that is still taking place in the world today.

Therefore I don't have to have no damn praise or be remembered by anybody about going to Spain. I'd go today. I'd go any other day, as old as I am. But nobody has to tell me about it. You don't have to praise me about it. It's something that I did. But I wasn't doing it just for Spain alone. I was doing it for Kilpatrick. I was doing it because I was a member of the movement that believes in that type of struggle. That's it. I was a Communist. A Communist fights oppression, and they fight tyranny everywhere. So that's the reason I went to Spain.

Vaughn Love

§ "We were all deep revolutionaries. We thought, 'We have to get to the front
and kill these Fascists!' . . . Most of the kids had some background in Marxist
education or in the trade union movement. My background in the
movement in Harlem gave me a certain outlook. I was through with the
system. I knew it didn't work, and I was thinking in terms of changing
society – to change the world."

*[The following text is excerpted from an interview conducted by Manny
Harriman for the Harriman Collection of oral history videotapes in the
Brandeis University Spanish Civil War Collection.]*

I was born in Dayton, Tennessee, December 5, 1907. Dayton, Tennessee, I
might add, is the place where they had the Scopes Trial in 1925. At that
time eastern Tennessee was one of the most progressive parts of the
United States. It was settled by Scotch-Irish people who had been volunteers in the American Revolution, and they were antislavery. They were
abolitionists.

This was the mountain region of Tennessee – Appalachia. And all
through that region people were more liberal with regards to race than
they were Georgia, Alabama, or Mississippi. There were no plantations in
this part of Tennessee. There was industry and mining and truck farming.
Some people would have a servant or two, but there was no plantation life
at all.

Later on, by the time I came along, the area around Chattanooga,
where Dayton is, was a great manufacturing center; it was called the
Dynamo of Dixie. It was a very open society.

My great-great-grandfather came into this region in 1824. He was
brought in there as the dowry in a marriage. His parents were two young

slaves who had been captured in Kenya, which was not where most of the slaves came from. My great-great-grandfather (my grandmother's grandfather) was their firstborn. When he came to Tennessee he was a 12-year-old boy; he was born in 1812. But the family that his mistress married into gave him his freedom because they were abolitionists. They gave him his freedom and then hired him as an apprentice. So that was old Sam McDonald, my great-great-grandfather.

In those early days, in that part of the country, there were a lot of free Negroes. It wasn't like in the Deep South, where you couldn't even free a slave because they didn't want them hanging around. My great-great-grandfather was one of those free Negroes. He was a horse trader. He could do anything with horses. And he had an old violin that he had found that he learned to play. He played all of the music of the time, the mountain music, hillbilly music. And he was very respected by everybody. He was all African, full-blooded 100 percent, but they say if you'd see him you'd have to say that all Africans were superior people, because he was a genius.

Now Sam married an Indian woman and had 19 children, one of whom was my great-grandmother, Katherine. She married a Clark, then she had a daughter, Vespy, who was my grandmother. Vespy married a fellow named Jim Love in 1892. Jim Love's mother was one of three daughters that her slave master fathered by a slave woman. Jim Love ran a saloon and a poolroom in Dayton and married Vespy.

My mother came along, and her parents tried to give her an education. They sent her off to a private school. But while she was there, when she was only 15 years old, she had a baby. That was me.

Now my father, my natural father, he was the son of a German baron. The baron had come to America in the 1860s to get away from the Franco-Prussian War or what the hell ever was going on there. And he took up with a black woman, and together they had my father. Now, the baron, he wanted to marry this woman, but you couldn't do that in Tennessee. But he gave this boy, my father, private everything–tutors and all. My father was very much loved by his father.

The baron didn't live to be a very old man, but he did eventually marry a German immigrant woman and had three other children by her. But they recognized my father as their brother. When they got married and grew up they lived off in Alabama, and they would sometimes come get me and take me off to visit with them for a few days. There was no big deal about it. It was a blood relationship. There was a lot of that. You've heard that saying, "blood is thicker than water." Well sometimes it is.

So my mother had me, she was 15 years old, and my grandmother raised me. My mother for some reason couldn't nurse me, and my grandmother had just had a son a year old. So I went on her breast and that was the end of it. I didn't care for my mother. There was two other girls in the house younger than my mother, and they just smothered me with love and care and everything – they'd just drag me around like a doll.

My mother married when I was about three years old. At that time my grandmother had about 11 children. They were quite prosperous, my grandparents. Old Papa Jim had a saloon and poolroom. When I was four years old all of these girls in the family taught me how to read and write. I was too young to go to school, so my grandfather used to take me to the poolroom with him, and I would read from my books. There was a guy there who thought I was just reading by heart, but I said no, I can read anything, so he got the newspaper, the *Chattanooga Times,* and I read that, and they almost died. My grandfather was beaming because he knew I could read. I did well as a child; I learned very quickly. But I was very small, so I had a tough time.

Now, in 1922 my grandmother died and I had to go to my mother, who was in West Virginia. She had married a man who ran a machine in the coal mines. When I went to West Virginia I was about 16. I had finished school up to the tenth grade. I was an athlete in Dayton. I was small, but I was tough.

At the school I went to in West Virginia, it was an all-black school in Montgomery . . . I boarded with a family there because it was too far from my mother's house to travel every day. There was a teacher there who had been to Fisk University, named Professor White, and he had been in the Army in France during World War I with my mother's brother, my uncle Walter. My uncle Walter was the dean at Tuskegee in Alabama, and they met off and on at different conferences for the schools. And they wanted me to go to Tuskegee. But I didn't want to be under Uncle Walter's supervision, because he was tough. And besides, I wanted to play football, and I was too small to play at Tuskegee. So I stayed at the school there in West Virginia. It was a good school. I joined the football team there.

After I graduated from high school I got a scholarship to Bluefield College, an athletic scholarship. I had an academic scholarship to Morehouse in Atlanta, but I didn't want to go to the South. I was afraid of the South. So I went to Bluefield in 1928 and played football. I was a quarterback.

The next year I went to West Virginia State, but I got hurt in the early part of the season, and I had to give up football. So what the hell, I thought, I might as well come to New York. So in the early part of September 1929 I came to New York. I was about 21. That was about three weeks before the Wall Street crash. The situation in New York at that time was already very bad, even before the market crashed.

I came to New York because everyone was telling me that if I could get to New York and get to Columbia or some of these bigger schools I could get a good education. But I got up there and I couldn't go to school, and I couldn't get a job that would give me the possibility to go to school. So I got a little job as an elevator operator in an apartment house in the Bronx.

Things were pretty rough after the Crash. I was working, but of course I wasn't getting any tips. I was able to keep my head above water. But within that year, I was having contact with different intellectual people around, students and so on. Some of them were radicals – progressive people – even in the apartment house where I worked.

I had a viewpoint, coming out of my education in black schools, that we were determined to get into the mainstream of American life. This was the idea of W. E. B. DuBois, for black students to get on the ball and improve themselves and improve their status. You had to speak that proper English. This is the sort of thing that we were working on at that time.

Now, after I've been in New York for a few years this Scottsboro thing comes up, in 1931. I had become renting agent for the building where I had run the elevator. I was making pretty good money. But when the Scottsboro thing came up I became interested in it, and I was instrumental in helping get people together to have demonstrations. I had no experience in this type of thing. But we would organize until finally all Harlem was out there on the Scottsboro case.

Then we developed the ILD, the International Labor Defense, to provide legal defense for blacks in the South. You couldn't get a black lawyer in the South. You couldn't get any kind of lawyer in the South. Then we developed an organization called the League of Struggle for Negro Rights (LSNR). And we were able to have cultural programs on Negro history and meetings and so on. This included church people.

At that time you had the very best of the black community in New York. These were the students who had come to New York. It was a wonderful climate there in Harlem. These people had never been able to participate in politics down in the South. But in New York what we needed at that time was politics. New York's politics was all Tammany Hall, and they had gerrymandered New York in such a way that there were no black officeholders in all New York. But we started organizing, and within a short time we had the American Labor Party, and people were participating – Adam Clayton Powell was involved.

It was a time when everybody was waking up among the student movement and the intellectuals. Because that Depression had scared the hell out of everybody. I mean, the bottom had fallen out. The system wasn't working like it was supposed to be working. The law of supply and demand. They were plowing under cotton and burying pigs out on the farms. At this time you had the American League against War and Fascism and different other organizations. There was a youth group there in Harlem called the Young Liberators. And the International Workers Order (IWO) [a mutual aid society] was one the big things that came into the field at that time because they had money. It offered insurance plans, and everybody needs insurance for medical expenses or burial expenses or dental expenses or whatever. This is something that everybody could have through the IWO, and it was cheap.

I became the secretary of Branch 691 of the IWO in Harlem. We had the biggest branch in the country because we had all the students and all the churches and even the fraternal organizations – the Knights of Pythias and all the lodges – because it was a better deal for insurance.

I also worked in the Federal Theater at that time, the WPA theater project, and we were able to get a lot of things going. For instance, the IWO used to have picnics and dances, and we used to have speakers from the NAACP and the Urban League; it was quite broad. We could get things done. We could have a meeting and have thousands of people. And of course, we'd had nothing before. We had the NAACP, but they had nothing of interest for the rank and file of blacks. They might get you in a college, but for the masses of people, they had nothing for you.

So that was the background for everything. We had branches of the IWO and the LSNR and the ILD all over the place, and that was the proving ground for the National Negro Congress. So the National Negro Congress comes in. The Negro Congress had people from all over, from the South and from the Unemployed Councils and from some of the progressive unions. It was really backed up.

We were coming back from the 1936 convention of the National Negro Congress out in Chicago when we got the news about the military revolt against the Spanish Republic. We were overjoyed because we just knew that the United States government was going to support the Republic. But we came to find out that it wasn't true. The United States starting doing business with Franco's side. So from that time on I started trying to figure out some kind of way to get to Spain.

At first I couldn't break loose from what I was doing. Everybody said we were doing well, that the black movement was going well. But I said to hell with it – this [Spain] is the most important thing to me. So I got in contact with some people, and regardless of who didn't want me to go, I went to Spain. I was with the second group, and we left in February of 1937.

We went to Le Havre, then we went to Paris, and from there we went to Marseilles, then on to Spain by boat on the *Ciudad de Barcelona*. We landed in Barcelona. We were the first Americans to get in there. But we were sidetracked. You see, we got picked up by the Anarchists, and they took us out on the town. Then one of our people got mixed up with a blonde woman in a nightclub – she spoke English. He went off with this woman, and later that night the police brought him back to our hotel. They found him in one of the sidestreets, and he had been drugged. Now, we didn't think much of it, but the next trip that the *Ciudad de Barcelona* made, the Fascists sunk the ship. See, they wanted information, and they drugged this fellow [who had] it.

From Barcelona we went on to Albacete and formed the first squads of the George Washington Battalion. We were all deep revolutionaries. We thought, "We have to get to the front and kill these Fascists!" You know. But the most revolutionary of all were the seamen; they had just come from a strike. Most of the kids had some background in Marxist education or in the trade union movement. My background in the movement in Harlem gave me a certain outlook. I was through with the system. I knew it pdidn't work, and I was thinking in terms of changing society – to change the world.

From Albacete we went on and fought at Brunete, at Perdillo, and at Mosquito. Then I was sent to military school, to officers' training. I was a section commander, and I had not been to school. So this gave me a chance to really get the hang of things. The instructors were Russian. The head one was called Captain Ramon, but I suspect he was a general. He was qualified to be a general. He had been through the Russian Revolution, and he had an answer for everything. After that training I came back to the unit, and we went to Teruel.

I was wounded at Teruel, and my wound hadn't really healed, but I was with a group that volunteered to go to hold the lines at the Ebro. And we held it. Every night we could go down to the river and see our people coming back across in the retreat. There was one guy from Buffalo, a black guy named John Hunter, and he had his machine gun. He had run away and crossed the river at night, all the while still carrying that machine gun. And this was after two weeks behind enemy lines.

The Fascists had great firepower in that war. But we knew how to take advantage of what we had, and we had great fighting spirit. Any time we were in an offensive, if we could get enough ammunition, we could keep going. But we couldn't get enough ammunition. They didn't want us to win that war, the Americans and the British didn't. Our own American naval intelligence and British intelligence were supplying intelligence to Franco's side during that war. They didn't want us to win. They didn't want democracy in Spain.

Crawford Morgan

> "From the time I arrived in Spain until the time I left, . . . I felt like a human being, like a man. People didn't look at me with hatred in their eyes because I was black, and I wasn't refused this or refused that because I was black. I was treated like all the rest of the people were treated, and when you have been in the world for quite a long time and have been treated worse than people treat their dogs, it is quite a nice feeling to go someplace and feel like a human being."

[*In September 1954 the Veterans of the Abraham Lincoln Brigade (VALB) were brought before the Subversive Activities Control Board (SACB) in response to a petition by U.S. Attorney General Herbert Brownell to classify the VALB as a subversive organization. On September 15 and 16, 1954, Crawford Morgan, an African-American veteran of the Abraham Lincoln Brigade, testified before the SACB on behalf of the VALB. Excerpts from that testimony follow. Morgan was questioned first by VALB's attorney, then cross-examined by SACB members, and then redirected by closing questions from the VALB attorney.*]

Did you have any understanding, Mr. Morgan, before you went to Spain, of what the issues were connected with that war?

I felt that I had a pretty good idea of what fascism was and most of its ramifications. Being aware of what the Fascist Italian government did to the Ethiopians, and also the way that I and all the rest of the Negroes in this country have been treated ever since slavery, I figured I had a pretty good idea of what fascism was.

We have quite a few fascist tendencies in this country. Didn't come to the point of taking up arms and killing a lot of people, but for the longest

175

time Negroes have been getting lynched in this country by mobs, and that was fascism on a small scale.

But over there [in Spain] it was one whole big group against the other. It was the Franco group that didn't like democracy. And they rebelled against the people after the 1936 elections and tried to stick their ideas down the throats of the freedom-loving people of Spain. So I, being a Negro, and all of the stuff that I have had to take in this country, I had a pretty good idea of what fascism was and I didn't want no part of it. I got a chance to fight it there with bullets and I went there and fought it with bullets. If I get a chance to fight it with bullets again, I will fight it with bullets again.

Mr. Morgan, were those thoughts in your mind before you went to Spain?

Ever since I have been big enough to understand things I have rebelled. As a small child of three or four years old I would rebel at human injustice in the way that I understood it at that age. And as long as I have been able to remember, up until now, the government and a lot of the people have treated me as a second-class citizen. I am 43 years old, and all my life I have been treated as a second-class citizen, and naturally if you always have been treated like one you start feeling it at a very tender age.

With Hitler on the march, and fascism starting the fight in Spain, I felt that it could serve two purposes: I felt that if we could lick the Fascists in Spain, I felt that in the trend of things it would offset a bloodbath later. I felt that if we didn't lick Franco and didn't stop fascism there, it would spread over lots of the world. And it is bad enough for white people to live under fascism, those of the white people that like freedom and democracy. But Negroes couldn't live under it. They would be wiped out.

Were you aware, at any time that you were a member of the International Brigade, of receiving any different treatment because of your race?

No, from the time I arrived in Spain until the time I left, for that period of my life, I felt like a human being, like a man. People didn't look at me with hatred in their eyes because I was black, and I wasn't refused this or refused that because I was black. I was treated like all the rest of the people were treated, and when you have been in the world for quite a long time and have been treated worse than people treat their dogs, it is quite a nice feeling to go someplace and feel like a human being.

Are you acquainted with an organization called the Veterans of the Abraham Lincoln Brigade?

Yes. I first became acquainted with it shortly after I returned [from Spain]. A lot of us came back together, a whole shipload of us, and a lot of the guys lived in New York. We went to Spain because we didn't like fascism, as I stated before. And when we returned to this country fascism was not licked, and so we banded ourselves together and we continued our fight against fascism wherever it was necessary.

Now Mr. Witness, I call your attention to an article entitled "Mixed Brigade" [Volunteer for Liberty, June 1942], which appears on the reverse side of the sheet "Respondent's Exhibition No. 2."

And I now invite the attention of the panel to the article just referred to by the witness, entitled "Mixed Brigade" [VALB attorney, Mr. Clay, reads article aloud].

The demands of the immediate formation of a mixed brigade of equal white and Negro soldiers is rapidly gaining strength. The proposal, though quite recently made, has already shown that it will receive widespread support. The Executive Committee of the Veterans passed a resolution calling for the formation of such a brigade on April 23, 1942. Almost at the same time the Reverend A. Clayton Powell, Jr., Negro councilman for New York City, wrote an editorial which appeared in the influential Negro newspaper, the *People's Voice*, also calling for the immediate formation of such a unit. Dr. Powell has even selected a name for the proposed brigade, Crispus Attucks. At a Victory Mass Rally attended by more than 2,000 NYU students, the demand for a mixed military unit was voiced again and again. Not only speakers but the student listeners were enthusiastically in favor of the idea.

In the great industrial sections of western Pennsylvania, the University of Pittsburgh's newspaper appeared with an editorial entitled "Black and White Democracy." The editorial was written in endorsement of the campaign being conducted by an organization called the Council Against Intolerance in America for the formation of a mixed unit.

The *Weekly Review*, a popular youth paper, devoted the major part of its issue of May 19th to the popularization of the slogan, "For Victory's Sake – A Mixed Brigade."

As a result of a meeting with Dr. Powell at which the Veterans pointed out that the Lincoln Brigade was such a mixed unit, two issues of the *People's Voice* have already featured stories and pictures of the Negro and white International Brigadiers in action. Indications are that future issues will continue to use the experiences of the Lincoln men.

The *People's Voice* is waging a real campaign for the formation of a Crispus Attucks Brigade and its naval equivalent, a destroyer bearing the name of Joe Louis, manned by a Negro and white crew. The paper is printing a coupon in its pages to be clipped by the reader. The coupon can be used to indicate whether one would or would not be willing to serve in a mixed military unit. So far, answers from Negro and white are overwhelmingly marked "yes."

All those who support the Crispus Attucks Brigade point out that the proposal is being made as a contribution to victory over the Axis, and not as a condition for all-out participation for the war. Neither is it being placed as a substitute for the complete elimination of Jim Crow from our Armed Forces.

The Veterans of the Abraham Lincoln Brigade, on the basis of their experience in Spain, are convinced that such a unit, composed of men who have indicated willingness to serve with it, would be a top-notch fighting outfit. Furthermore, the Veterans believe it would be a most effective example to show why Jim Crow has no place in America.

The Veterans have expressed their determination to do everything possible to bring about the formation of the Crispus Attucks Brigade, so that American can improve its fight for democracy both abroad and at home.

Do you agree with the policy concerning segregation as expressed in that article?

Yes, I agree, and I would like to state why I agree. I agree with that policy because anything to the contrary is not living up to the Constitution of the United States; it does not guarantee that each guy is free and equal as provided under those articles in the Constitution. But the laws pertaining to the guaranteeing of freedom and those sections that regard Negroes – the Thirteenth and Fourteenth amendments – were stringently violated as far as the Negroes were concerned, ever since I have been on this world. And the government is abetting it, and one instance is the segregation of the Negroes in the United States Army. For the 47 months that I was in there, not only were we Jim Crowed into Jim Crow units, but all of the nasty jobs, all of the worst jobs, were handed to the majority of the Negroes, to my people, when they were in the army.

[From cross-examination by SACB attorneys] I believe, sir, you stated to us, and you stated to the panel, sir, that you had a good idea about what fascism was, and that you knew most of the ramifications of fascism; is that correct, sir?

Yes.

I wonder if you would tell the panel, or give this panel a definition of fascism.

Well, just briefly, my idea of fascism is of certain things happening. For instance, we do not have fascism now in our country. We would have fascism in our country if the government broke all the trade unions and we didn't have any say-so at all in what was right and wrong in our government, if we didn't have free elections and all of the Americans was ruled by the iron fist, so to speak – a real police state, with all of your rights took away from you. Then you would have fascism.

Tell me, then, based on your definition of fascism, do we have any fascist tendencies in the United States?

Yes. One of the fascist tendencies in the United States–I am an offset printer, and in New York City most shops that need an offset printer, I will go in, and because I am a Negro they won't give me the job. And because I am a Negro in New York City–the bulk of the Negroes are segregated in Harlem, where the worst conditions are, worst meats on the market, and the highest rent. And outside of Harlem most landlords will not rent them apartments. For instance, I was born in North Carolina. Right now, when I leave here, if I go to North Carolina and some white woman I have never seen says I raped her, I will probably get hung before I get to court; and even after I go to court, then I will get legally hung.

After World War II was over, two Negroes, servicemen in Atlanta, was lynched. The government didn't do nothing about it. When we were in the army in Mississippi, the crackers shot us up, and never did the government do nothing about it. And the company next to me–Negroes–were shot up between Jackson, Mississippi, and Camp Shelby by civilians. And those that got back to camp–all Negroes–the army busted them and gave them time.

Those are fascist tendencies. But there are a lot of people in the United States like myself and other people that is going to fight with all we have to see that the Constitution of the United States is upheld. When that happens–those lynchings and the other discrimination–that is a violation of the Constitution, and it is not being a good American if you don't fight to uphold those things.

I wonder if you would tell the panel if you would take up arms against this government of the United States since it does have fascist tendencies?

I took up arms against the Fascists in 1937 where the legal government of Spain was recognized as the legal government of that country by our government and by the other governments in the world. There was an armed fight against fascism. But what you are asking me is, why don't I go out and be a stupid anarchist and get a machine gun and shoot any government official down if I don't like what they are doing. That is what you are asking me. Now, maybe a lot of people would like for guys like us to do things like that, but we are only interested in freedom of speech, freedom of religion, and equality. That is all any person requires, and we don't have it. But going out with arms, that is not the way to get it.

Sir, I believe you stated of the time you spent in Spain that you were treated just like everybody else and that it was the time that you felt like a human being?

Yes, sir.

Has there been any other time in your life when you felt like a human being?

Yes. When I first arrived in England with the U.S. Army.

Does that mean that you don't feel like a human being with the friends and society you are living in?

That's right. I would like to explain that a little deeper. For instance, Milton [Milt Wolff, a white Lincoln Brigade veteran also testifying at the hearing] is my friend, but if I take him home where I was born, then he wouldn't be allowed to stay at my house because of anti-Negro laws which prohibit races from mingling. I can't go with him and he is my friend, and that is one law that is going to be enforced, and it is going to be enforced to the letter.

Were you ever convicted of any offense involving moral turpitude?

I don't understand the question.

Were you ever convicted of any offense involving dishonesty? Such as theft or something of that nature?

Yes.

Would you tell the board where that was, and when?

During the Depression, around 1931 or 1932, when we had about 19,000,000 people unemployed and starving, no place to live – I was one of those people. I was living in a vacant slaughterhouse; I believe it was on West 40th Street. It had been vacant for years, and falling apart. I wasn't the only one. There was a lot of people living in there. So we began to take the copper out of the building that was falling down, and a policeman arrested four or five of us, and I think it was six months I got for petty larceny.

Is that the only offense?

No. As near as I can remember – what I am speaking about is all along the time of the Depression – back in the early thirties I was locked up several times. I was locked up in front of the home relief bureau because we were fighting for people to get relief. We were successful in getting a pretty good sizable check for a number of people, but when we got on the outside some slap-happy cop hit me, and I knocked him down, and . . .

Where was this?

This relief bureau, as near as I can remember, was on West 48th Street. And I went before the judge, and I didn't serve any time. I don't know if it was dismissed or I got a suspended sentence or which.

Were you ever in the state of California?

Yes. That was during the Depression also. A bunch of us fellows left New York on a freight train and was trying to get to where they were building this dam out there. I forget if it was Boulder Dam or what it was. So on this train going out, when we crossed on this train, there were hundreds of people, Negro and white, on the train, whole families, some coming toward Chicago and others going toward the coast. And when we got in, I think it was Fresno, California, every Negro on the train was arrested. No white person was arrested, but all the Negroes were arrested, and we resented it very much.

It seems, if I can remember correctly, that some white man or white woman was killed, and somebody had said they saw some Negro 'round the car or something. Anyway, that was the basis for locking up every Negro on the train and throwing him in jail. And we were in jail four or five days. The people that locked us up said, "We know you don't want to be in jail, but we got orders; they told us to lock up every colored person on the train."

How many days did you spend in jail for this?

Approximately four or five days.

[Redirect by VALB attorney Clay] Mr. Morgan, I will call your attention to the time when you stated you were convicted for petty theft in New York City. How old were you at that time?

I would have to check back. It has been a long time ago. It was the early part of the thirties, and I was born in 1910.

You testified that you were living in a slaughterhouse at that time?

Yes.

Was that the only place you had to live at that time?

Yes, that is right.

You testified also on cross-examination that you had been locked up several times. Was there any other occasion when you were arrested that you have not already related in response to questions from the government?

Yes. One night I wasn't sleeping in the slaughterhouse, and I went to sleep in Central Park. I and another person. And it began to rain about 12 or 1 o'clock, and we got up to leave the park and ran into three policemen. They grabbed me and slapped me in the face a few times with a blackjack. They took me to the stationhouse, and I think I got ten days, charged with loitering in the park.

Did you have any bed to sleep in anywhere at that time?

No.

Patrick Roosevelt

> "I could see just what was taking place [in Ethiopia] . . . I got very angry. I said, 'Now here's Hitler. He just wants to try his war machines here on this little country, and kill thousands and thousands of people for what? Just for his own selfish motives.' And that's why I got interested in Spain. I wanted to see if I could help these little people out against a big war machine."

[The following text is an excerpt from the Abraham Lincoln Brigade Film Project interview.]

You grew up in Washington State?

The state of Washington, yeah, and California.

Did you go to school in Washington?

Yeah, I went to school there. But I didn't finish there. I finished high school in California.

And what did you do after high school?

Well, I loused around for some time. I went to the California Institute of Technology for two and a half years. And then I got interested in flying, and that went ahead. I got more interested in that than anything else. And so that's what I followed up.

To learn to fly?

Yes. And it was tough too. Especially when you didn't have the money. You see, I've known as long as six months in a stretch when I never got a chance to see the bed. That was because I slept on the airplane wings of the guy we used to barnstorm around with in order to learn to fly. That's how serious it was.

183

You were barnstorming?

Yeah, barnstorm, yeah. But there were certain parts of the country I couldn't fly in.

Why was that?

Well, you don't know anything about the Southern states do you?

Back then did you ever hear about people who were fighting against that? People who were opposed to racism and so on? Were there any groups?

Well, no, the nearest thing I heard about at that time, and they was beginning an organization in San Francisco, was the IWW [Industrial Workers of the World]. I don't know if you ever heard of 'em or not. But that was the nearest thing I ever heard of that was pertaining to it.

And how did you hear of the IWW?

Well, I've always had an open mind to listen and I was searching for something that was politically and economically better than what was existing.

How did you learn that? Did the IWW help you?

No, no, no. . . . I was a great reader. And it helped to kind of steer me to different things I could read, to get further knowledge of things I wanted to accomplish. But I never was a member of the IWW. At that time I just wasn't stable enough to join any type of organization. But by reading their literature, one thing led to another, and it caused me to start to read things like *Political Economy* by Marx and Engels. One thing just led to another. Understanding about the exploitation of man by man. I used to get a lot of pleasure out of reading that because it was so clear.

Did you know people who were radical at that point?

Well, not then, but later on I did, yeah.

How did you meet them?

Well, you see, one thing always leads to another. You understand what I mean? A few years previous to that, Karl Marx and Lenin or any of those things like that didn't mean nothing to me. But you see, one thing led up to another.

Tell me when you first heard about Spain.

Let's see. That was before, before they started to fight in Spain. You see, what turned my head that way was Mussolini. When he was going to go and just actually rape poor Africans in Ethiopia after they didn't have enough to fight with. And still there is this. I was very angry with the Africans. I said, why talk so loud? And what do you have to defend yourself with? There they go, with high powered airplanes and everything. And the thing that got me completely turned around was that the United States and Great Britain had an embargo against Ethiopia.

I could see just what was taking place there, what was speeding these things on. I got very angry. I said, "Now here's Hitler. He just wants to try his war machines here on this little country and kill thousands and thousands of people, for what? Just for his own selfish motives." And that's why I got interested in Spain. I wanted to see if I could help these little people out against a big war machine. And I will always remember the little Spaniard, he had the guts to stand up even though the odds were against you.

When did you go into Spain?

It was in 1937. I don't recall the day now. You see, after I lost this leg I did something wrong. I prayed to have all the past extracted from my mind, which is wrong. But I just don't retain things like that. The nineteenth of August was when I got this leg shot off.

The nineteenth of August in '38.

That's right.

So you were there a long time.

Yeah, I was there a long time. I was a machine gunner. But we didn't have enough firepower to win that war.

We didn't have enough firepower to conquer the Germans, and the Germans was bringing all that heavy, new artillery equipment in there. And so that was it, you know. I was surprised that everybody over there didn't get hurt. If I had stayed there one more day where I was, in the Sierra Pandols, I'd have been relieved by the British anyway.

So how many battles were you in Spain? Do you remember the names of them?

I can't recall them all. I was just here trying to think of the number of skirmishes I had.

Were you in the Ebro offensive?

Yeah, I think – let's see, I think that was the next-to-the-last offensive I was in, because I came down with a fever in the stomach. And the next one was the Pandols, that was the last one.

So it was in the Sierra Pandols that you got hit?

Yeah. They called it 666. That's the hill, that's the mountain – 666.

That was a tough battle.

Oh my God. That was. I can remember that hill was taken seven times to my knowing and was lost seven times. The toughest division in Spain was the Listers, and they [had] taken that hill more than any individual division that I know of. Now, the English moved up there on the next day. See, I got hit on a Thursday and the English moved up there on a Friday.

Did you know how badly you were wounded, or were you unconscious when this happened to you?

Well, I tell you, I wasn't unconscious, but I knew it wasn't good, because in a machine-gun nest, when they got the range of this nest and started to firing on it, I knew it wasn't going to be but a few seconds before we were going to be right inside that range there, and all the guys there had a pit dug, and they could jump in the pit, and I had to be on the top.

And that's why you got it.

No, no. You should have seen that. There was only one other guy out of there that was halfway alive, and he was split open.

Oh, so you were lucky.

Yeah, all because I was up on top, and the shell that did the most damage came down under me a few meters away, see, and hit one guy and ripped his head wide open and so on. There were seven guys in that nest. And me, it only got to my foot, see, and I didn't know what happened. I know it was burning down there a little bit. And so I got to the place where I could get it straightened out, there I saw that the shoe was split wide open. I knew it couldn't leave a foot in that shoe.

So were you operated on in Spain, or did they send you back home right away?

I was operated on there. That was a brutal invitation because those poor doctors were worked to death there. You know what I mean, there were such few doctors they had. And so I got angry at the first place they took me, and at the next I couldn't because they tried to put me to sleep with chloroform. But they couldn't put me to sleep. So they gave me a spinal shot right here. And when I woke up, the amputation was done.

So tell us what happened to you when you got back.

Well, when I got back to France I stayed in an American hospital for a little while and . . . everything was fine when I got back. Everything was fine.

When you got back to the U.S., what help did the Friends of the Lincoln Brigade give?

Any kind of help that they could. I had no place to stay. They paid for me a room at the hotel. And then got me a room uptown in Harlem. And they had some people that was connected well enough to get me set up to get on relief. And so that helped out considerably.

They helped you find work? Or were you not able to work at this point?

See, this was before I got the [artificial] leg on. After I got this leg on, with my electrical background, I didn't have too much trouble getting a job.

Were you unhappy? It must have been pretty upsetting to be wounded like that.

Well, I tell you something. That's what most people think. But I wanted to stay as normal as possible. And I would always keep in my mind positive thinking. Because what's under the bridge is under the bridge. You can't pull it back.

How did you support yourself after you got back?

First I went with the Approved Technical Apparatus concern. Making instruments for testing. Then from there I was with the Fenmore Engineering Company on Madison Avenue. And from there, the war had broke out. And I was two and a half years as a machine shop foreman in New Jersey.

Did you ever join the Communist party?

No.

You weren't interested in being more active with the Party?

Well, look. I'll tell you what. To me, joining the Party is just like joining the church. See I'm not a church member, but if I was contemplating on going to heaven, then I think I would go out and just as well join the church. Now, I'm saying that in order to say this. I've had my fill of political economy and dialectical materialism and other things. I've read that as much as reading the Bible. More than I've read the Bible.

But you didn't want to join the Party even after reading all those books?

No. It's not a matter of joining. That's not going to make me any different. It's only going to cause me to go out when I don't feel like going out. Do you follow me? It would just confine me more.

Were you a trade unionist?

Oh yeah. I was a trade unionist. I was in the Machinists, in the CIO, the UEMWA [United Electrical and Machine Workers of America].

Did you get harassed during the fifties, during the McCarthy era? Did you get bothered? Did the FBI come?

No, they didn't. See, the only way they didn't was because I had this artificial limb. They started asking me questions and I said no, I couldn't go no place. They just came to me once, and that's all.

EPILOGUE

The reader or researcher new to the topic of this volume – African-American participation in the Spanish Civil War – may at first find it obscure, even eccentric. Indeed, a strange and remarkable picture emerges from these pages. It is a picture of a tumultuous time, more than 50 years ago, when scores of African-American workers and students, professionals and unemployed, left their communities, where freedom was still little more than a promise, to go to Spain. There they joined with others of almost every race and nation in defending the freedom of another people.

One might wonder how significant a role these African Americans could have played in the distant political feuds of a European nation. Furthermore, one might wonder, what relevance could that long-ago incident possibly have for us at the turn of the twenty-first century?

Despite the diversity of the stories represented here, whether in documentation, in photographs, or in first-hand testimony, a few common themes consistently emerge. One of the strongest is that these African-American fighters were not anomalous or eccentric creatures cast adrift on the shores of Spain; they were all firmly rooted in the centuries-old African-American tradition of struggle against oppression. Many variables of time and place led these particular black people to take up arms in Spain. But for each one, the road to Spain ultimately led back to the tradition of struggle that began with the slaves.

The African Americans who fought in Spain also emerged from the experience of America's Great Depression. Almost all of them had known poverty. Many of them had known unemployment and destitution; some of them had been homeless. The Depression was a time of suffering and injustice for the majority of white Americans, but its impact on black Americans was even harsher. The circumstances of economic collapse and deprivation led African Americans to renew their fight for equality and freedom. It also led many of them to seek equality in the founding of a new economic order that would put peoples' needs before the demands of profit.

This economic struggle brought black Americans into alliance with their counterparts from other races and led to the formation of labor organizations, unemployed councils, and tenant unions. Many of these organizations were linked with the Communist party, the Socialist party, or other radical groups. Others were of an independent or New Deal liberal cast. Through participation in this broad-based movement for social change, many Americans of all races found themselves in close alliance with their counterparts from other lands. Through participation in this movement, many African Americans came to see links between their own struggle and those in other nations, such as Spain.

While some whites were moved by the hardships of the Depression to join interracial and international alliances for economic justice, others fell prey to groups who made ethnic and religious minorities scapegoats for the economic problems of the times. In Europe this led to the formation of fascist movements that gained power in Germany and Italy and were on the rise elsewhere. In America this development was mirrored by the growing activity of the Klan and other racist and anti-Semitic organizations. The first-hand experience of racist persecution by African Americans led many to identify strongly with the victims of European fascism.

Still, even as they joined interracial alliances for democracy and justice, the African Americans who went to Spain were at the core motivated by a long-range concern for the welfare of their own African-American and Pan-African communities. Again and again, that message is brought home in the testimonies of black Lincoln Brigade veterans who said the fascist invasion of Ethiopia was a key factor in determining their decision to go to Spain. These men knew that in Spain they would have the opportunity to do battle with troops of the same Italian fascist army that had butchered the people of Ethiopia.

Finally, the African Americans who went to Spain stood firmly in a long and often heroic tradition of black military service. In all of America's battles, from the Revolutionary War to Operation Desert Storm, African Americans have fought and died with honor. They often saw themselves as fighting not only to defend whatever degree of democracy and freedom existed in America but also to extend the boundaries of American democracy to their own communities.

Until the 1950s, despite a history of distinguished service, African Americans in uniform were forced to serve in segregated, all-black units. These units, usually under white command, were given the dirtiest and most dangerous assignments. Their contributions to the nation's defense were never properly recognized by the broader public. The blacks who joined the Lincoln Brigade were fighting to defend democracy in Spain, but they also saw their participation in the antifascist struggle as part of a larger campaign to extend black Americans' claims to equality and self-determination. The African-American members of the Lincoln Brigade waged the good fight in Spain not as soldiers in a Jim Crow auxiliary but as full and equal partners with their white compatriots, with the democratic Spaniards, and with like-minded allies from around the globe. As an embodiment of the principle of equal partnership in a fight for freedom, the Lincoln Brigade uniquely represented the best of American democratic values. As an interracial group of men under arms, and even under black command, they also represented an unprecedented American social reality.

The relevance of the African-American volunteers' role in Spain, however, does not rest solely upon their status as pioneers of military integration. What African Americans did in Spain is at least as important as those with whom they did it. The African Americans who went to Spain stand today as shining examples of the belief that freedom and justice for all peoples can be a reality. These 90 or more black Americans believed that the freedom of one person or one nation was linked with the freedom of all. They believed that until every person, community, race, and nation enjoyed justice and democracy, the humanity of all would be diminished. They believed in these ideals so deeply that they were prepared to travel across the ocean to a foreign land to fight and even to die for them. They took personal responsibility for acting to make the promises of democracy a reality for themselves and for others.

The story of the African Americans of the Abraham Lincoln Brigade, until now largely unexplored, is one rich with unrecognized black heroes and heroines, with examples of sacrifice and solidarity, and with the lessons of commitment. We hope the volume before you is only a beginning in the recovery of that story and those lessons.

DANNY DUNCAN COLLUM
Editor, Executive
Director, ALBA

VICTOR A. BERCH
Chief Researcher,
Archivist, ALBA

SOURCES

ALBA's project on African-American participation in the Spanish Civil War began as an attempt to identify the available sources of information on this topic. We conducted our search with an eye toward making the source materials more accessible to scholars and researchers and toward encouraging broader scholarly interest in the subject.

We began by searching the Spanish Civil War materials in the Special Collections Department at Brandeis University Libraries. Because the blacks in the Lincoln Brigade were a fairly small part of the group and were thoroughly integrated within the unit, materials relevant to their story were scattered throughout the collection. Using the list of black veterans supplied by the Veterans of the Abraham Lincoln Brigade, we began checking the name indexes of photograph and correspondence files and surveying the books and pamphlets collection. We also identified the material related to black participation found in the film and tape audiovisual collections.

The Friends of the Abraham Lincoln Brigade (and later VALB) kept extensive scrapbooks of newspaper clippings on the Lincoln Brigade throughout the war years and on into the 1950s. Early in our search we read through all of these scrapbooks for references to African-American veterans. Next we borrowed microfilm of the Communist party newspapers the *Daily Worker* and *People's World* and of the African-American newspapers the *Pittsburgh Courier*, the *Afro-American*, the *Amsterdam News*, the *Atlanta Daily World*, and the *Chicago Defender*. We read through all of these newspapers for the peak war years of 1937 and 1938.

We also looked in the National Archives for State Department documents related to the presence of African Americans in the Spanish conflict. Much valuable material also came from some of the approximately 300 surviving veterans of the Lincoln Brigade. They passed on reminiscences, clippings, and photographs previously unknown.

To assemble these materials we decided early on to take a predominantly biographical (rather than topical) approach. That is, we sought primarily to organize the material according to the black veteran (or veterans) to whom it pertained. By this method we hoped to assemble a biographical sketch of each veteran and to supply the opportunity for further research into their lives. The first result of this effort is the "Roll of African American Veterans" found in part 2 of this volume. As Robin D. G. Kelley notes in his introduction in part 1, books have been written about African Americans and the U.S. Communist party or the American Left and the various issues raised in and by that encounter. But the lives of these African-American heroes from the Spanish Civil War have remained mostly unexplored. We hoped, by our research, to begin the process of giving these men and women back to African-American, and American, history.

Having chosen a biographical approach, we then decided to order sources first by type (i.e., book, article, archival, etc.) and then chronologically, so that one could follow the documentation through the life story of the individual. Regarding the individual listings, those using this list will also note that in some cases one or more black Lincoln Brigade veterans were discussed in an article headlined about another, or about another topic altogether. Sometimes the same article will also be listed under more than one subject, or name, heading. Our researchers read the entire articles and determined that there was material in them justifying their inclusion under more than one category.

In the course of our research a few topical headings also suggested themselves as supplements to the biographical listings. A number of articles dealt in general terms with the phenomenon of black Americans in Spain. Some of these included discussions of the role played by a large number of the individuals, others integrated the subject of black participation into overall discussion of the war effort. In the source listings that follow, these are found under the heading "The Battlefront."

Support for the Spanish Republican cause was a highly visible component of political and cultural life in America's black communities in the 1930s, especially in the big cities. Under the heading "The Home Front," we list sources of information on fund-raising, political, and other activities in solidarity with Spain undertaken by African Americans in the United States.

The African-American press covered the Spanish Civil War in the years 1936-39. The coverage in these papers, of course, emphasized black participation. But it also dealt with the whole range of national and international political issues and conflicts raised by the war, usually from a position of overt sympathy with the Loyalist cause. We found the perspective in these articles to be unique and worthy of further examination by future scholars. For that reason we have included a listing of articles from the papers cited above under the heading "The Spanish Civil War in the African-American Press."

Finally, our files on a few African-American supporters of the Spanish cause who were not Lincoln Brigade veterans became so voluminous that they warranted subheadings of their own. These are James Ford, Langston Hughes, and Paul Robeson. Ford was an African-American leader of the U.S. Communist party in the 1930s who visited Spain and agitated prominently for Spanish democracy. Langston Hughes, known in his day as the African-American poet laureate, covered the war for the *Afro-American* and wrote extensively for the *Volunteer for Liberty*, the battlefield newsletter of the International Brigades in Spain. Paul Robeson, the singer, actor, and political figure, entertained the troops in Spain and was extremely active in Republican support activities in the United States and abroad.

This source list is offered as only a starting point for work in this subject area. We look forward to additions to it.

ABBREVIATIONS

BUSCW: Brandeis University Spanish Civil War Collection
ALB: Abraham Lincoln Brigade
USSDA: United States State Department Archives (at National Archives Washington, D.C.)
ALBA: Abraham Lincoln Brigade Archives (at Brandeis University Libraries, Waltham, Mass.)
VALB: Veterans of the Abraham Lincoln Brigade

THE VETERANS

FRANK EDWARD ALEXANDER
Photographs
BUSCW C247; *Seattle Post-Intelligencer*, April 16, 1982.
Audiovisual
BUSCW ALB Film Project. Preproduction interview. Four and a half hours, cassettes. Tapes 236-38, box C.
Archival
BUSCW World War II letters.

AMOS ARCHER
No sources.

WILLIAM BAKER
Photographs
BUSCW B352.

THADDEUS ARRINGTON BATTLE
Articles
"Student Volunteers in Spain Radio Armistice Greeting." *Columbus* (Ohio) *Dispatch,* November 18, 1937.
"Howard University Greets Student Who Fought in Spain." *Daily Worker,* November 10, 1938.
"D.C. Boy Who Fought Fascists Greeted by H.U. [Howard University] Faculty." *Washington* (D.C.) *Tribune,* November 19, 1938.
Photographs
Daily Worker, November 10, 1938.
Archival
USSDA file #852.2221. Documents on the welfare of Battle, dated June 7, 1938; June 24, 1938; September 10, 1938; October 4, 1938.

VERNOLD MASTEN BEEBE
Archival
USSDA file #351.1121. Regards Bernard Kaplan and other stowaways on the SS *Normandie;* mentions Beebe in documents dated August 25, 1938; August 29, 1938; August 31, 1938; September 21, 1938.

TOM BROWN
Archival
BUSCW Prisoner of War Commission files.

WALTER P. CALLION
Photographs
"Wounded Lincoln Boys Home." *People's World,* September 7, 1938.
Archival
BUSCW World War II letters.

COUNCIL GIBSON CARTER
Articles
"Negro Committee Aids Spain." *Daily Worker,* December 23, 1938.
Photographs
Daily Worker, December 23, 1938.
Archival
Letter from Sandino to Carter (State Department document; photocopy at BUSCW).

SOURCES

ALBERT EDWARD CHISHOLM
Photographs
BUSCW B99, B119, C144.
Audiovisual
BUSCW ALB Film Project. Preproduction interview. Three hours, cassettes. Tapes 231-32, box C.
Archival
BUSCW interview with Chisholm in 1984.

MICHAEL CHOWAN
No sources.

ROLAND CLEVELAND
Photographs
BUSCW B481.

MACK COAD
Articles
"Foster Salutes Seamen Fallen in Spain." *Daily Worker,* December 17, 1938.
"The Stake of the Negro People in Fight against Fascism Took Mack Coad to Spain." *Daily Worker,* February 11, 1939.
Photographs
BUSCW B500, E437, E439, P45, P347.
Daily Worker, December 17, 1938.

WALTER COBBS
Photographs
BUSCW P46, P347.

LEROY COLLINS
Articles
"Salud." *Project Educator,* April 22, 1938.

JAMES COX
Photographs
BUSCW B95, P347.

BASILIO CUERIA Y OBRIT
Books
Cuba y la defensa de la República Española (1936-1939). Havana: Editora Politica, 1981, 233-36.

Articles

"De Nuestro Deportistas." *La Prensa* (New York), May 7, 1937.

Ross, Adolph. "Bringing Matters Up to Date." *Volunteer* 12, no. 2 (December 1990). (Letter regarding Basilio Cueria.)

Photographs

Cuba y la defensa de la República Española (1936-1939). Havana: Editora Politica, 1981, 184-85.

TOMAS DIAZ COLLADO

Books

Cuba y la defensa de la República Española (1936-1939). Havana: Editora Politica, 1981, 294.

WALTER DICKS

No sources.

NATHANIEL DICKSON

No sources.

ARNOLD BENNETT DONOWA

Articles

"Sails for Spain Today." *Daily Worker*, July 21, 1937.

"To Aid Spain." *Atlanta Daily World*, July 23, 1937.

"Local Doctor Goes to Spain." *Amsterdam* (New York) *News*, July 24, 1937.

"To Aid Spain." *Pittsburgh Courier*, July 31, 1937.

Davis, Ben, Jr. "A Small Man from the Cape with a Big Record in Spain." *Daily Worker*, September 27, 1937.

"Loyalists Foil Toledo Thrust of 8,000 Moors." *New York Herald Tribune*, October 20, 1937.

"Medico Norteamericano es herido en Port Baou." *La Prensa* (New York), October 21, 1937.

"Dr. Arnold Donowa, Former Dean at Howard University, Shot in Spain." *Pittsburgh Courier*, October 30, 1937.

"Surgeon in Spain." *Chicago Defender*, March 26, 1938.

Rolfe, Edwin. "American Negro Surgeon at Spanish Front Appeals for Medical Supplies for Loyalists." *Daily Worker*, September 23, 1938.

_____. "Ex-Howard Dean at Spanish Front." *Afro-American*, October 1, 1938.

"Eight Medical Volunteers to Return December 31." *Daily Worker*, December 30, 1938.

Herbert Rosen. "Noted Harlem Doctor, Returned from Spain." *Daily Worker*, January 4, 1939.

"Found Only AFRO in Spain." *Afro-American*, January 7, 1939.

"Harlem Honors Donowa at Spain Meeting Sunday." *Daily Worker*, February 17, 1939.

Eugene Gordon. "Negro Dentists Hit Anti-Semitic Report." *Daily Worker*, February 9, 1945.

Photographs

BUSCW P281, P312.

Atlanta Daily World, July 23, 1937.

Daily Worker, July 21, 1937.

Chicago Defender, March 26, 1938.

Daily Worker, December 30, 1938; January 4, 1939.

LARRY STRATFORD DUKES

Photographs

BUSCW B100, B571, B572.

RAY (RAMON) DUREM

Books

Walrond, Eric, and Rosey E. Pool, eds. *Black and Unknown Bards: A Collection of Negro Poetry.* Aldington, Kent (England): Hand and Flower Press, 1958.

Durem, Ray. *Take No Prisoners.* London: Paul Breman, 1962; reprint 1971.

Pool, Rosey E. *Beyond the Blues: New Poems by American Negroes.* Lympne, Kent (England): Hand and Flower Press, 1962.

Hughes, Langston, ed. *New Negro Poets: USA.* Bloomington: Indiana University Press, 1964.

_____. *The Book of Negro Humor.* New York: Dodd, Mead & Co., 1966.

Major, Clarence, ed. *The New Black Poetry.* New York: International Publishers, 1969.

Adams, William, Peter Conn, and Barry Slepian, comps. *Afro-American Literature: Poetry.* Vol. 3. Boston: Houghton Mifflin, 1970.

Adoff, Arnold, comp. *Black Out Loud: An Anthology of Modern Poems by Black Americans.* New York: Macmillan, 1970.

Hughes, Langston, and Anne Bontemps, eds. *The Poetry of the Negro, 1740-1970.* New York: Doubleday, 1970.

Jordan, June. *Soulscript.* New York: Doubleday, Zenith Books, 1970.

Lomax, Allan, and Raoul Abdul, eds. *3000 Years of Black Poetry.* New York: Dodd, Mead and Co., 1970.

Randall, Dudley, ed. *The Black Poets.* New York: Bantam Books, 1971.

Adoff, Arnold, comp. *The Poetry of Black America: An Anthology for the Twentieth Century.* New York: Harper and Row, 1973.

Colley, Ann C., and Judith K. Moore, comps. *Starting with Poetry.* New York: Harcourt, Brace, Jovanovich, 1973.

Rush, Theressa Gunnels, Carol Fairbanks Myers, and Esther Spring Arata. *Black American Writers Past and Present: A Biographical and Bibliographical Dictionary.* Metuchen, N.J.: Scarecrow, 1975.

Articles
Crisis, April-May 1971.
Phylon 16, no. 3 (1955).

PIERRE DUVALLE
Audiovisual
Videotaped oral history in the Manny Harriman Collection, BUSCW.

KANUTE OLIVER FRANKSON
Articles
Wright, Richard. "American Negroes in Key Posts of Spain's Loyalist Forces." *Daily Worker*, September 29, 1937.
Archival
USSDA file #811.111. Documents (dated August 9, 1938; August 20, 1938; August 23, 1938; September 10, 1938; September 12, 1938) show that Frankson was a naturalized citizen from Jamaica, born circa 1890. This file lists his name as Canute Stoddard Frankson.

DOMINGO GAMIS Y CABRERA
Articles
"Five Heroes of Cuba Who Fell at Jarama." *Daily Worker*, April 3, 1937.
"De Nuestro Deportistas." *La Prensa* (New York), May 7, 1937.
Photographs
Daily Worker, April 3, 1937.

WALTER BENJAMIN GARLAND
Articles
"Negro Commanding a Machine-gun Company." *Daily Worker* (BUSCW clipping; no date).
"Harlemites Taking Part in Conflict." *Amsterdam News* (New York), June 26, 1937.
"Negro Heroes in Loyalist's Gallant Stand." *Richmond* (Virginia) *Planet*, July 24, 1937.
Rochester, Sterling. "Negro Ex-serviceman behind a Machine Gun on the Jarama Front Was with the First American Soldiers on the Battlefront." *Daily Worker*, July 25, 1937.
Matthews, Herbert. "Americans Gain Loyalist Heroes." *New York Times*, July ?, 1937.
"Bard, Haywood, Hughes Speak on Radio Friday." *Daily Worker*, August 26, 1937.

"Three American Negroes to Broadcast from Madrid." *Washington* (D.C.) *Tribune,* August 28, 1937.

"American Negroes in Key Posts of Spain's Loyalist Forces." *Daily Worker,* September 29, 1937.

Wright, Richard. "Walter Garland Tells What Spain's Fight against Fascism Means to Negro People." *Daily Worker,* November 18, 1937.

Rushmore, Howard. "Miners Welcome Steve Nelson Home from Fighting in Spain." *Daily Worker,* November 19, 1937.

"Boys from Spain Will Be Honored at Benefit on Saturday." *Daily Worker,* December 1, 1937.

"Lincoln Vets to Organize at Parley." *Daily Worker,* December 20, 1937.

Garland, Walter. "An Answer to Lynching." *People's World,* February 2, 1938.

Garland, Walter. "An Answer to Lynching." *Among Friends* 1, no. 1 (Winter 1938).

Shields, Art. "Heroes of Two Wars against Fascism." *Daily Worker,* December 10, 1944.

Photographs

BUSCW P79.

Daily Worker, November 19, 1937; December 10, 1944.

Archival

BUSCW World War II letters. August 8, 1942; December 20, 1942; March 27, 1943; December 9, 1943; December 14, 1943; February 5, 1944; February 10, 1944; March 9, 1944; March 14, 1944; March 19, 1944; March 26, 1944; April 12, 1944; May 23, 1944.

EUGENE VICTOR GAVIN

Archival

USSDA file #852.2221. Document dated October 13, 1937, on the death of Dinsmore Finley, also mentions the welfare of Gavin. Documents (dated July 22, 1937; July 29, 1937; October 13, 1937; October 14, 1937; May 7, 1938; May 11, 1938; May 31, 1938; June 2, 1938; June 28, 1938; December 22, 1938) on the welfare of Gavin and his brother, Robert Owen Gavin. His mother claimed Eugene was an American Indian.

ROBERT OWEN GAVIN

Archival

USSDA file #852.2221. Documents (dated May 2, 1938; May 17, 1938; July 8, 1938; July 27, 1938; August 1, 1938; August 4, 1938; August 25, 1938; September 23, 1938) concerning the welfare of Robert Gavin, from his wife; report that Gavin is missing in action.

Archival
Photocopied correspondence of Ben Gardner (BUSCW).

THEODORE GIBBS
Articles
"Chicago Holds Law Memorial." *Daily Worker,* August 7, 1937.
Smith, Peter. Untitled article, *AMI,* no. 9, February 1938.

MEREDITH SYDNOR GRAHAM
Archival
USSDA file #852.2221. Documents (dated September 17, 1937; September 22, 1937; September 23, 1937; October 8, 1937; October 14, 1937; November 15, 1937; May 19, 1938; May 24, 1938; June 3, 1938) on the death of Graham.

CENTURIO GUTIERREZ DIAS
Articles
"Heroes Everyone: The Men Who Went to Spain." *Toronto* (Canada) *Clarion,* August 23, 1937.

PHILIP E. HALL
No sources.

GEORGE HARVEY
No sources.

HARRY HAYWOOD
Books
Haywood, Harry. *Black Bolshevik: Autobiography of an Afro-American Communist.* Chicago: Liberator Press, 1978.
Articles
"Bard, Haywood, Hughes Speak on Radio Friday." *Daily Worker,* August 26, 1937.
"Three American Negroes to Broadcast from Madrid." *Washington* (D.C.) *Tribune,* August 28, 1937.
Davis, Ben, Jr. "A Small Man from the Cape with a Big Record in Spain." *Daily Worker,* September 27, 1937.
Wright, Richard. "American Negroes in Key Posts of Spain's Loyalist Forces." *Daily Worker,* September 29, 1937.
"Americans Mainstay of Loyalist Offensive at Brunete, Belchite: Haywood Tells 'Daily,' Praises Negroes in Ranks of Spain's 'New Army.' " *Daily Worker,* October 12, 1937.

Photographs
"The Spirit That Won Herndon's Freedom." *Daily Worker*, May 1, 1937.

MILTON HERNDON
Articles
"Herndon's Brother Writes Him." *Daily Worker*, June 23, 1937.
"Dr. Barsky to Speak for Spain on July 19." *Daily Worker*, July 16, 1937.
"Milton Herndon Dies in Loyalist Attacks." *Daily Worker*, October ?, 1937.
"Herndon Brother Is Killed in Spain." *New York Post*, October 13, 1937.
"Loyalists Foil Toledo Thrust of 8000 Moors." *New York Herald Tribune*, October 20, 1937.
"Milton Herndon Died in Loyalist Attack." *New York Times*, October 20, 1937.
"Milton Herndon Killed in Action at Sargossa." *Daily Worker*, October 20, 1937.
"A Real Patriot." *Chicago Defender*, October 30, 1937 (unsigned editorial).
"In Memoriam." *Volunteer for Liberty* 1, no. 23 (November 11, 1937).
Wright, Richard. "Walter Garland Tells What Spain's Fight against Fascism Means to the Negro People." *Daily Worker*, November 18, 1937.
Edwards, Thyra. "Kill Kin of Herndon in Civil War." *Chicago Defender*, November 20, 1937.
"Memorial for Milton Herndon Next Sunday." *Daily Worker*, November 22, 1937.
White, David McKelvy. "The International Brigade of 1938." *Daily Worker*, July 4, 1938.
North, Joseph. Review of *Volunteer for Liberty*. In *Masses and Mainstream*, June 1949.
Photographs
Volunteer for Liberty 1, no. 23 (November 11, 1937).
Daily Worker, May 20, 1938; July 4, 1938.
Archival
USSDA file #852.2221. Documents dated April 19, 1939, and April 26, 1939, on the death of Herndon.

JOHN PORTER HUNTER
Articles
Matthews, Herbert. "Americans Gain Loyalist Heroes." *New York Times*, July ?, 1937.
"Negro Heroes in Loyalist's Gallant Stand." *Richmond* (Virginia) *Planet*, July 24, 1937.

Photographs
BUSCW B61, B63, B188, B373.

Archival
USSDA file #852.2221. Documents (dated July 19, 1937; July 26, 1937; August 10, 1937; August 11, 1937) concerning the welfare of a John Dudley Hunter, reportedly killed in Spain.

OSCAR HENRY HUNTER

Articles
Davis, Ben, Jr. "Small Man from Cape with Big Record from Spain." *Daily Worker,* September 27, 1937.
Wright, Richard. "American Negroes in Key Posts of Spanish Loyalist Forces." *Daily Worker,* September 29, 1937.
_____. "Walter Garland Tells What Spain's Fight against Fascism Means for the Negro People." *Daily Worker,* November 18, 1937
Pickens, William. "What I Saw in Spain." *Crisis* 45, no. 10 (October 1938).

Audiovisual
BUSCW ALB Film Project. Preproduction interview. Three hours, ¼-inch tape. Tapes 124-27, box A. (ALBA oral history audiocassette.)

BURT EDWARD JACKSON

Articles
Wright, Richard. "Walter Garland Tells What Spain's Fight against Fascism Means to the Negro People." *Daily Worker,* November 18, 1937.
Carter, Art. "Ex-Loyalist Fighter Heads Ordnance Section of 99th." *Afro-American,* March 1944.
Shields, Art. "Heroes of Two Wars against Fascism." *Daily Worker,* December 10, 1944.

Photographs
BUSCW A225, B171, E221, E250, P103.

Archival
BUSCW World War II letters. August 12, 1942; October 1, 1942; May 17, 1943; November 15, 1943; March 23, 1944; May 12, 1944; July 12, 1944; October 5, 1944.

AARON BERNARD JOHNSON
No sources.

EDWARD JOHNSON
Archival
BUSCW Prisoner of War Commission files.

RICHARD JOHNSON
No sources.

SALARIA KEE

Pamphlet

The Negro Committee to Aid Spain, with the Medical Bureau and North American Committee to Aid Spanish Democracy. *A Negro Nurse in Republican Spain.* New York, 1938. BUSCW.

Articles

"8000 March in Harlem Demonstration." *Daily Worker,* March 30, 1937.

"Negro Nurse Will Aid Spain." *Daily Worker,* March 30, 1937.

"Sails for War Duty in Spain." *Pittsburgh Courier,* April 17, 1937.

Davis, Ben, Jr. "Small Man from Cape with Big Record in Spain." *Daily Worker,* September 27, 1937.

"Americans Earn High Posts with Loyalists." *Afro-American,* October 1937.

Poston, Ted. "Louise Thompson Returns with Glowing Report of Negro in Spanish War." *Washington* (D.C.) *Tribune,* October 9, 1937.

Hughes, Lanston. "New York Nurse Weds Irish Fighter in Spain's War." *Afro-American,* December 11, 1937.

"Fascists Won't Win, Declares Negro Nurse." *Daily Worker,* May 18, 1938.

Cooke, Marvel. "Salaria Kee, Harlem Hospital Volunteer, Back in New York." *Amsterdam* (New York) *News,* May 21, 1938.

"150 Nurses Attend Banquet Honoring Salaria Kee." *Amsterdam* (New York) *News,* May 28, 1938.

"Six Famous Writers Hit Fascist Set." *Amsterdam* (New York) *News,* May 28, 1938.

"Salaria Kee Speaks at Spain Meeting in Harlem Thursday." *Daily Worker,* June 1, 1938.

"Drive Planned for Americans with Loyalists." *Buffalo Courier Express,* June 6, 1938.

"Here on Tour." *Chicago Defender,* June 18, 1938.

"Negroes Send Ambulance to Boys in Spain." *Daily Worker,* August 5, 1938.

"Salaria Kee Leaves on Tour to Rally Negro Aid for Spain." *Daily Worker,* August 16, 1938.

"Nurse Aids in Ambulance Drive." *Afro-American,* August 20, 1938.

Patai, Frances. "Heroines of the Good Fight: North American Women Volunteers in the Spanish Civil War." BUSCW manuscript, 1989.

Photographs

BUSCW P320.

Daily Worker, March 30, 1937.

Chicago Defender, April 17, 1937.

Pittsburgh Courier, April 17, 1937.

People's World, January 10, 1938 ("Photo of Salaria Kee").

AMI, no. 9, February 1938 ("Some of the American Nurses").

Daily Worker, May 18, 1938.

Chicago Defender, June 18, 1938.

Audiovisual

BUSCW ALB Film Project. Original sound for filmed interview. One hour, 45 minutes; ¼-inch tape. Tapes 159-163A, box B.

_____. CAs (picture without sound); 500 feet of 16mm color film. CR 192, 199, box J.

_____. Wild sound; 25 minutes, 16mm tape. Box J.

_____. Filmed interview (sound and picture); 3,600 feet of 16mm color film and tape. CR 191-199, box J.

_____. Preproduction interview. Three hours, cassettes. Tapes 209-10, box C. (ALBA oral history audiocassette.)

Archival

BUSCW May 21, 1979. Information on tribute to Salaria Kee in Seattle, Washington.

USSDA file #138/SPAIN/185, dated April 8, 1937. Lists Salaria Kee's nurse registration number, training, and date of graduation.

ADMIRAL KILPATRICK

Articles

"Cleveland CIO Hits Ban on Vets." *Daily Worker,* June 12, 1943.

Photographs

BUSCW Ro55. (*Ro* signifies the Edwin Rolfe Collection.)

Audiovisual

BUSCW ALB Film Project. Preproduction interview. Three hours, cassettes. Tapes 212-13, box C. (ALBA oral history audiocassette.)

OLIVER LAW

Books

Brandt, Joe, ed. *Black Americans in the Spanish People's War against Fascism, 1936-1939.* New York: VALB, 1980. BUSCW.

Articles

Rochester, Sterling. "Negro Ex-serviceman behind a Machine Gun on the Jarama Front." *Daily Worker,* 1937 (BUSCW clipping; month, day unknown).

Marion, George. "Oliver Law, Hero of Jarama Front." *Daily Worker,* April 17, 1937.

"El 'Batallon Lincoln' Forma una Aldea Norteamericana en El Frente Del Jarama." *La Prensa* (New York), May 18, 1937.

"Ball Player Hurls Grenades for Spain." *Afro-American,* June 5, 1937.

"Harlemites Taking Part in Conflict." *Amsterdam News,* June 26, 1937.

"Air Armada Is Turned Loose upon Capital." *Appleton* (Wisconsin) *Post Crescent,* July 10, 1937.

"Chicagoan Killed in Spanish War." *Chicago* (Illinois) *American,* July 10, 1937.

Rochester, Sterling. "Big Welcome Planned for Lincoln Boys." *Daily Worker,* July 10, 1937.

"Three Americans Killed in Madrid Fighting." *St. Louis* (Missouri) *Post Dispatch,* July 10, 1937.

"Report Negro Commander Killed in Action." *Daily Worker,* July 13, 1937.

"American Battalion Head, Killed in Madrid Action." *New York Times,* July 14, 1937.

"Negro Fighters in Spain." *Daily Worker,* July 15, 1937.

"Abe Lincoln Battalion Leader Killed in Spain." *Pittsburgh Courier,* July 24, 1937.

"Negro Heroes in Loyalist's Gallant Stand." *Richmond* (Virginia) *Planet,* July 24, 1937.

"Chicago Holds Law Memorial Sunday, 6 P.M." *Daily Worker,* August 7, 1937.

"Wounded Soldier in Hospital Pays Last Tribute to Negro Comrade." *Daily Worker,* August 10, 1937.

"Heroes – Everyone." *Toronto* (Canada) *Clarion,* August 23, 1937.

"In Memory of Our Fallen Leaders." *Volunteer for Liberty* 1, no. 12 (August 30, 1937).

Davis, Ben, Jr. "A Small Man from the Cape with a Big Record in Spain." *Daily Worker,* September 27, 1937.

"In Memoriam." *Volunteer for Liberty* 1, no. 18 (October 11, 1937).

"Americans Earn High Posts with Loyalists." *Afro-American,* October 13, 1937.

Cunard, Nancy. "Negro Captain of Spanish Unit Killed in Battle." *Atlanta Daily World,* December 20, 1937.

_____. "Tells How Negro Commander of Spanish Battalion Dies." *Washington* (D.C.) *Tribune,* January 1938.

"100 Negroes Fighting with Loyalists, Robeson Says." *Daily Worker,* February 4, 1938.

"Robeson Says Negroes Are Fighting in Spain." *New York Herald Tribune,* February 4, 1938.

"Negroes at Teruel Hail Lincoln Day in Letter to U.S.." *Daily Worker,* February 12, 1938.

"Oliver Law in a Filmstrip of Rare Pictures Shown." *Compass,* February 9, 1951.

"Will Show Film on Negro Hero in Spain." *Daily Worker,* February 9, 1951.

Photographs

Volunteer for Liberty 1, no. 18 (October 11, 1937).

Audiovisual

Taped interview with Charles Nusser for radio station WNYC. BUSCW.

BUSCW footage in the film *A Day with the Lincoln Brigade.*

ABRAHAM LEWIS

Books

Brandt, Joe. *Black Americans in the Spanish People's War against Fascism, 1936-1939.* New York: VALB, 1980. BUSCW.

Articles

Wright, Richard. "Walter Garland Tells What Spain's Fight against Fascism Means to the Negro People." *Daily Worker,* November 18, 1937.

Pickens, William. "What I Saw in Spain." *Crisis* 45, no. 10 (October 1938).

"92 Vets to Arrive Home on Saturday." *Daily Worker,* January 31, 1939.

"Three More Local Vets to Return from Spain." *Cleveland Press,* February 2, 1939.

"Mourn Cleveland C. P. Leader." *Daily Worker,* March ?, 1949 (BUSCW clipping).

Photographs

BUSCW B213, B262, B314, C293.

CHARLES HOWARD LEWIS

No sources.

NORMAN LISBERG

Photographs

BUSCW B261.

Archival

USSDA file #352.113. Documents dated April 5, 1939, and April 17, 1939, concerning the death of Norman Lisberg.

VAUGHN LOVE

Articles

Wright, Richard. "American Negroes in Key Posts of Spain's Loyalist Forces." *Daily Worker,* September 29, 1937.

Rolfe, Edwin. "American, Canadian, Spain Volunteers Study, Relax as They Train for Civilian Life Home." *Daily Worker,* November 28, 1938.

North, Joseph. "Returned Lincoln Vets Place Wreath at Lincoln's Statue: Vow Lasting Fight for Spain." *Daily Worker,* December 21, 1938.

"Wounded Spanish Civil War Veteran Says Conflict Is Question of Life or Death." *Daily Worker,* 1942 (BUSCW clipping; month, day unknown).

"Patient Fought Nazis in Spain." BUSCW VALB Scrapbook, May-December, 1945.

Photographs

BUSCW B260, P139.

Audiovisual

BUSCW ALB Film Project. Preproduction interview. One and a half hours, cassettes. Tape 254, box C.

BUSCW oral history videotape, Manny Harriman Collection.

Archival

BUSCW World War II letters. July 29, 1942; August 2, 1942; August 29, 1943; January 30, 1944; March 13, 1944; April 23, 1944.

ELUARD LUCHELL McDANIELS

Books

Nelson, Steve. *The Volunteers.* New York: Masses and Mainstream. BUSCW.

Articles

Quince, Peter. "No 'White Man's' Army." *People's World,* February 9, 1938.

"California Boys Heroes in Spain." *People's World,* August 26, 1938.

Pickens, William. "What I Saw in Spain." *Crisis* 45, no. 10 (October 1938).

Battman, John. "Spanish, Negro Peoples Fight Same Foe, Loyalist Vet Says." *People's World,* February 13, 1939.

McDaniels, Luchell. "One Returned Vet Tells Need of the Rest." *People's World,* March 16, 1939. (Letter by McDaniels.)

Quin, Mike. "A Negro Seaman Sees the World at War." *Daily Worker,* May 3, 1942.

_____. "This American Negro Set South Africa Back on Its Heels." *Daily Worker,* May 4, 1942.

Photographs

BUSCW B324, E229, E1196, P325.

"Photo of Luchell McDaniels." *People's World,* January 28, 1938.

"The Volunteer Presents." *Volunteer for Liberty* 2, no. 31 (September 5, 1938).

"Photo of Luchell McDaniels." *People's World,* February 13, 1939.

Audiovisual

BUSCW ALB Film Project. Preproduction interview. Three hours, cassettes. Tapes 170-71, box C.

Archival

BUSCW Radical Elders Oral History Project transcript (copy).

ANDREW MITCHELL

Books

Bessie, Alvah. *Men in Battle: A Story of Americans in Spain.* New York: Charles Scribner's Sons, 1939.

Photographs

BUSCW B325.

CRAWFORD MORGAN

Articles

"Plan to Honor Norfolkians Fighting in Spanish War." *Norfolk Journal,* January 15, 1938.

Photographs

BUSCW B332, D99, D100, D101, P316.

Archival

BUSCW World War II letters. September 2, 1942; June 19, 1944; January 1945; February 11, 1945.

Transcript of testimony before the Subversive Activities Control Board. BUSCW.

THOMAS PAGE

Articles

"With the Lincoln-Washington." *Volunteer for Liberty* 2, no. 30 (August 26, 1938).

Kennedy, William. "Rockville Boy Home from Spain after Fighting with Loyalists." *Nassau Review-Star,* December 23, 1938.

Photographs

BUSCW B709, E221

"The Volunteer Presents." *Volunteer for Liberty* 2, no. 31 (September 5, 1938): 7.

Audiovisual

BUSCW ALB Film Project. Original sound for filmed interview, 65 minutes, ¼-inch tape. Tapes 191-93, box B.

_____. Preproduction interview. Three hours, cassettes. Tapes 260-61, box C.

_____. Transcript of filmed interview. Blue looseleaf notebook, 37 pages, box ZC.

_____. Filmed interview (sound and picture); 2,400 feet of 16mm color film. CR 247-52, box K.

SOURCES

Archival

BUSCW World War II letters. November 12, 1942; December 6, 1942; February 23, 1943; April 21, 1943; May 20, 1943; May 27, 1943; July 31, 1943; August 5, 1943; November 17, 1943; January 12, 1944; May 19, 1944; November 19, 1944; January 19, 1945.

CHARLES AUGUSTUS PARKER

Books

Yates, James. *From Mississippi to Madrid: Memoir of a Black American in the Abraham Lincoln Brigade*. New York: Shamal Books, 1986; reprint, Seattle: Open Hand Publishers, 1989, 145. BUSCW.

Articles

"9 Americans Killed in Lincoln Brigade." *New York Evening Post,* October 25, 1937.

"List the Names of 9 Killed in Spain Fighting." *Daily Worker,* October 27, 1937.

JAMES LINCOLN HOLT PECK

Books

Peck, James. *Armies with Wings.* New York: Dodd, Mead & Co., 1940.

Hastie, William H. *On Clipped Wings: The Story of Jim Crow in the Army Air Corps.* New York: NAACP, October 1943.

Yates, James. *From Mississippi to Madrid: Memoir of a Black American in the Abraham Lincoln Brigade*. New York: Shamal Books, 1986; reprint, Seattle: Open Hand Publishers, 1989, 155A. BUSCW.

Articles

"Interview with James Peck." *People's World,* January 13, 1941.

Misrahi, Joe. "Phantom Brigade: A Volunteer in Spain, a Combat Tour with an American Fighter Pilot in the Spanish Republican Air Force." *Wings* 2, no. 2 (April 1972): 20-41.

CLAUDE PRINGLE

Articles

Shields, Art. "Back of Franco's Lines." *People's World,* May 20, 1939.

Photographs

BUSCW B89, C307.

Archival

BUSCW Prisoner of War Commission files.

ALPHEUS DANFORTH PROWELL

Articles

Quince, Peter. "No 'White Man's' Army." *People's World,* February 9, 1938.

Cassidy, Henry. "Slaughter of Americans in Spain Shatters Ideals of Volunteers." *Cincinatti Times Star,* April 7, 1938.

MARCUS RANSOM
Books
Brandt, Joe, ed. *Black Americans in the Spanish People's War against Fascism, 1936-1939.* New York: VALB, 1980. BUSCW.

OTTO COLEMAN REEVES
Photographs
BUSCW C247, D228.
Archival
Brier, Morris. "Three Friends." Unpublished manuscript. BUSCW.

VIRGIL RHETTA
Articles
O'Kein, Robert. "200 Americans Escape Insurgents." *San Francisco Examiner,* April 11, 1938.
"Hail Negro Who Died to Emancipate Spain." *People's World,* July 4, 1938.
"Memorial for 3 Americans Dead in Spain." *People's World,* July 19, 1938.
"Presides at Memorial to War Martyr." *L.A. Courier,* July 30, 1938.
Photographs
"Photo of Virgil Rhetta." *People's World,* July 23, 1938.

DOUGLAS BRYAN ROACH
Books
North, Joseph. *Men in the Ranks: The Story of 12 Americans in Spain.* With a foreword by Ernest Hemingway. New York: Friends of the Abraham Lincoln Brigade, 1939. BUSCW.
Articles
Davis, Ben, Jr. "A Small Man from the Cape with a Big Record in Spain." *Daily Worker,* September 27, 1937.
Albee, George. "300 Wounded Americans on Way Back from Spain." *St. Louis Co. Independent,* November 5, 1937.
"300 Wounded Americans on Way Back from Spain." *Lansing Industrial News,* November 19, 1937.
"300 Wounded Americans Returning from Spain." *Eau Claire Advocate,* November 19, 1937.
"Lincoln Vets to Organize at Parley." *Daily Worker,* December 10, 1937.
"Americans Have Died Fighting for Democracy in Spain." *Life,* April 1938.
"Boston Gunner 'Best in Spain.'" *Pittsburgh Courier,* April 23, 1938.
Davis, Ben, Jr. "Doug Roach, Negro Hero of Lincoln Brigade Dies Here." *Daily Worker,* July 14, 1938.

S O U R C E S

"Funeral for Doug Roach on Saturday." *Daily Worker*, July 14, 1938.
"Funeral for Doug Roach on Saturday." *Daily Worker*, July 15, 1938.
"Roach Is Mourned by New England Communist Party." *Daily Worker*, July 15, 1938.
"Douglas Roach Services." *New York Herald Tribune*, July 16, 1938.
"Lincoln Vets Pay Final Tribute to Doug Roach Today." *Daily Worker*, July 16, 1938.
"Douglas Roach, 28, in Spanish War." *Boston Transcript*, July 18, 1938.
"Home Town Pays Roach Final Tribute." *Daily Worker*, July 19, 1938.
"Minor Praises Roach at Funeral." *Daily Worker*, July 21, 1938.
"Bury Spanish War Hero with Honors." *Boston Chronicle*, July 23, 1938.
"Of Whom the Race Can Well Feel Proud." Reprint of editorial from *Boston Chronicle*, December 24, 1938, December 29, 1938.

Photographs
BUSCW P322, P325.
Boston Chronicle, December 24, 1938.

JAMES ROBERSON
Books
Yates, James. *From Mississippi to Madrid: Memoir of a Black American in the Abraham Lincoln Brigade*. New York: Shamal Books, 1986; reprint, Seattle: Open Hand Publishers, 1989, 72, 73. BUSCW.

STERLING TAYLOR ROCHESTER
Articles
"Negro Machine Gunner Returns from Spain." *Daily Worker*, July 6, 1937.
"Big Welcome Planned for Lincoln Boy." *Daily Worker*, July 10, 1937.
"New Yorker with Loyalists Praises Democratic Army." *New York City World Telegraph*, July 12, 1937.
Rosen, Herbert. "Lincoln Battalion Heroes Describe Fighting in Spain." *Daily Worker*, July 14, 1937.
"Negro Fighters in Spain." *Daily Worker*, July 15, 1937.
"What's on Tonight." *Daily Worker*, July 15, 1937.
"Race Machine-Gunner Home from Spain to Lecture on the War." *New York City Age*, July 17, 1937.
"Negro to Talk on Spain." *Atlantic City* (New Jersey) *Press*, July 24, 1937.
"Negro Ex-serviceman behind a Machine Gun on the Jarama Front Was with the First American Soldiers on the Battle Front." *Daily Worker*, July 25, 1937.
"Negro to Tell of Spanish War." *Wilkes-Barre* (Pennsylvania) *Record*, July 30, 1937.
"Negro Loyalist Fighter Begins Speaking Tour." *Daily Worker*, August 2, 1937.

"Spanish Major in Pittsburgh Tomorrow." *Daily Worker,* August 3, 1937.

"Spanish War Hero to Tour." *Pittsburgh Courier,* August 7, 1937.

"Heroes – Everyone." *Toronto* (Canada) *Clarion,* August 23, 1937.

"Spain Meeting to Hear Negro Loyalist Hero." *Daily Worker,* September 8, 1937.

"Sterling Rochester to Speak September 13 in Indiana Harbor." *Daily Worker,* September 9, 1937.

"Lincoln Battalion Man to Describe Spanish War." *St. Louis* (Missouri) *Star,* September 10, 1937.

"Crown Heights YCL to Hear Rochester Speak on Spain." *Daily Worker,* September 22, 1937.

"Soldiers Back from Spain Tell Why They Dared Death." *Philadelphia* (Pennsylvania) *Record,* October 30, 1937.

Tucker, William. "28 Philadelphia Boys Died in Spanish War." *Philadelphia Bulletin,* May 11, 1938.

"Communist Party Convention Pays Homage to Americans Who Died for Freedom, Democracy." *Daily Worker,* May 31, 1938.

"Reds Dispute Dies Witness." *Afro-American,* September 3, 1938:

Photographs

Daily Worker, July 14, 1937.

Afro-American, July 24, 1937.

Daily Worker, May 31, 1938.

Archival

USSDA file #811.00B/1787. Documents dated November 21, 1939, concerning membership in CPUSA (Philadelphia).

JULIUS RODRIGUEZ

Photographs

"Ambulance Driver at the Front."*AMI,* no. 9, February 1938.

PATRICK ROOSEVELT

Articles

"15 Americans in Spain Cross French Border." *Chicago News,* February 2, 1939.

"Spain Evacuates Last of American Fighters." *Johnson City* (Tennessee) *Press,* February 2, 1939.

"Yanks Cross Frontier." *Duluth* (Minnesota) *Herald,* February 2, 1939.

"Pat Roosevelt Lost Leg in Spain but Proud He Followed Lincoln Order." *Daily Worker,* February 13, 1939.

"Tribute to Spanish War Vets." *People's Voice,* April 21, 1945.

Photographs

BUSCW P196, P282, P353, P717, P817.

People's Voice, April 21, 1945.

   Audiovisual

BUSCW ALB Film Project. Preproduction interview. One and a half hours, cassette. Tape 259, box C.

CONRADO FIGUEROS ROSARIO

No sources.

OLIVER CHARLES ROSE

   Audiovisual

BUSCW ALB Film Project. Preproduction interview. Three hours, cassettes. Tapes 141-42, box A.

WEST SWANSON

   Articles

"Spain Meeting to Hear Negro Loyalist Hero: Chicago Steel Leader Killed in Spain to Be Honored." *Daily Worker*, September 8, 1937.

DANIEL BEDE TAYLOR

   Photographs

BUSCW P309.

JOSEPH TAYLOR

   Articles

North, Joseph. "Franco Defense Desperate; Loyalists Encircle Gandesa." *Daily Worker*, July 29, 1938.

"Franco Bombers Fail to Halt Ebro River Drive." *Daily Worker*, August 3, 1938.

Pickens, William. "What I Saw in Spain." *Crisis* 45, no. 10 (October 1938).

   Photographs

BUSCW B118, B385, C304, E221, E250, E790.

   Archival

BUSCW World War II letters. May 17, 1943.

RALPH THORNTON

   Photographs

BUSCW B55.

Pittsburgh Courier, December 4, 1937.

   Audiovisual

BUSCW ALB Film Project. Preproduction interview. One and a half hours, cassette. Tape 219, box C.

HERBERT VERDIER
  Archival
USSDA file #852.2221. Documents dated June 11, 1939; June 21, 1939; July 5, 1939; contains letter from stepmother seeking whereabouts.

FRANK WARFIELD
  Articles
"Langston Hughes Speaks on Spain." *People's World,* December 13, 1938.

GEORGE WALTER WATERS
  Photographs
BUSCW B237, C155, P639.
  Archival
USSDA Name Index.

ALONZO WATSON
  Articles
"Fallen Members of Lincoln Battalion: Honor Roll." *Daily Worker,* May 12, 1937.
"Harlem Negro Dies Fighting for Spain." *Daily Worker,* May 14, 1937.
"Chicagoan Is First American Negro to Die in Spanish War." *Pittsburgh Courier,* May 22, 1937.
"Harlem to Honor Negro Killed in Spain; Ford to Speak on Negroes in Front Line at Madrid." *Daily Worker,* June 9, 1937.
"To Honor Negro Hero." *Daily Worker,* June 12, 1937.
"To Honor Negro Killed in Spanish Civil War." *New York City Age,* June 12, 1937.
"Harlem Lincoln Boy's Friends Plan Big Push." *Daily Worker,* June 18, 1937.
"Alonzo Watson." *Boston Chronicle,* June 19, 1937.
"Harlemites Taking Part in Conflict." *Amsterdam* (New York) *News,* June 26, 1937.
"Heroes – Everyone." *Toronto* (Canada) *Clarion,* August 23, 1937.
Davis, Ben, Jr. "A Small Man from the Cape with a Big Record in Spain." *Daily Worker,* September 27, 1937.
"Louis Thompson Returns with Glowing Account of Negro in Spanish War." *Washington* (D.C.) *Tribune,* October 9, 1937.
  Photographs
Daily Worker, June 12, 1937.
New York City Age, June 12, 1937.

SOURCES

WILLIAM EDWARD WHITE

Archival

USSDA file #852.2221. Documents (dated October 22, 1937; October 23, 1937; October 26, 1937) concern return of White to the United States.

MORRIS HENRY WICKMAN

Books

Brandt, Joe, ed. *Black Americans in the Spanish People's War against Fascism, 1936-1939.* New York: VALB, 1980. BUSCW.

Articles

"Ten from State Leave Spain." *Lancaster* (Pennsylvania) *New Era,* December 8, 1938.

JEFFERSON WIDEMAN

Articles

" 'Loyalists Will Win' Veterans Say Here." *Philadelphia Bulletin* (no date).
North, Joseph. "Crowds Roar Welcome to Lincoln Veterans." *Daily Worker,* December 19, 1938.

Photographs

BUSCW P307.
Daily Worker, December 16, 1938.

FRED WILLIAMS

Archival

USSDA file #852.2221. Documents (dated May 11, 1938; May 18, 1938; July 19, 1938; Aug 8, 1938; November 12, 1938; December 2, 1938; June 30, 1939; July 11, 1939; August 2, 1939; August 7, 1939) concern the whereabouts of Williams.

PAUL ELISHA WILLIAMS

Articles

Steiner, Herbert. "Bailing Out." *Daily Worker,* March 5, 1938.
Williams, Paul. "Why Do They Crash?" *People's World,* June 4, 1938.

SAMUEL CONWAY WILLIS

Photographs

BUSCW B83, B240.

JAMES YATES

Books

Yates, James. *From Mississippi to Madrid: Memoir of a Black American in the Abraham Lincoln Brigade.* New York: Shamal Books, 1986; reprint, Seattle: Open Hand Publishers, 1989.

SOURCES

Articles

Meldon, John. "Democracy's Vets Lead May Day Line." *Daily Worker,* May 2, 1938.

"Army Punishes Veteran Fighters." *New World* (Seattle), March 19, 1943.

Audiovisual

BUSCW ALB Film Project. ALB Poetry Reading. Filmed event. 350 feet of 16mm color film. Box L.

_____. Preproduction interview. Three hours, cassettes. Tapes 153-54, box C.

Archival

BUSCW World War II letters. November 24, 1942; February 20, 1943; January 4, 1943.

CHARLES YOUNGBLOOD

Articles

"A Boy Home from War." *Kansas City Star,* October 18, 1938.

" 'Would Give Other Eye' to Halt Fascism, Says Injured Yank Captive of Franco." *People's World,* October 27, 1938.

THE BATTLEFRONT: GENERAL SOURCES ON AFRICAN AMERICANS IN THE SPANISH CIVIL WAR

Books

Brandt, Joe, ed. *Black Americans in the Spanish People's War against Fascism, 1936-1939.* New York: VALB, 1980. BUSCW.

Articles

"Spanish Reds Offer Independence to Moors: 'We Fight for Our Liberty and Yours' Says Leaflet: Proclamation Issued in Arabic." *Chicago Defender,* February 13, 1937.

"37 Americans Land in France on Way to Spain." *Chicago Defender,* February 13, 1937.

"A Negro in Spain: 'I Am the Town Pet.' " *Daily Worker,* April ?, 1937 (BUSCW clipping).

"Negro Leaders Ask Action in Fascist Spies." *Daily Worker,* May 13, 1937.

Ehrenburg, Ilya. "Ethiopian Fights on Guadalajara Front: Son of Ras Imru in Front Rank of Spain's Army." *Daily Worker,* May 21, 1937.

"New Complications Aggravate Spanish Crisis." *Atlanta Daily World,* June 5, 1937.

Ingram, Rex. "De Lawd." *Amsterdam* (New York) *News,* June 26, 1937.

"Two Worlds at War in Spanish Revolution: So States Logan." *Atlanta Daily World,* July 11, 1937.

"Two American Machine Gun Leaders Wounded in Spain: John Hunter and Walter Garland." *Pittsburgh Courier,* July 17, 1937.

218

"Lincoln Battalion Boys at the Front in Spain." *Daily Worker*, July 19, 1937.

Lightfoot, Claude. "Chicago Holds Law Memorial." *Daily Worker*, August 7, 1937.

"France Denies German Charge that Senegalese Troops Fight in Spain." *Pittsburgh Courier*, August 14, 1937.

Wright, Richard. "American Negroes in Key Posts of Spain's Loyalist Forces." *Daily Worker*, September 29, 1937.

_____. "Bates Tells of Spain's Fight for Strong Republican Army." *Daily Worker*, October 1, 1937.

"Negroes Heroes in Spanish War Says I.W.O Head." *Pittsburgh Courier*, October 9, 1937.

Poston, Ted. "Louise Thompson Returns with Glowing Account of Negro in Spanish War." *Washington* (D.C.) *Tribune*, October 9, 1937.

_____. "Louise Thompson Returns with Glowing Account of Colored Men in Spanish Civil War." *Atlanta Daily World*, October 11, 1937.

"Americans Mainstay of Loyalist Offensive at Brunete, Belchite, Haywood Tells Daily." *Daily Worker*, October 12, 1937.

Americans Earn High Posts with Loyalists." *Afro-American*, October 13, 1937.

"Moors Reported to be 'Cheating On' Chief of Rebel Army in Spain." *Pittsburgh Courier*, October 16, 1937.

"Negro Paper Pays Tribute to Herndon, Other Negroes in Spain." *Daily Worker*, November 1, 1937.

"No Discrimination against Negroes Fighting in Spain." *Atlanta Daily World*, November 1, 1937.

"No Discrimination against Negroes Fighting in Spain." *Pittsburgh Courier*, November 6, 1937.

Rushmore, Howard. "Miners Welcome Steve Nelson, Home from Fighting in Spain." *Daily Worker*, November 19, 1937.

"The Robert Weavers Fete Thyra Edwards." *Pittsburgh Courier*, November 27, 1937.

"Spanish Volunteer Returns to U.S.A." *Chicago Defender*, December 4, 1937.

"Spain's War Has Group Fighter." *Atlanta Daily World*, January 24, 1938.

"100 Negroes Fighting with Loyalists, Robeson Says." *Daily Worker*, February 4, 1938.

Amlie, Hans. "With the Americans Fighting Fascism." *New York Evening Post*, February 7, 1938.

Quince, Peter. "No 'White Man's' Army." *People's World*, February 9, 1938.

Edwards, Thyra. "Social Worker Visits Spanish Loyalist Men." *Chicago Defender*, February 12, 1938.

"Negroes at Teruel Hail Lincoln Day in Letter to U.S." *Daily Worker,* February 12, 1938.

Ford, Henry. "For Peace and Democracy." *Crisis,* March 1938.

"Caught behind the Fascist Line in Spain – Kaye Tells Vivid Story of Food Transport." *Daily Worker,* April 23, 1938.

"U.S. Blacks in Spain Called Hard Fighters." *Chicago Defender,* May 21, 1938.

"Fight against Fascism Joined by Six Writers." *Atlanta Daily World,* May 23, 1938.

"Spain Medical Vets Organize." *Daily Worker,* June 29, 1938.

"Colored Soldiers Called 'Toughest in Spanish War.' " *Atlanta Daily World,* June 30, 1938.

White, David McKelvey. "The International Brigade of 1938." *Atlanta Daily World,* July 4, 1938.

"26 Wounded Lincoln Vets Arrive from Spain on Wednesday." *Daily Worker,* July 19, 1938.

"Moors Refuse to Fight in Spanish War." *Atlanta Daily World,* July 23, 1938.

Lawrence, Will. "Max Yergan, Progressive Leader, Says Negroes Aiding Spain Are in Fight for Liberty." *Daily Worker,* July 26, 1938.

"Eight American Heroes Give Lives in Spain." *Daily Worker,* July 30, 1938.

North, Joseph. "2 Loyalists 'Talk' 25 Fascists into Laying Down Arms." *Daily Worker,* August 1, 1938.

"Wounded Spain Vets on Ship with Corrigan." *Daily Worker,* August 2, 1938.

Lawrence, Will. "From the Stock Yards and Steel Mills." *Daily Worker,* August 5, 1938.

"Wounded Vets Arrive Here from Spain." *Daily Worker,* August 6, 1938.

North, Joseph. "Lincoln Boys Hold Vital Lines on Ebro under Vicious Assault of Franco Planes." *Daily Worker,* August 24, 1938.

"2 Ships Bring Lincoln Boys to New York." *Daily Worker,* August 25, 1938.

North, Joseph. "How's the Union Back Home? – That's the First Question of Lincoln Boys." *Daily Worker,* August 26, 1938.

"Pickens to Visit Spain." *Pittsburgh Courier,* August 27, 1938.

"Wounded Lincoln Boys Home." *Daily Worker,* August 29, 1938.

"36 Wounded Vets Arrive Here September 24." *Daily Worker,* September 21, 1938.

Pickens, William. 'What I Saw in Spain." *Crisis,* October 1938.

_____. "Pickens Says." *Atlanta Daily World,* October 6, 1938.

"Lincoln-Washington Battalion Is Leaving Spain to Carry on Fight for Democracy on Another Front." *Daily Worker,* October 11, 1938.

"Captured Vets to Be Greeted on Wednesday." *Daily Worker,* October 24, 1938.

"2 Sets of Prisoners: Fascists Cringe, Loyalist Would Give 'Another Eye' to Stop Fascism." *Daily Worker,* October 25, 1938.

"Immigration Head Says Must Exclude 10 Spain Vets." *Daily Worker,* October 26, 1938.

"U.S. Boys Reach Paris on Way Home." *Daily Worker,* October 27, 1938.

" 'Would Give Other Eye' to Halt Fascism, Says Injured Yank Captive of Franco." *People's World,* October 27, 1938.

Rolfe, Edwin. "Bombs Fail to Halt Barcelona Fetes for Lincoln Boys." *Daily Worker,* November 3, 1938.

_____. "American, Canadian, Spain Volunteers Study, Relax as They Train for Civilian Life Home." *Daily Worker,* November 25, 1938.

North, Joseph. "Pasionaria 'Will Never Forget' Herndon, Negro Americans Who Carried Stars and Stripes in Vet Parade: Spain Mourns Doug Roach." *Daily Worker,* December 2, 1938.

"Americans Evacuated from Spain." *New York Times,* December 4, 1938.

"Second Group of 147 Vets Sail for U.S." *Daily Worker,* December 10, 1938.

"Friends Give List of 149 Vets Arrived from Spain Thursday." *Daily Worker,* December 14, 1938.

"Spain Group Will Honor Negro Leader." *Daily Worker,* December 19, 1938.

Davis, Ben, Jr. "Struggles in Spain, China Vital for Negro Americans." *People's Daily World,* February 8, 1939.

Battman, John. "Spanish, Negro Peoples Fight Same Foe, Loyalist Vet Says." *People's World,* February 13, 1939.

Shields, Art. "Back of Franco's Lines." *People's World,* May 20, 1939.

McSorley, Edward. "Dr. Ward, Yergan, Robeson Speak Commemorating I.B.'s [International Brigade's] Fight for Spanish Democracy." *Daily Worker,* February 29, 1940.

"National Negro History Week." *Volunteer for Liberty* 12, no. 1 (March 7, 1951).

Photographs

Daily Worker, July 19, 1937; November 19, 1937.

Chicago Defender, December 4, 1937.

Fight for Peace and Democracy, April 1938, 45.

Daily Worker, July 18, 1938 (unidentified ALB member); July 26, 1938 (Max Yergan); August 6, 1938 (includes Leroy Collins); August 29, 1938 (includes Walter Callion); December 2, 1938 (Milton Herndon, Douglas Roach, Salaria Kee).

THE HOME FRONT: SOURCES ON
AFRICAN-AMERICAN SOLIDARITY WITH SPAIN

GENERAL SOURCES

<u>*Articles*</u>

"Youth Leader Returns from European Tour." *Chicago Defender,* October 17, 1936.

"War in Spain." Ruth Pearson Koshuk, *Chicago Defender,* October 24, 1936.

"Hughes, Cullen Aid Ambulance Corps for Spain." *Pittsburgh Courier,* February 27, 1937.

"Negro Group Gives to Spain Supplies Raised for Ethiopia." *Daily Worker,* March 2, 1937.

"Spain Gets 25% of Proceeds of Dance at the Savoy." *Daily Worker,* March 6, 1937.

"Harlem to Parade for Spain and Ethiopia." *Daily Worker,* March 22, 1937.

"March Today for Spain, Ethiopia." *Daily Worker,* March 27, 1937.

"What's on Sunday: Harlem Swing Club." *Daily Worker,* May 29, 1937.

"Race Becomes Ally to Spain in War Crisis." *Chicago Defender,* April 10, 1937.

"AME [African Methodist Episcopal] Union Hears Rayford Logan Talk of Spanish Civil War." *Atlanta Daily World,* April 29, 1937.

"Aids Spanish Kids." *Daily Worker,* June 5, 1937.

"March for Spain in Harlem Saturday." *Daily Worker,* June 8, 1937.

"A Significant Rally for Ethiopia Tonight." *Daily Worker,* June 11, 1937.

"What's on Sunday." *Daily Worker,* June 26, 1937.

"Browder Will Speak at Garden Tonight." *Daily Worker,* July 14, 1937.

Herndon, Angelo. "Herndon Urges Protest on Invasion of Spain." *Daily Worker,* July 17, 1937.

"Robeson Makes a Thrilling Speech in Behalf of Spain." *Pittsburgh Courier,* July 17, 1937.

"Rochester Tells of Heroism of Negro Fighters at Front in Spain." *Daily Worker,* July 17, 1937.

Herndon, Angelo. "Herndon Urges Protest on Invasion of Spain." *Daily Worker,* July 18, 1937.

"Rex Ingram Asks America to Free Scottsboro Boys." *Daily Worker,* July 18, 1937.

Winston, Henry. "Harlem YCL Honors U.S. Boys in Spain." *Daily Worker,* July 1937 (BUSCW clipping).

James, William. "Baltimore to Hear Galleano Sunday." *Daily Worker,* August 7, 1937.

"Spanish Solidarity Meet in Odessa in Colorful Incident." *Atlanta Daily World*, August 16, 1937.

"Pretty Champions Who Will Perform for Spain." *Daily Worker*, August 18, 1937.

"Black Sailors Rally against Fascist Spain." *Pittsburgh Courier*, August 21, 1937.

"3 American Negroes to Broadcast from Madrid This Friday." *Daily Worker*, August 24, 1937.

"U.S. Race Men to Broadcast from Madrid." *Chicago Defender*, September 4, 1937.

Thompson, Louise. "IWO [International Workers Order] to Hold Meeting for Spain October 2." *Daily Worker*, September 8, 1937.

Ingram, Rex. "Concert for Spain at Town Hall." *Daily Worker*, September 14, 1937.

Bias, Lawrence. "The Black Volunteer." *Afro-American*, September 18, 1937 (fiction).

"Our Brothers in Spain." *Chicago Defender*, September 18, 1937.

"Screen Director Leaves for Spain, Hopes to Produce Another Film." *Atlanta Daily World*, September 20, 1937.

"Chicago Negro Paper Hails Role of Negro in Spain's War on Fascism." *Daily Worker*, September 24, 1937.

Rochester, Sterling. "Race Must Help Spain to Rescue Freedom." *Chicago Defender*, September 25, 1937.

"IWO Leaders to Report on Spain Visit Tonight." *Daily Worker*, October 2, 1937.

"Negro Pianist to Play at Philadelphia Concert for Lincoln Boys." *Daily Worker*, October 8, 1937.

"Day Star's Anger over War Forced Il Duce's Son to Leave West." *Atlanta Daily World*, October 10, 1937.

"A Year of the International Brigade." *Volunteer for Liberty* 1, no. 18 (October 11, 1937).

"2 Chicagoans in Spain to Make Survey." *Chicago Defender*, October 30, 1937.

"Louise Thompson Speaks on Spain." *Chicago Defender*, November 6, 1937.

Wright, Richard. "Negro Social Worker Hails Housing, Education in Spain." *Daily Worker*, November 12, 1937.

"Negro Congress Resolution for Boycott of Japan against Fascism Released by Yergan, Leader at Session." *Daily Worker*, November 18, 1937.

"Honor Herndon at Harlem Rally Sunday." *Daily Worker*, November 27, 1937.

"Boys from Spain Will Be Honored at Benefit on Saturday." *Daily Worker*, December 1, 1937.

SOURCES

"Welcome Jewish Volunteers Tonight at 8:30." *Daily Worker*, December 4, 1937.

"Thyra Edwards Speaks of Issues, Programs, Actions." *Chicago Defender*, December 18, December 25, 1937; January 1, 1938.

"Harlem Dances to Mark Victory at Teruel." *Daily Worker*, December 24, 1937.

"Spain Vets to Hold National Parlay February 12." *Daily Worker*, February 8, 1938.

"Harlem to Mark Spain Anniversary." *Daily Worker*, February 16, 1938.

"Harlem Group Meet Tomorrow on Embargo Fight." *Daily Worker*, February 25, 1938.

"Negro Group to Sponsor Benefit Dance Tonight." *People's World*, February 26, 1938.

"Black American with Mexican, Philipino, Cuban and Japanese Volunteers." *Volunteer for Liberty* 2, no. 7 (February 28, 1938).

"Ask Aid for the Spanish Loyalists." *Chicago Defender*, March 5, 1938.

"Langston Hughes to Be Heard on Spain." *Afro-American*, March 5, 1938.

"Robeson's Back in Spain." *Afro-American*, March 5, 1938.

"Thyra Edwards Urges Spanish Loyalist Aid." *Afro-American*, March 5, 1938.

"Spain's Woman Leader Praises Race Fighters." *Chicago Defender*, March 12, 1938.

"Negroes in Spain Call on People to Spur Aid." *Daily Worker*, March 15, 1938.

"Harlem Groups Join in Spain Meeting Wednesday." *Daily Worker*, March 29, 1938.

"Harlem C.P. [Communist party] to Honor Americans in Spain: Ford among Speakers." *Daily Worker*, April 11, 1938.

"Loyalist Veteran Leads May Day Parade Group." *New York World Telegram*, April 30, 1938.

"Friends Send Funds to 87 U.S. Boys Held Prisoner at Franco Concentration Camps." *Daily Worker*, August 30, 1938.

"Ask Medics to Give Aid to Loyalists." *Atlanta Daily World*, September 6, 1938.

"Ambulance of Mercy to Stop in St. Louis." *Pittsburgh Courier*, September 10, 1938.

"People of U.S. Back World Aid in Spain." *Daily Worker*, September 23, 1938.

"To Give Milk, Soap for Spain." *Atlanta Daily World*, September 23, 1938.

"Crisis Shows Need for Spain Relief Ship." *Daily Worker*, September 27, 1938.

"Tennessee Faculty Organizes to Aid Republican Cause in Spain." *Atlanta Daily World*, October 25, 1938.

"Negroes Give Supplies to Spain Relief Ship." *People's World,* November 2, 1938.

" 'Mercy' Ambulance En Route to Spain." *Pittsburgh Courier,* November 12, 1938.

McCall, Martin. "A Handy Birthday Concert: Father of the Blues to be Honored Next Monday Night at Carnegie Hall Is Benefit for Spanish Children's Milk Fund." *Daily Worker,* November 17, 1938.

"Campaign for Lifting of Embargo." *Atlanta Daily World,* November 17, 1938.

McCall, Martin. "A Handy Concert for Milk Fund: W. C. Handy Birthday Concert for the Benefit of the Spanish Children's Milk Fund, under the Joint Auspices of Harlem and Musicians' Committee to Aid Spanish Democracy; All Performing Artists Were Negro." *Daily Worker,* November 24, 1938.

"The W. C. Handy Birthday Concert: *Daily Worker* Editorial Board Issues Statement on Review of Last Thursday." *Daily Worker,* December 2, 1938.

Hammond, John. "A Concert-goer also Writes His Opinion of McCall's Review and of Concert." *Daily Worker,* December 2, 1938.

"Negro Leaders Call Conference on Spain of Fascist Menace." *Daily Worker,* December 30, 1938.

"Declare Need of Negro People to Cooperate with All Forces Struggling for Democracy: Labor Church, NAACP Leaders Urge Unity." *People's World,* January 3, 1939.

"Negro Leaders Call Spain Aid Conference." *People's World,* January 3, 1939.

"Spain's War Victims Aided by Monthly Donations from New York's Social Workers." *Pittsburgh Courier,* January 21, 1939.

"Negro Leaders Meet Today for Spain Aid Drive." *Daily Worker,* January 28, 1939.

"Negro Leaders Join Drive against Embargo of Spain: Almost 100 Endorse Campaign of Negro Committee to Aid Spain." *Daily Worker,* February 8, 1939.

"Lincoln Brigade to Dance Tonight." *P.M.,* December 24, 1942.

Powell, Adam Clayton, Jr. "Vets Rally Tonight to Urge Freedom for Anti-Fascists in North Africa." *Daily Worker,* March 4, 1943.

"Republican Spain Rally Set for January 2 in Garden." *P.M.,* December 13, 1944.

Wilkerson, Doxey. "Toward Freedom: New Year Opens with Rally Against Franco." *Daily Worker,* January 1, 1945.

Tobias, Channing, Jr. "Rally Demands Break with Franco." *P.M.,* January 3, 1945.

Powell, Adam Clayton, Jr. "To Mark 14th Anniversary of Spanish Republic." *Daily Worker,* March 1945 (BUSCW clipping).

"Lincoln Vets Dinner April 11." *Daily Worker,* March 2, 1945.

Powell, Adam Clayton, Jr. "They Fought against Fascism in Two Wars: Lincoln Vets Pledge Fight to Free Spain." *Daily Worker,* April 13, 1945.

———. "Lincoln Brigade First People's Army – Powell." *People's Voice,* April 21, 1945.

"New Yorkers Blast Franco." Charles Collins, *Daily Worker,* May 18, 1945.

  Photographs

"Game for Spain." *Daily Worker,* February 13, 1937.

"Famous Race Singer at Spanish Hospital." *Chicago Defender,* April 23, 1938.

"Working to Help Loyalists." *Pittsburgh Courier,* September 3, 1938.

Daily Worker, December 2, 1938.

THE SPANISH CIVIL WAR IN THE AFRICAN-AMERICAN PRESS

  Articles

"Moslems Keeping Aid from Spanish." *Chicago Defender,* September 12, 1936.

Lochard, T. P. "Panorama of the World News." *Chicago Defender,* September 19, 1936.

"Moroccans Revolt against Fascists." *Chicago Defender,* September 19, 1936.

"700 Cubans Fight for Spanish Red Loyalists." *Chicago Defender,* September 19, 1936.

"Madrid's Passion Flower." *Chicago Defender,* November 28, 1936.

"Musician Is out of Spain." *Afro-American,* January 2, 1937.

"Ethiopian Troops May Aid Spain." *Afro-American,* February 20, 1937.

Jones, Joseph. "Ethiopians Aid in New Italian Rout." *Afro-American,* February 20, 1937.

"Ethiopian Student Fights on the Side of Spanish People." *Chicago Defender,* April 3, 1937.

"Spanish Loyalist Pledges Fealty to Ethiopian Cause." *Afro-American,* April 3, 1937.

"Loyal Victory Called Key to Ethiopian War." *Afro-American,* June 19, 1937.

Cunard, Nancy. "Black Moors Fighting for Spanish Fascists, Given Demoralizing Treatment." *Atlanta Daily World,* July 15, 1937.

"Italy Sends Badoglio to Spain." *Chicago Defender,* August 14, 1937.

"No African Troops in Spanish Conflict." *Chicago Defender,* August 14, 1937.

"Moorish Troops in Spain's Rebellion." *Chicago Defender,* August 21, 1937.

Cunard, Nancy. "Claim Moors Deserting Franco: African Fighters in Spanish War to Report." *Atlanta Daily World,* September 27, 1937.

Pickens, William. "What I Saw in Spain." *Crisis* 45, no. 10 (October 1938).

"Son of Ethiopian Jailed as Fascist Agent." *Chicago Defender,* October 23, 1937.

Powell, Adam Clayton, Jr. "Demand Release of Imprisoned International Brigade Heroes." *People's Voice,* February 21, 1943.

JAMES FORD

Articles

Harrison, George. "Ford Makes a Stirring Appeal for Lincoln Boys in Short Wave Broadcast from Madrid." *Daily Worker,* May 12, 1937.

"Miaja Sees Victory for Spanish People." *Daily Worker,* May 17, 1937.

Marion, G[eorge]."Ford on Way Home from Spain; Saw Lincoln Boys in Trenches." *Daily Worker,* May 19, 1937.

Davis, Ben, Jr. "Ford Returns from Spain Confident of Loyalist Victory." *Daily Worker,* May 26, 1937.

"Ford Appeals from Madrid for Support." *Chicago Defender,* May 29, 1937.

"5000 Honor Lincoln Boys at Meeting–Ford and Minor Speak." *Daily Worker,* June ?, 1937.

"Ford Talks in Harlem on Spain Tonight." *Daily Worker,* June 4, 1940.

"Ford to Speak at Big Chicago Rally for Spain." *Daily Worker,* June 5, 1937.

"Glory Rally for Spain to Hear James Ford." *Daily Worker,* June 5, 1937.

"The Spanish People Are Achieving It, Says Negro Leader Just Returned from Madrid." *Sunday Worker,* June 6, 1937.

"U.S. OK's Smoke Fund for Lincoln Battalion." *Daily Worker,* June 7, 1937.

"Afro-Americans to Honor Ford in Washington." *Daily Worker,* June 10, 1937.

"Ford Speaks to 3000 at Chicago Rally." *Daily Worker,* June 10, 1937.

"Fate of Ethiopians Bound Up with Spanish Struggle." *Daily Worker,* June 11, 1937.

"Ford Praises Negroes in Spanish War." *Daily Worker,* June 11, 1937.

"Ford to Speak on Spain Trip in Baltimore." *Daily Worker,* June 12, 1937.

"Ford Praises Negroes in Spanish War." *Daily Worker,* June 14, 1937.

"Ford to Speak on WHCA [radio station] from Spain Rally." *Daily Worker,* October 6, 1937.

LANGSTON HUGHES

Articles

"Langston Hughes Hails Negroes in Spain." *Daily Worker*, March 19, 1937.

Cunard, Nancy. "Langston Hughes Poem Aids Spanish Loyalists." *Atlanta Daily World*, June 1, 1937.

Hughes, Langston. "Too Much of Race." *Volunteer for Liberty* 1, no. 11 (August 23, 1937).

"Bard, Haywood, Hughes Speak for Radio Friday." *Daily Worker*, August 26, 1937.

"Three American Negroes to Broadcast from Madrid." *Washington* (D.C.) *Tribune*, August 28, 1937.

Hughes, Langston. "Roar, China!" *Volunteer for Liberty* 1, no. 13 (September 6, 1937).

"Negro Poet to Broadcast from Madrid." *Daily Worker*, September 7, 1937.

Hughes, Langston. "Negroes in Spain." *Volunteer for Liberty* 1, no. 14 (September 13, 1937).

_____. "The Voice of 15 Million." *Daily Worker*, September 23, 1937.

Wright, Richard. "American Negroes in Key Posts of Spanish Loyalist Forces." *Daily Worker*, September 29, 1937.

Pastor, Ted. "Louise Thompson Returns with Glowing Account of Negro in Spanish War." *Washington* (D.C.) *Tribune*, October 9, 1937.

Hughes, Langston. "October 16th." *Volunteer for Liberty* 1, no. 19 (October 11, 1937).

"Hughes Finds Moors Being Used as Pawns by Fascists in Spain." *Afro-American*, October 30, 1937.

Hughes, Langston. "Letter from Spain." *Volunteer for Liberty* 1, no. 23 (November 15, 1937).

_____. "Madrid's Flowers Hoist Blooms to Meet Raining Fascist Bombs." *Afro-American*, November 27, 1937.

_____. "New York Nurse Weds Irish Fighter in Spain's War." *Afro-American*, December 11, 1937.

"Song of Spain." Langston Hughes, *Daily Worker*, December 13, 1937.

"Langston Hughes Sees Victory for Loyalists." *Daily Worker*, January 22, 1938.

Hughes, Langston. "Addressed to Alabama." *People's World*, January 23, 1938 (poem).

"Rose Freed and Langston Hughes, the Negro Poet." *AMI*, no. 9 (February 1938).

"Negro Poet to Speak on Spain at IWO Center." *Daily Worker*, March 1, 1938.

"Hughes Speaks on Spain's War." *Afro-American*, March 12, 1938.

"Poet Calls Fascism Threat to Negroes." *Milwaukee Leader*, April 5, 1938.

"Hughes Speaks." *Atlanta Daily World*, April 8, 1938.

"Langston Hughes Delivers Stirring Chicago Message." *Atlanta Daily World*, April 11, 1938.

"Langston Hughes Putting on Play." *Afro-American*, April 23, 1938.

"Spanish Folk Songs of the War." Translated by Langston Hughes. *Volunteer for Liberty* 2, no. 21 (June 15, 1938).

"U.J. Delegates Sail for Paris Parley: Spain Relief Sessions also Objective of Dreiser, Hughes." *Daily Worker*, July 13, 1938.

"Langston Hughes Speaks on Spain." *People's World*, December 13, 1938.

Bessie, Alvah. "The Lessons of the Spanish Civil War." *People's World*, March 1949.

Peterson, Ralph. "Against the Night." *National Guardian*, April 11, 1949.

Review of *Volunteer for Liberty*. *Compass*, July 5, 1949.

Review of *Heart of Spain*. *National Guardian*, December 11, 1952.

Review of *Heart of Spain*. *Sunday Worker*, December 21, 1952.

Photographs

BUSCW P316.

Ro152, Ro153, Ro154, Ro155, Ro164, Ro166, Ro168. (*Ro* signifies the Edwin Rolfe Collection.)

Daily Worker, September 7, 1937.

Volunteer for Liberty 2, no. 7 (February 28, 1938).

PAUL ROBESON

Articles

"Harlemites Taking Part in the Conflict." *Amsterdam* (New York) *News*, June 26, 1937.

"Robeson Given Ovation over Spanish Stand." *Chicago Defender*, July 17, 1937.

"Intellectuals Confused about Struggle in Spain, Declares Paul Robeson." *Pittsburgh Courier*, June 26, 1937.

"Robeson, baritono americano canta para los leales." *La Prensa* (New York), January 29, 1938.

"Robeson in Spain for Concerts; Robeson Will Cheer Troops at War Front." *Chicago Defender*, January 29, 1938.

"Robeson's Voice Hails War in Spain." *Atlanta Daily World*, January 29, 1938.

"Robeson Acclaims Spanish People." *Daily Worker*, February 2, 1938.

"Robeson Hero of Spanish War Picture, to Portray Oliver Law." *Chicago Defender*, February 26, 1938.

"What Negroes Are Doing: Robeson to Portray Oliver Law in Film." *Birmingham* (Alabama) *News*, February 27, 1938.

"Robeson Adds Spanish Songs to Repertory." *Pittsburgh Courier,* March 19, 1938.

"Spanish Songs Added to List of Robeson." *Afro-American,* March 19, 1938.

"Great American Negro Visits Spain." *Daily Worker,* April ?, 1938.

"International Letter from Paul Robeson, Jr." *Daily Worker,* April 26, 1938.

Robeson, Paul. "An American Boy Writes from Russia." *Afro-American,* June 18, 1938.

"160 Musicians Join Plea to Lift Embargo." *Daily Worker,* January 26, 1939.

"Robeson Warns of Fascist Peril to Negro in Cable." *Daily Worker,* February 21, 1939.

"Robeson in Plea to Lift Embargo." *People's World,* February 25, 1939.

"Paul Robeson Breaks with Movie Trust." *People's World,* March 10, 1939.

"Dr. Ward, Yergan, Robeson Speak Commemorating IB's (International Brigade's) Fight for Spanish Democracy." *Daily Worker,* February 29, 1940.

"Spanish Fighters Feted." *Los Angeles Times,* February 5, 1945.

"Pour Funds to Aid Spanish Vets into a Captured Nazi Flag." *Daily Worker,* February 13, 1945.

"Spanish Appeal Sponsors Salute to Show Business." *Daily Worker,* May 23, 1945.

"238 Appeal for Ban on Arms to Franco." *New York Times,* May 17, 1951.

Photographs

BUSCW P586, P777.

AMI, no. 10, March 1938.

Daily Worker, April 6, 1938.

Chicago Defender, April 9, 1938; April 16, 1938.

"Paul Robeson in Spain." *People's World,* May 2, 1938.

INDEX

THE CONTRIBUTORS

Robin D. G. Kelley is a professor in the Department of History at the University of Michigan, Ann Arbor. He is a specialist in African-American radicalism and author of the book *Hammer and Hoe: Alabama Communists in the 1930s,* published in 1990 by the University of North Carolina Press.

Danny Duncan Collum was executive director of the Abraham Lincoln Archives from fall 1988 to spring 1991. He is now a writer and editor living in New Orleans.

Victor A. Berch was head of Special Collections at Brandeis University Libraries. He is now ALBA's archivist and curator of the Spanish Civil War Collections at Brandeis.